EIGHTH AIR FORCE
BOMBER STORIES

Patrick Stephens Limited, a member of the Haynes Publishing Group, has published authoritative, quality books for enthusiasts for more than twenty years. During that time the company has established a reputation as one of the world's leading publishers of books on aviation, maritime, military, model-making, motor cycling, motoring, motor racing, railway and railway modelling subjects. Readers or authors with suggestions for books they would like to see published are invited to write to: The Editorial Director, Patrick Stephens Limited, Sparkford, Nr Yeovil, Somerset, BA22 7JJ.

EIGHTH AIR FORCE
BOMBER STORIES

EYE-WITNESS ACCOUNTS FROM AMERICAN AIRMEN AND BRITISH CIVILIANS OF THE PERILS OF WAR

Ian McLachlan & Russell J. Zorn

PSL

Patrick Stephens Limited

First published in 1991
Reprinted in January 1992
Reprinted in March 1992
Reprinted in July 1992

British Library Cataloguing in Publication Data
McLachlan, Ian
  8th Air Force bomber stories: Eye-witness
  accounts from American airmen and British
  civilians of the perils of war.
  I. Title.
  940.54

  ISBN 1 85260 367 4

Patrick Stephens Limited is part of the Haynes Publishing Group P.L.C., Sparkford, Nr Yeovil, Somerset, BA22 7JJ

Printed in Great Britain by J. H. Haynes & Co. Ltd.

Contents

Preface

I HOPE THIS book will interest, teach, and remind the reader of young American bomber crews who faced tremendous adversities with great valour and, sometimes, human failings. If it does, full credit must go to my co-author, Russell J. Zorn, who died before seeing completion of his project. His energy was unabated, even though he recognised the risks of overworking with a weak heart. Only hours before that expected, yet unexpected, final heart attack, I phoned to say that PSL were publishing our book, and I fondly recall the satisfaction he felt, knowing that his work would present the courage of his countrymen to a wider audience.

Russ was born in Buffalo, New York, and served with the New York Central Railroad before World War Two. When his country became embroiled in that conflict, Russ worked as a publicity director for the US Draft Board and, seeing so many friends making their own contribution for a freer world, he enlisted in the Army Air Force. His chosen role was photographer, and initial training started at Rome Air Base, New York. He then moved to Ten Mile Station, Charleston, South Carolina, for a further five months before proceeding to Warner Robbins Air Base at Macon, Georgia, prior to an overseas posting. Like many others, Russ routed through the port of embarkation base at Camp Kilmer and then boarded the British troopship, *Aquitania*. On 12 August 1943, the converted liner anchored off Gourock, Scotland, and Russ began the final phase of a journey to the 1st Strategic Air Depot at Honington in Suffolk, England. He would be there for more than two exciting years.

An Air Depot issued supplies and provided in-depth maintenance, modification and repair facilities for bases in its area. Subordinated to the central depot were numerous, lesser stations established on operational airfields within the jurisdiction of the parent organization. As a photographer, Russ carried his 4 in x 5 in format Speed Graphic camera like an extension of his arm although, on one occasion, his 'arm' fell off during a difficult aerial photography session. A major role for Russ and his colleagues was photographing downed bombers for damage assessment and official records. Sometimes, up to fifteen prints might be made, and Russ sent some home through the censor. As will be seen, he journeyed throughout England and Wales, riding an open jeep in strange countryside denuded of signposts. However, the proliferation of bases, and crashes, in East Anglia kept him primarily in that region, travel-

Russ in relaxed mood at Honington, 1944.

ling along twisty roads through tiny villages. Orders also focused his attention on bombers of the Third Air Division, although others were covered if
1 SAD photographers were in the vicinity. Not all the crash pictures that follow
were taken by Russ – his contribution was the presence of mind to preserve
them. At the war's end, activities wound down when the Eighth Air Force
began its retreat into British and American history. Masses of material were
moved home, but some equipment and records were destroyed, sometimes being
buried on bases which were themselves soon abandoned. Towards the end
of 1945 Russ was ordered to destroy the pictures taken by 1 SAD photographers; the incidents were closed, the bombers obsolescent.

Contemplating more than 2,000 crash negatives and pictures, plus hundreds
more prints of repair techniques and specialist tools created by ingenious
airmen, Russ realised that they might, one day, have historical significance.
Also, from the seemingly mundane, the collection extended to pictures of
famous personalities from that era – Vera Lynn, Bob Hope, Glenn Miller,
General Eisenhower, and many others. Russ felt he would regret their destruction and, making a special compartment in his trunk, he arranged to ship
them home. In December 1945 Russ bade farewell to a cold, ration-sombred
Britain and embarked on the *Europa* at Southampton. Two days before
Christmas he was discharged from the Army and resumed a civilian career.
This, plus marriage to a tolerant and loving Ruth, two sons, church work,
and golf kept the wartime photographs in the background for over 20 years.

During that time, the tranquillity of East Anglia lost even the echo of the mighty aerial armadas. Tales from those epoch-making times settled into a mixture of fact and folklore, upon which a post-war generation of aviation enthusiasts fed avidly. Farmworkers told of battle-damaged bombers bellying into fields, and of others falling violently in surrounding countryside or, occasionally, into the communities themselves. Spurred by research into such events, a new aspect of aviation enthusiasm emerged, aviation archaeology, and my book, *Final Flights* – also published by PSL – reveals dramatic incidents where research was initiated by these activities. Tracing American bomber crash sites, I would try to imagine how they appeared at the time. Often, fragments of history were found, eyewitnesses interviewed and survivor accounts gleaned, but I never realised that pictures of the incidents existed.

During the late 1960s Russ Zorn blew the dust from his boxes of negatives. Looking back, he felt haunted by ghosts of broken bombers and almost forgotten fliers whose downfall his photographs recorded. As a young sergeant with a job to do, Russ paid little heed to what had happened to the bombers he portrayed, and had deliberately closed his mind to the more horrific images. Contemplating the collection after the passage of years, he now knew that the pictures yielded only part of the story: their historical significance was devalued without further facts. The first, hesitant, step taken towards this book was a letter to the Bury Free Press, enclosing some photographs. An active response signified that memories of the 'Mighty Eighth' were very much alive in England, and his pictures caused real excitement among British aficionados. One, Stewart Evans, wrote to Russ, triggering an exchange of material and early plans for this book. Sadly, personal circumstances forced Stewart to leave the project and, as a close friend, I was invited to replace him. When Russ died, his son Ray took up the baton, concluding his father's research and helping to complete the tribute Russ intended for the men whose courage had been captured by his camera.

For myself, the book is not only a tribute to those airmen, but is now dedicated to a fine friend. On his behalf, I hope the following pages give some reward.

Ian McLachlan

Acknowledgements

THIS BOOK WAS created from special relationships. Firstly, that between America and Britain – two democratic nations bonded by similar freedoms and prepared to defend them. Secondly, that between the authors' families – Ruth Zorn and her son Ray; Julie, Bethan and Rowan McLachlan, who gave encouragement, support and tolerance. Thirdly, the kindred spirits of fellow writers, researchers and enthusiasts who generously provided additional information.

In addition, and above all, I acknowledge the veterans whose accounts modestly represent their own unclaimed heroism but also the many, many young airmen unable to speak for themselves.

Thanks are due to the following: C.E. Adams, N.G.T. Adams, S. Adams, C.E. Anderson, R. Andrews, Ashford and Tenterden Recovery Group, E. Avery, H.A. Ayres, S. Balls, T. Balls, J.E. Baker, G. Barker, R. Barker, G.W. Barnett, *Beccles and Bungay Journal,* N. Beckett, M.H. Bennett, J.Blackham, D. Blake, S.B. Blakeman, R. Bowden, M. Bowman, C. Bowyer, R.C. Boyer, W.E. Bradford, J.B. Brinegar, J.E. Brown, S.G. Bryant, P.B.Burgess, L.J. Burrows, F.W. Buschmeier, R.L. Butters, A.M. Caffyn, Cambridge American Military Cemetery, C. Cansdale, J. Carless, A.M. Carter, C.H. Carter, P.G. Cheal, R.G. Chilton, M. Clark, F. Coker, C.H. Collins D.D.S., R.J. Collis, L. Correia, P.M. Dean, R. Debenham, E.M. Demaray, F.J. DiMola, *Diss Mercury and Advertiser,* P.A. Dodd, E. Doylerush, K.S. Dropek, Eastern Counties Newspapers Group Ltd., A. Elias, T.G. Emms, S.P. Evans, K. Everett, J. Felton, R.A. Freeman, L.O. Gamma, D and R Garnham, I. Garstka, B. Gaustad, A.R. Gearing, W.A. Geigle, J.R. Gerba, V. Gilbert, J. Gill, G.M. Gipson, S. Goldstein, D. Grainger, M. Grant, R.J. Graves, A.G. Green, L. Green, V. Grimble, D.E. Groom, R.G. Guidi, Dr H.V. Hagerty D.M.D., R. Haines, C. Hall, F. Halm, B. Hammerton, R. Handforth, K. Harbour, C.R. Harden, *Hastings News,* L. Hatch, M. Harvey, G. Hawes, I. Hawkins, K. Hayward, R. Heart, F.A. Hendrick, H.L. Heyneman, I.A. Higgons, N. Hochberg, H. Hoehler, B.J. Holman, G.E. Holmes, G. Howe, R.F. Hughes, R. Humphreys, J. Hutchinson, B.A. Hyland, F. Irwin, G.W. Irwin, W. Jeffries, J. Johnson, Kent Aviation Historical & Research Society, N.C. Kiefer, A.E. King, E. King, L. King, J. Knight, A. Korothy, R.A. Krahn, E.F. Langholz, E.J. Lapthorne, J.P. Lawsky, H. Lawson, Dr B.B. Layl, J.K. Leonard, R.A. Lincoln, K. Lockwood, H.C. Lohff, L.G. Lonsway, W. Lundy, D.M. MacGregor,

J. MacMillian, G.R. Madley, S.A. Mandel, A.R. Manuel, R.E. Martin, Maxwell Air Force Base, J.F. McCallum Jr., E. Meeks, J. Meen, M. Meierhenry, *Mendlesham Memories,* F.R. Merkley, G. Meyer, UK Ministry of Defence, D.S. Monroe, A.J. Moor, S. Moore, C.G. Morgan, E.T. Moriarty, R. Murphy, I.R. Nelson, E. Newton, D.J. Noe, R.H. Nolan, Norton AFB HQ USAF Inspection and Safety Centre, N.E. Offord, J. Palmer, C.W. Parke, J. Partridge, G. Patrick, W. Paxon (Member of Congress), D.J. Payne, T.A.J. Payne, R. Penovich, Dr. K. Percival-Barker, M. Pestell, R & B Pleasance, L.R. Pote, N. Powell, G.M. Pratt, M. Prestia, J. Quinn, M.F. Radtke, N.C. Raeber, P. Ramm, M.J. Read, E.K. Reeder, A Ringhofer, M. Rogers, J.M. Rossman, P. Ruplenas, J.E. Saunders, N.B. Schlors, P.J. Schmitt, K. Seibert, R. Simons, J. Simpson, H. Slater, M.H. Smith, Col R. Smith, P.L. Speronis, G. Stebbings, R. Steel, K.S. Steele, L. Steele, N.L. Struchen, Suffolk Constabulary, R.L. Summa, T. Sutcliffe, L. Swedlund, H. Templeton, C.D. Terry, P. Thrower, K.H. Trimble III, F.P. Uhlein, R. Urich, USAF Historical Division, J. Vasco, D. Wade, G.D. Ward, R. Ward, G. Warren, C.V. Weber, S.O. Wellman, D.W. Wilkinson, A. Williams, M. Wood, D. Woodland, *Worthing & Lancing Guardian,* A.M. Wright, R & R Zorn.

100 BG MAM, 385 BGMA, 390 BGMAN, 447 BGA (UK), 486 BGA.

Finally, appreciation is expressed to the backroom girls, Julie McLachlan and Sue Balls, for word-processing the manuscript and suffering the writer and his corrections.

Ian McLachlan
Norwich, England
August 1991

1: Pathfinder

WEDNESDAY, 10 NOVEMBER, 1943, started like any other day for housewife Rose Wingfield. Despite work under way for a new bomber base at Eye, the war had impinged little on her life, although she welcomed the extra money earned by laundering for American airmen. Such tranquillity would shatter that day in circumstances Rose would never forget.

Having washed and cleared the breakfast dishes, Rose tidied the house before deciding she needed some items from Brome village store. Gathering bag, purse and ration books, she cycled the short distance to the shop run by sisters Ethel and Violet Fulcher. Chatting for a few minutes, Rose remarked on the mild weather – she still wore a summer dress and the mid-morning sun had made her journey from Number 20, Brome, very pleasant. It had gone 10.30 a.m. when Rose left the shop and began pedalling homewards past the Old Rectory, now a country house named *Oaksmere*. Here, the evidence of war was strangely signified by an avenue of stunted lime trees whose tops had been lopped off because they lay on the

Rose Wingfield – a young housewife so nearly caught in the catastrophe. (Rose Hart.)

Labourer, Charlie Burridge became embroiled in a wartime tragedy. (Mrs F. Watling.)

approach to the new airfield. Work on the big base, which was still under construction, had levelled woodland, demolished two cottages and obliterated Potash Lane. This spoiled surrounding drainage, and Rose was not surprised to see four workmen ditching alongside the road. One of them stood at the roadside with a horse and tumbril, while the others laboured in the ditch itself. Rose recognised old Charlie Burridge from Langton Green and called out a cheerful 'Morning Charlie' as she went by, adding jokingly. 'You aren't digging your own grave, are you?' Charlie paused. 'I hope not, Ma'am', he laughed.

Scarcely had she left the scene when Rose was frightened by a tremendous roar, overhead but behind and near the workmen. Leaping from her bicycle, Rose turned and stood as transfixed as a rabbit, a terrified spectator powerless to prevent any of the rapidly-happening horror, and barely safe herself. Less than fifty feet above and diving directly at the workmen was a huge bomber. Four anguished engines seemed to scream their last moments, and one was blazing fiercely. In those moments before the crashing crescendo of fire and death, Rose saw workmen fleeing for their lives, but their very existence was overwhelmed by 25 tons of doomed bomber. As the bomber smashed directly on to the road-gang, its propellers knifed cleanly through the rearing, terror-stricken horse, chopping the animal in half. Rose saw its head and shoulders tossed bloodily aside as the rest vanished into a hellish fireball of noise and destruction. Charlie Burridge, Walter Clarke and William Dixon died instantly. Charlie's body lay in the ditch from which he had joked with Rose only a few minutes earlier. One of the workmen, possible Ernie Barker, almost escaped. Rose saw a figure leaping for safety, only to be scythed down by the bomber's wingtip. Ernest Barker died from his injuries two days later.

Stunned by the speed of events, Rose had hardly gained any composure before rescue vehicles hurtled on the scene. A huge pall of acrid, black smoke billowed into a clear blue sky from the intense and angry phosphorous-fed flames. Within the inferno, ammunition cooked and exploded, sending stray bullets zinging with dan-

Wedged beneath the left elevator were the remains of Dixon's tumbril . . . Hours after the crash, wisps of smoke still drift from the Pathfinder's burnt port aileron. A twisted propeller blade rests in the foreground. (Russell J. Zorn.)

This Flying Fortress had been the first H2S Pathfinder for the Eighth Air Force. Note the bulbous radar dome beneath the nose of B-17F 42-5793. (Stewart P. Evans.)

gerous random across the landscape. Coloured signal flares showered wildly into the countryside as the bomber literally melted into the furrows, cremating both crew and contents. Rose realised she could help no one, and Military Policemen ushered shocked eyewitnesses and other spectators to safety.

Later that day Rose felt compelled to return, if only to convince herself of the shocking reality of the incident she had witnessed. Recognizing Lt McKinney because of her laundry-work, Rose and her husband were allowed nearer the smouldering remains. The only major portions still identifiable were the severed wingtips, both swept back towards the burnt remains of a fin and port tailplane. Wedged beneath the left elevator section were the remains of Dixon's tumbril. The smell of hot metal and burnt flesh stung the nostrils. Rose did not envy the airmen sifting through ashes of the fuselage for human remains and dog tags. She saw some charred bodies removed, and her husband picked up a dog-tag and gave it to the officer in charge. Surprisingly, Rose saw the scorched remains of a white nylon parachute and, appreciating how useful this was for petticoats, picked up the crumpled folds, which were strangely heavy. Rose wondered why, then recoiled, horror-stricken when she saw the reason. Clinging to the molten material was an airman's boot, still containing a badly-burned foot. Shocked, she threw it down and wondered how many young men had perished so horribly.

Understandably, civilians were not told of cause or casualties, but rumours circulating soon after the crash said that the aeroplane was special. Just how special only became known in later years, when security surrounding secret equipment on board was reduced. This Boeing Flying Fortress had been the first H2S Pathfinder for the Eighth Air Force.

Developed by the British, H2S was the coded identity of an independently-functioning, airborne radar which provided an image of the terrain below. American proponents of daylight bombing had been forced to admit that operational conditions in Europe often prevented use of the sophisticated Norden bombsight. Battling through fighters and flak to reach 'socked in' targets frustrated and demoralized airmen, as well as reducing operational efficiency. Technical aids to target location became vital to improve utilisation of air power on days which precluded visual bombing. To the radar image night or day were unimportant, and borrowing British night-bombing technology enabled the Eighth to increase the frequency of attacks where overcast targets evinced a suitable radar footprint. With typical irreverence to the brains behind such technology, the Americans nicknamed their radar 'Stinkey', but such familiarity was a long way off when the bomber which fell at Brome was chosen as the first B-17 to carry the new equipment.

During March 1943 a B-17F Flying Fortress, serial number 42-5793, from the 92nd Bombardment Group at Alconbury flew to RAF Defford for installation of the 10 cm frequency H2S radar. While technicians planned the layout, Britain helped train American airmen to use H2S at the top-secret Telecommunications Research Establishment at Greater Malvern. A plan to replace the B-17's ball turret with a radar dome was unwelcome because it reduced protection for the aircraft. The ferocity of Luftwaffe attacks demanded maximum defensive firepower, and losing the ball-turret would be highly unpopular with aircrews. At this time the Flying Fortress lacked the chin turret, so interference with standard armament was minimised by siting the radar below the bomber's nose. Concealed in a housing moulded from an early form of plastic, the radar scanner's position maximised performance and image clarity. Thus modified, B-17 42-5793 became the test bed for systems development and did not return to Alconbury until August.

By then, the Eighth had formed a specialist Pathfinder Force (PFF) unit, the 482nd Bombardment Group, to which 42-5793 was now assigned. The following month, this aircraft was a planned Combat Wing Leader for the first Eighth Air Force, H2S-led attack, but the temperamental set malfunctioned and B-17 *Finger M-Mike* remained on *terra-firma* while aircraft modified later stole her glory over Emden. Several missions followed with varying success for the new equipment and then, on 10 November, 42-5793 was readied for another operation. With so few PFF aircraft available, it was customary for the 482nd crew to leave Alconbury in the early hours and attend

A former farm-boy from South Carolina, radar technician M/Sgt Robert G. Levi died in the crash of 42-5793 at Brome, Suffolk, England. (Robert Morgan.)

briefing with the Group whose aircraft they would lead that day. The early hours of 10 November found pilot Lt Arthur J. Reynolds and crew flying the short hop from Alconbury to Thorpe Abbotts, home of the 100th Bomb Group, famed as the 'Bloody Hundredth'. Despite clear conditions over East Anglia, continental weather patterns proved unfavourable for planned targets and the mission was cancelled. Lt Reynolds and crew could go home. Normally, a B-17 crew comprised ten men, but H2S required attention and technician Master Sergeant Robert G. Levi was on board to look after the radar. A farm-boy from South Carolina, Levi was among the first airmen to learn the idiosyncrasies of early H2S units. Robert's skills would not be needed, and the flight to Alconbury would be low enough to enable him to enjoy the countryside. Most crew members uninvolved in take-off procedures usually gathered in the radio room for safety reasons. This was nearer the bomber's centre of gravity and had bulkheads against which the crew could brace themselves in the event of a crash. Reynolds, assisted by co-pilot Lt John J. Russell, taxied the B-17 to its take off position. Navigator Lt Sheldon V. McCormick could easily find his way home and Bombardier Lt Alfred L. Rolnick would save his ordnance for another day. Watching over the relevant dials and gauges was Tech Sgt Amos H. Behl, whose other role as top-turret gunner would not be required today. Equally, the other sergeant-gunners, Laurie C. Evans, Leslie N. Boling, William H. Landers, Andrew J. Allison, and John D. May could relax and look forward to chow instead of combat. Nonetheless, any take-off had its own tensions as the gunners gathered with Tech Sgt Robert B. Holmes in the confines of his radio compartment. The thirteenth crew member was Corp Herman J. Kolousek, another radar mechanic.

Cleared for departure, the B-17 began its final flight. Somewhere, beyond the point of no return, the bomber's number one engine caught fire. With the aircraft struggling to stay airborne but too low for parachutes, the best chance was the runway under construction at Eye. This lay almost directly ahead, and was closer than Thorpe Abbotts. Events overruled both skill and courage as flames seared through essential control cables and determined the fates of both warriors and workers. The casualties, British and American at Brome, became part of the terrible toll levied for defeating the evil afflicting Europe. The loss of top-secret apparatus was replaceable: 17 lives were not.

2: Bob the bullfighter

FOR LT ROBERT M. Simons, Saturday, 13 November 1943, turned out to be one of *those* days. It started with the usual combat qualms, but, as an experienced 388th Bomb Group pilot, Bob had coped with these through several very rough missions. Four weeks earlier they had crash-landed at RAF Lichfield and, while his navigator, Lt Ralph C. Boyer, still had his leg in a cast, no-one else was hurt although both wheels of their B-17 had been torn off and its nose had been smashed open. On another mission, over Bremen, they had been scared by a runaway number three propeller, but Bob and co-pilot Lt Al Marcus had feathered the unit and pushed the remaining throttles wide open to hold formation beyond enemy territory and reach the protection of RAF Spitfires before landing safely at Knettishall. Bob was dismayed to find that their target was again the port of Bremen – but let him take up the story.

Bob the bullfighter, an Eighth Air Force Matador, Lt Robert M. Simons parachuted into a new set of problems when he abandoned his B-17 over England.

'I should have known that taking off in an aircraft with the last two numbers 13 (42-30213) and on the thirteenth of the month was not going to bring the best of luck to my crew, but we were supposed to fly that aircraft. We were assigned a very good B-17G model and had named it *Return Engagement* but, just as I was ready to take off, it had the left tyre blow out. The aircraft was pulled out of the way so the rest of the Group could take off. We were told to get all of our gear and machine-gun barrels over to No. 213, *Lil One*. With such a changing of planes and getting all of our gear in the right place and the guns in working order, we were about fifteen minutes late in taking off. Operations thought we could catch up because we could head straight for the 'Splasher', where the Group would depart for the enemy

The nose art of Li'l One – *B-17F-90-BO of the 388th BG, Knettishall.*

coast. (A 'Splasher' was a radio beacon over which bombers could rendezvous). We were at about 23,000 ft and almost over the enemy coast, again trying for Bremen, Germany, and could still not see any of the Group, nor, for that matter, any of the entire Eighth Air Force.

'This time it was equipment failure that did us in. While cruising around trying to locate our own Group, or any other Group that we could tie in with, the number three prop started to run away. This was not a new experience . . . However, this time, no matter what we did, the prop kept winding up faster and faster until I read the RPM's over thirty-six hundred. We were all waiting for the prop to spin off by heating up and fall under the left wing. All the while this was going on, in the cockpit the navigator (Lt Robert L. Gudgel) was getting us a heading back to base and I told the crew to get ready to abandon aircraft if necessary, and to keep on the intercom and look out for bailout lights and bells.

'While Gudgel got us a heading, the co-pilot (Al Marcus) was shutting everything down on number three. I was heading back to the English coast and losing altitude. When we hit the tip of the coast we were about 19,000 ft and the prop still had not fallen off, but was starting to cause pieces of the engine cowling to fly off and hit the right side of the fuselage, just like flak was hitting us. Up to that time I thought I could bring the aircraft back safely to our base but the bombardier (Lt John D. Pond) called up on intercom and told me we had one big fire going on all around the engine and in the back of it. The B-17 was a good aircraft and could take a lot of punishment, but one thing it could not take was fire. Sometimes they blew up like a Fourth of July firecracker; other times the fire went in to the wing and the gas tanks took the whole wing off.

'This all took place in about thirty seconds after the fire really got started and, from what the bombadier told me, we had a fire going for more time than was safe to hang around. I saw that we were just over the coast, so I ordered the crew to bail out. I pushed every bailout button, both mine and the one on the co-pilot's side. On the intercom I gave the abandon ship order as fast as I could say it, over and over again. In a matter of split seconds I was left alone in the cockpit and turned the aircraft towards the sea. I knew I was just about over the water, so I planned a delayed jump so I would not blow out to sea. When I saw the aircraft was just about at the coast and headed seawards, I bailed out and delayed the jump.

'I was at 18,000 ft when I left the aircraft, and delayed pulling the rip-cord until I estimated my altitude at around the height of turning on to my final approach when coming in for a landing.

'Everything they told me about parachuting was true: except for the first ten seconds, when you felt as if you were being turned inside out and going in every direction at once from hitting the slipstream. With the combat chest pack you fell on your back with your feet raised a little above your head and you could look over each shoulder and see the ground. Everything else seems to be moving except you. It's just like laying on a big air cushion unless you let one of your legs separate from the other. If the left leg goes off to the left, you spin left in a violent manner. The same for the right leg. I did the whole trip, spun to the left and the right, before I made a point of keeping both legs close together. The chute opened just like they said it would and I came to a rough stop. Before, everything was moving except me and there was this rushing noise as I passed through the air. Now that the chute was open there was a strange silence, almost as if you could hear a pin drop. When I was approximately 100 to 200 feet above the ground, gusty winds hit the chute, part of it collapsed, and I went into the middle of a hedgerow. Everything happened so fast I did not have time to realize what was going on until I saw that I was upside

'I fell out of the hedgerow into a pasture that was the private property of one of the largest English bulls ever born . . .' (Ian Z. Garstka.)

down and tangled in the chute. I fell out of the hedgerow into a pasture that was the private property of one of the largest English bulls ever born, and he did not like my intrusion into his brunch ...

'By the time I was halfway out of my chute harness I noticed the bull starting towards me in a most unfriendly attitude. I could not move about, being half in the harness and still caught somewhat in the hedgerow. Then I remembered my .45 Colt Automatic which I carried in the old-style Cavalry Hip Holster. It was still with me, staying right in the holster through the bail-out, spinning left and right then crashing through the hedgerow. This says a lot for the designer of this type of gear. I pulled out the automatic and put three or four shots right in front of the bull and he stopped, began to think about me and then started to come closer. I emptied my clip, again shooting in front of his nose. This time he stopped and began to think hard about the situation. While we were in a Mexican standoff, a young English boy of about twelve years old stuck his head through part of the hedgerow and, with eyes as big as saucers, said, 'Are you a German?' I told him I was American. He really looked relieved. I said I thought I was hurt, and asked if he could go for help. It seemed that the farm I landed on was deserted except for the bull that still looked menacing and definitely wanted me out of his territory. I put my second clip into the Colt and fired five or six shots in his direction. This time he went over to the other side of the pasture and stood there. I got through the wire and hedge to the other side and he immediately came charging up to where I was, taking complete control of his pasture again.

'In the distance I heard the ringing bells of British Police car being driven at full speed in my direction. A police officer from Beccles picked me up and drove me back to the police department, which was part of his home. He immediately gave me two drinks of some strong Scotch, which settled me down quite a bit. While he was making calls to British and American air bases, telling them about a crew coming down in parachutes all over their areas, a British girl dressed in WAAF uniform came into the room and offered me another drink of Scotch. It turned out that she was the policeman's daughter. She told me she was stationed at RAF Lichfield, near Birmingham, and about a month ago a B-17 had crash-landed at her base, torn up the place and knocked out their telephone service for a few hours. I said, 'My God! That was me!' She told me her base was a fighter training field, and I had given the personnel an exciting afternoon. By this time an ambulance from a nearby B-24 Group arrived and I was transported to its base.

'When I arrived I was met by Chaplains from all three Western religions. They had heard someone was coming in hurt but did not know how bad. I was able to walk from the ambulance, and thought maybe they were a little disappointed that I was not just a bit more in need of their services ...

'I started to feel rough the next day. The Scotch from the British policeman kept me in good shape until then. My back, legs and right hip hurt when I walked, and I started to urinate blood, so was sent to base hospital and from there to the 5th General Hospital at Salisbury for about six months and then back to the States for another three months.'

Bob's crew landed safely, although his radioman, S/Sgt Irwin W. Rehder had a slight head wound. John Pond had watched the Cyclone engine burn until the front casing turned cherry red. As the vibrations became more violent, oil lines broke and flames spread back from the cowling across the wing. John needed no encouragement to get out, and immediately pulled his rip-cord, which resulted in a fifteen-minute descent. Drifting towards Beccles, he became alarmed by nearby power cables and then frightened at the prospect of falling from one of the rooftops. Finally he was deposited

A smoking smear on Norfolk heathland near East Wretham – all that remained of the Flying Fortress Li'l One. (Russell J. Zorn.)

gently into someone's flower garden. The back door opened and a woman politely enquired whether her unexpected guest would like a cup of tea. Releasing his harness, John followed her indoors while workers from a factory nearby pulled his parachute from the power lines and bundled it up for him. After tea and cakes, his hostess asked whether he was American or German, and relaxed considerably on learning his nationality. *Lil One* failed to behave as Bob intended. Far from vanishing into the North Sea, the Fortress swung about and trailed her blazing coat inland some thirty miles, crashing harmlessly on heathland within the Stanford Battle Area at 9.40 a.m. Her cargo of M47 incendiary bombs ignited, completing the destruction initiated by a runaway propeller.

3: Liberty Belle

AMERICAN AIRMEN PERSONALISED their aircraft with nose-art, sometimes adding aspects of themselves and their national character in the choice of illustration and name. Many aeroplanes carried light-hearted caricatures, others were adorned with pin-ups, and some bore patriotic artwork. The Flying Fortress *Liberty Belle* combined patriotism with pin-up, and her pilot, Robert C. Smith, was justifiably proud of his aircraft and the men of his Lead Crew, 549th Squadron, 385th Bombardment Group. As a standard B-17F, serial 42-30096, the Fortress was like any other, but, given her colourful nose-art, hard-earned mission score and tally of fighter claims, callsign 'Walpole V-Victor' became their *Liberty Belle*, a symbol of freedom over tyranny.

   As part of the Group's original cadre, Smith's crew trained in Montana before bringing their brand-new Boeings across the Atlantic to the village of Great Ashfield, Suffolk, England. Not all of Bob's crew would survive, but, years later, his affection for the men with whom he served remained strong. Paul Lindsay, his co-pilot, flew

Nose art for the proud 385th BG Flying Fortress Liberty Belle *proclaimed patriotism with pin-up. Captain Robert Smith is in the cockpit.*

many missions while suffering from tuberculosis, but beat both bacillus and human foes to succeed in the teaching profession. Navigating *Liberty Belle* was Nathan Ungar, a handsome young airman who demonstrated tremendous heroism on the famous Schweinfurt mission of October 14, 1943. Savaged by flak and enemy fighters, *Liberty Belle* had the superchargers of two engines knocked out, part of her oxygen system destroyed, and two gunners seriously wounded. Even as German fighters homed in again, Nate ferried oxygen bottles for the injured crewmen, keeping them alive until the safety of lower altitude was reached. The most boisterous officer in Bob's crew was Charles A. Stevens from Florida, whose skill as a bombardier contributed sig-

Liberty Belle *at rest on her Great Ashfield hardstanding on 15 October 1943, the day after Schweinfurt.* (Henry C. Lohff.)

nificantly to their selection as a Lead Crew entrusted with critical responsibilities for mission effectiveness. Technical Sergeant George L. Lilburn was the crew's 'father figure', and Bob selected him as First Sergeant for the enlisted men. The 2nd Tech Sgt was radio operator Edwin F. Randig, who collected a German bullet over Schweinfurt. This one did not have his name on it in the traditional sense, because it was spent when it hit him, causing only a bruise and lodging in his leather jacket. Squeezed into the ball turret was S/Sgt Troy M. Roberts, whose handling of his twin-fifties added to the swastika tally on *Liberty Belle's* nose. That they came home from Schweinfurt at all was attributed to S/Sgt Samuel S. Litt. When the aircraft was holed in her number three tank, Sam manipulated the fuel tank transfer system with swift dexterity, saving enough fuel for *Liberty Belle* to get home. An effective bomber crew needed combined skills, but all failed if bombs did not reach the target, and S/Sgt Henry C. Lohff was their armament expert and left waist gunner. On three occasions the release mechanism malfunctioned. Each time, Carl Lohff leant over the open bomb bay without a parachute, triggering free the hang-ups.

Providing the sting in the bomber's tail was S/Sgt Louis G. Lonsway. In the punishment over Schweinfurt, a 20 mm cannon shell burst in Lonnie's left-hand ammunition pannier. The explosion bowled him backwards into the fuselage and set fire to some material and a portable oxygen bottle. Had the fire taken hold, *Liberty Belle* and her crew would have become part of Schweinfurt's horrific statistics, but Lonnie rapidly beat out the flames with his hands, which were badly burned. He also had shrapnel in his left arm, thigh and buttock. On the intercom he informed Bob he had been 'hit in the ass', but kept at his guns as another, twin-engined fighter closed in. Only his right gun fired, but Lonnie blew the enemy's number one engine clean out of its nacelle and the German fighter fell earthwards in pieces. For his courage, Lonsway received the Distinguished Service Cross. Yes, Bob Smith could be proud of his crew. The last flight they made saw equipment failure do what German flak and fighters failed to achieve – destroy *Liberty Belle* on their nineteenth mission.

With their wounds healed and repairs to the aeroplane complete, nine of Bob's boys climbed aboard to attack industrial targets in Solingen. Of the regular crew, only Lindsay was not with them, and the co-pilot's seat was occupied by a young

Lt Col Elliot Vandevanter Jr presents Louis Lonsway with the DSC for his courage. (Louis G. Lonsway.)

Bob Smith could be proud of his crew. Standing, L to R: Robert Smith, Paul Lindsay (not on board that day), Nathan Ungar and Charles Stevens. Kneeling, L to R: Edwin Randig, George Lilburn, Samuel Litt, Troy Roberts and Henry Lohff. Louis Lonsway is absent. (Edwin Randig.)

Lieutenant, James D. McKee, who had not flown with them before. *Liberty Belle* was tasked with leading the low squadron, but thick cloud handicapped assembly. Leaving Great Ashfield, Bob climbed steadily through the overcast, heading for the 385th's assembly area south of Ipswich. At 19,000 ft they surfaced into a sharp blue-and-white world seemingly unrelated to the dark earth below. Other Fortresses emerged, and Bob told Sam Litt to fire red flares signalling them to form up on *Liberty Belle*. Moments later Bob heard a sharp explosion in the aircraft. Startled, he turned right, towards the noise, and a blazing flare hit him right between the eyes, bounced off, and ricocheted wildly around the flight deck. He was shocked and dazed, but his experience and training had imbued enough presence of mind to enable him to make split-second decisions almost instinctively. The entire top-turret area was engulfed in flames and already beyond any possibility of being extinguished. With her mixed load of 500 lb bombs and incendiaries, *Liberty Belle* could explode at any moment.

Engaging autopilot on an easterly heading, Bob was reaching to switch the radio to interphone when McKee abruptly throttled back all four engines. Bob never knew why he did so, but the B-17 sagged earthwards before Bob grabbed the controls and levelled off. This cost precious seconds, and *Liberty Belle* had turned into a fiery cocktail of flares, fuel and bombs, ready to eviscerate herself and crew in one final, astral flash. Bob's vision was still blurred from burns around his eyes and face, and he squinted, struggling to see the bail-out bell. His right hand was painfully scorched but, reaching the bell, he held it and held it and held it, doing the best he could for his crew. Strangely, McKee did not budge, and although Bob yelled at him to go the young flier remained immobile as flames roared about them with increasing ferocity. Bob could not lift him, and decided to lead, hoping to bring McKee to his senses. Only later did Bob learn that his co-pilot feared parachuting – a phobia which cost his life. Choking on cordite smoke and trying to shield his face, Bob staggered to the hatch and leapt clear before he passed out.

Presumably he opened his parachute, perhaps a greater deity helped, but Bob regained consciousness floating through a snow-storm. The gentleness of myriad, dancing flakes was lost on him – his descent seemed interminable. Suddenly he smacked into hard ground and heard his leg 'snap with a sound like a breaking board'. Unable to use his right hand or leg, he struggled, trying to collapse the now unwanted parachute, but the wind dragged him painfully for some distance before he disentangled himself. Sense told him he was in a dangerous state of shock. Remembering two morphine syrettes given by Doc Kuhn, Bob decided that this was enough of an emergency to justify their use. (Syrettes were injections of morphine in a miniature disposable tube.) He was squeezing one into his arm when an English farmworker ran up. As Bob's senses faded the man exclaimed 'Oh, my God!', and Bob passed out. Hazily, he remembers an ambulance and a doctor administering the second syrette – the first, formal medical action of a long treatment. Apart from burns and a broken leg, Bob had compression fractures of three vertebrae and spent eighteen months recovering. How had his crew fared?

Edwin Randig was monitoring his radio receiver, wondering if they would be recalled because of bad weather. Then he noticed a greyish-white smoke apparently drifting in through the roof hatch. Switching to intercom, he was startled by a loud, excited, garbling voice which alarmed him thoroughly, and he leapt to his feet. Opening the door to the bomb bay, Edwin was enveloped by clouds of smoke billowing aft, and he recognized the pungent odour of flares. Grabbing an extinguisher he clambered into the bomb bay – this meant disconnecting both oxygen and interphone lines, so he had no contact with other crew members. Looking down between the bombs, Edwin saw red flames through a crack in front of the left bomb-bay door. Suddenly, the aeroplane dived (as McKee cut the throttles) and Edwin pitched forward, luckily falling astride the narrow catwalk but losing the extinguisher. Even as *Liberty Belle* levelled off Edwin knew she was finished. Hastily climbing back to get his parachute, a chest-pack always kept on the floor in front of his transmitter, Edwin snapped it on and retreated aft. Amidships, he passed Troy Roberts climbing from his position.

Navigator Nate Ungar with his personal nose art on the port side of Liberty Belle. *Nate's body was found near Wake's Colne in Essex.*

The barely recognisable tattered nose section from Liberty Belle *lies near Wormingford.* (Russell J. Zorn.)

Lohff was putting on his parachute and Lilburn, already wearing his, was releasing the waist door. George motioned Edwin to jump, but the radio operator hesitated, and then a burst of flame through the radio room door decided matters. *Liberty Belle* would explode any second, and Edwin dived headfirst through the door. His parachute popped perfectly and he saw the B-17 dive into the overcast; then came the explosion.

Litt, McKee, Stevens and Ungar died. Nate's body was found near Wake's Colne – either he had jumped without a parachute or it did not open.

Liberty Belle exploded in mid-air, showering pieces over a wide area. The bulk of the wreckage fell near Penlan Hall, Wake's Colne, close to the 362nd Fighter Group base of Wormingford. An Ordnance Report mentions two 'high order' detonations, undoubtedly from the eight M43 500 lb bombs she carried. Two unexploded bombs were found buried 250 yards from the main impact point. The remains of McKee, Litt and Stevens lay in the burnt forward fuselage – they died fighting for the liberty their bomber represented.

4: So near – so far

RADAR TECHNOLOGY WAS not a monopoly of the Allies, and German scientists achieved major, independent developments. Daylight bombing by PFF was countered by radar-controlled flak of notorious repute in a war where you might not see your enemy or know the damage done. When a bomber fell, jubilant units of the *Fliegerabwehrkannonen* — 'Flak' for short – could place victory rings on gun barrels. What they could not claim were crippled victims vanishing into the North Sea or crashing on return, and there were many of these.

Flak certainly gave Eighth Air Force units an uncomfortable time on December 13 1943, when over 600 bombers attacked North German targets, most hidden by

George Fabian's crew, 96th BG. Standing, L to R: Jay Epright, Frank Alioto, unknown: Joe Tonko, John Yuhas. Kneeling, L to R: Robert Hughes, Tom Scanlan, George Fabian, unknown.

cloud. Nearly 170 aircraft sustained flak damage. The 96th Bombardment Group from Snetterton Heath sent 54 Fortresses. Flak wounded *Dry Run 4th* near the Frisian Islands and marauding Junkers JU 88s finished her off. Anti-aircraft fire blew *Short Stride* to pieces over the target, but some parachutes were reported. *Dottie J. 2nd* put up a valiant struggle when hit by flak, and it is her story which follows.

Despite shrapnel tearing through her thin aluminium fuselage skin, not one of her ten crew was injured. However, damage to the bomber's vital organs was severe, and both Cyclone engines on the port side were smashed into silence. Unable to hold formation, pilot Lt John Fabian and co-pilot Lt Thomas J. Scanlon feathered both airscrews and fell away. The drag of the six heavy propeller blades and two dead engines on one side slewed the bomber round, making both pilots fight for control. Additional woes were heaped upon them as one of the starboard engines faltered and *Dottie J. 2nd* slid nearer to the merciless North Sea, hidden but menacing beneath dense cloud. The only benefit of such diabolical weather was the scarcity of German fighters, and the crew concentrated on getting home. Staff Sergeant Truman P. Starr transmitted a stream of Mayday signals. The four other S/Sgt gunners, Frank Alioto, Robert P. La Robardiere, James W. Mabry Jr, and Jay E. Epright, busied themselves dismantling anything the Boeing did not need for essential flight and tossing it overboard. Most of the guns, ammunition, flak-jackets, excess radio equipment – all tumbled into the icy sea. Steadily the bomber lost height: a single engine insufficient for survival.

On the flight deck, engineer and top-turret gunner Tech Sgt Joseph M. Tonko worked with the pilots, anxiously trying to restart the least-damaged engine. They were now below cloud, and it seemed to navigator Lt John A. Boyd that his efforts to find the best course home were pointless. Also in the nose, bombardier Lt Robert F. Hughes had thrown out everything he could but, when he peered through the

Plexiglass, the water seemed perilously close and both officers were ready to take ditching stations. Just then, the miracle happened and the failed starboard engine picked up, giving them new life. Pulling as many revolutions as they dared, the pilots of *Dottie J. 2nd* regained some lost altitude and held steady at 300 ft until the sand-flats of Norfolk slipped beneath her wings.

The decision was made to land at Snetterton Heath, but joining the landing circuit provided fresh hazards. Other B-17s, some damaged, were also attempting to land. With her dead left engines *Dottie J. 2nd* had to fly a safer, right-hand landing pattern. Turning into the dead side could create catastrophic instability, causing the unbalanced bomber to roll out of control. Ordering the crew to crash stations, Fabian and Scanlon nursed the bomber earthwards. The safe haven of Snetterton seemed tantalising with individual, trees, hedges and farm buildings growing steadily larger.

Braced against the radio room bulkhead, Bob Hughes watched from the starboard window as their swelling shadow danced swiftly over hedges and raced across fields. Suddenly, terrifyingly, the shadow changed attitude and Bob felt the bomber's nose rear upwards. They were crashing. Bob's last recollection was of pressing his hands behind his head.

Frank Alioto thought they had been forced to turn into the dead engines to avoid another bomber. To him, the aeroplane just 'drove into the ground'. Six of the crew were in the radio room when it hit. One engine was torn off and bounced into the radio room hatch, killing three airmen instantly. Frank was tossed from the wreckage and survived, but other crewmen who were thrown out did not. Boyd, Starr, La Robardiere and Mabry died. Bob Hughes regained consciousness fifteen feet from the fuselage and grateful. *Dottie J. 2nd* did not explode or burn, but the B-17 was a ghastly sight. Somehow, the entire forward section finished upside down facing towards the torn-off tail.

Surprisingly, the survivors quickly returned to combat after hospitalization and a week's rest and recuperation at a coastal resort. During this period both pilots wrote to their comrades' next of kin. To Boyd's parents, Thomas Scanlon said; 'I feel that John's spirit will still be up there on future missions guiding us'. Trying to ease their grief, John Fabian explained how their son had given the survivors an extended lease of life.

This lease risked termination on 4 February, 1944, when the crew were again attempting to reach home after suffering flak damage over Frankfurt. This time, German fighters caught the straggler, but Boyd's spirit may well have flown with them, for all parachuted to safety. The discomfort of captivity would be endured, the lease was extended, and the memory of fine friends would never be forgotten.

Dottie J. 2nd, wrecked near Snetterton Heath. Somehow, the entire forward section finished lying upside down facing towards the torn-off tail. (Russell J. Zorn.)

5: Gremlins

LONG BEFORE MOVIES were made about them, gremlins did great dis-service in the RAF before transferring in unwelcome numbers to the USAAF. Defined as 'mischievous sprites alleged to cause mishaps', they probably concealed human tiredness and inefficiency, but gremlins feasted easily on man's mistakes. Nearly 50 years later, Frederic W. Irwin relates how, when he was a young lieutenant, he and his crew had a close encounter with a persistent species.

'To gain a proper understanding of the events which led to the crash at St Mary's in the Marsh on 30 December, 1943, it is necessary to give some background. We were part of the 333rd Bomb Squadron, 94th Bomb Group (H) stationed at Rougham Airfield, Bury St. Edmunds, Suffolk. Our crew comprised:

Pilot and Aircraft Commander	2nd Lt Donald D. Sharps
Co-Pilot	2nd Lt Thomas P. Sheedy
Navigator	2nd Lt Frederick W. Irwin
Bombardier	2nd Lt Orin D. Gurley
Engineer and Top Turret Gunner	S/Sgt Edward Deutsch
Radio Operator	S/Sgt August J. LoBone
Left Waist Gunner	S/Sgt Kenneth F. Majeski
Right Waist Gunner	S/Sgt William C. Nall
Ball Turret Gunner	S/Sgt John L. Fees
Tail Gunner	S/Sgt Joe Miksic

'On 29 December the 94th group flew a practice mission. These were quite boring for everyone in the crew except the two pilots. The Air-Exec was flying in the lead

Frederic W. Irwin when he was an air cadet in 1943.
(F. W. Irwin.)

aircraft, maintaining a running and caustic commentary over the radio. The truth was that, lacking fighter escort, the best defence the bombers had was a good tight formation. Sad to say, for a great deal of the time it was their only defence, as drop tanks for the P-47 Thunderbolt were only just being introduced, and the P-51 Mustang would not be seen in any significant numbers for another month. Any deep penetration of Germany was therefore fraught. We had already discovered this over Schweinfurt and Regensburg, and would have another grisly reminder early in the next month at Brunswick.

'Returning to the practice mission of the 29th . . . Well into the mission it was noticed that the oil pressure on number three engine was dropping precipitously, whilst simultaneously the head temperature was rising. The engine was cut and the prop feathered. We radioed the lead that we were returning to base with an engine out. Upon return we taxied to our hardstand and turned the aircraft over to the crew chief to investigate and rectify the problem. This ended our aerial activity for that day.

'That evening a battle order came through, and we were alerted to fly. The following morning, after a pre-dawn breakfast and briefing, we learned that the target was a complex of I.G. Farben plants in the Ludwigshafen-Mannheim area, strung along the east bank of the Rhine. We also discovered that we would be flying the ailing aircraft of the previous day.

'The specialized briefings followed the main briefing, and we proceeded to the flight line to draw our parachutes, guns etcetera, and were carried out to the flight line in the standard GI truck. Arriving at the hardstand, our pilots perused the Form 1 of the aircraft. They were not completely convinced that the trouble, whatever it had been the day before, was adequately repaired.

'The Squadron Engineering Officer would stop by each of his squadron aircraft and check with the various crew chiefs for problems before engine start. When he came by our hardstand, the two pilots pounced on him for details concerning our problem of the previous day. He dismissed it in a cavalier fashion and informed us that the problem was so minor that it had been repaired in a trice, the engine started, and run up on the ground. He further stated that it did not even warrant a flight check.

'We had been briefed to assemble after take-off as Group, Wing, and finally Division, and to make good a specified departure time from Beachy Head en route to France and beyond to Germany. We were almost due south over the Thames Estuary, bound for our departure point. I was checking my watch intently and began to wonder why we had not begun to turn . . . suddenly someone in the lead aircraft realized they were about to pass their departure point to the port, and racked the B-17 around the tightest turn possible, doing an almost vertical turn, carrying full fuel, bomb, and ammunition load. In the not-so-successful effort to follow our leader (I can no longer remember what group was leading) there were B-17s all over the English Channel as each successive group, squadron, and element tried vainly to maintain a cohesive formation. Complete squadrons were over and under each other as they were ploughing through the prop wash of the units that had preceded them. Our own aircraft was engaged in the most ridiculous manoeuvre one can imagine for an aircraft of that size and weight. Whilst maintaining constant heading and airspeed, we were sliding laterally through an ever-increasing arc until it felt as if we were easily approaching the 90° mark, which, to put it mildly, was viewed with some consternation, as the chance of going right over on our back seemed a distinct possibility. The aircraft was never built for such stresses, and should it occur we would be in the same position as Icarus on his fabled flight – wingless. However, the fate that sometimes guards foolish young warriors intervened, things simmered down, and we resumed the semblance of formation at a point north of Paris.

'We had penetrated the French coast south of Abbeville but north of Le Havre, I would guess in the area around Fecamp or St Valery-en-Caux, heading south-east and passing north of Paris but headed almost directly for the Mannheim-Ludwigshafen plant. We kept our fingers crossed at the coastline as we did not wish to encounter the 'Abbeville kids', they of yellow-nose fame, although as our escorts kept increasing the Abbeville kids seemed to lose their aggressiveness. We now know, in hindsight, that the original unit had lost most of their experienced flying personnel and were used as a cadre around which the Germans built their formidable interceptor force.

'We proceeded after our little fiasco over the Channel without further incident. Whilst en route I had what were, for me, rather fascinating occurrences. I remember that the callsign for fighter control on VHF was 'tackline', and apparently Eighth Fighter Command had a lone observer very high over the target area who kept up a running commentary to fighter control, which I found quite fascinating. The other phenomenon which intrigued me was listening to the German radar. Every time the beam passed over the aircraft you would hear what sounded like an incomplete musical phrase, and if you listened long enough you felt like shouting: "For Christ's sake play the rest of it".

'We were navigating that day by a combination of dead reckoning and map reading. I can no longer remember what our initial point was, but I do remember that, by my reckoning, we had ten minutes to run to the IP. I reckon we were making good 200 k over this ground, which would put us about 37 n.m. from the IP. Had Hollywood been doing this, at this point the brasses would strike a prolonged ominous chord, backed by a continuous roll from the tympani. However, all I heard on the intercom was: 'There goes that son-of-a-bitch again'. Simultaneously, I was conscious of a change in the sound of the engines, and made inquiries on the intercom. Receiving no answer, I crawled back through the tunnel from my desk in the nose, popped up between the two pilots on the flightdeck, and discovered that number three engine had repeated its performance of the previous day, only this time we lost oil pressure so rapidly that we were unable to feather the prop. The bomb bay was awash in oil and the prop was windmilling. The engine, of course, had been shut down. All of these events transpired in seconds.

' "Give us a course for home," chorused the pilots, starting a diving turn to the left as we departed the formation, losing altitude and picking up speed. After a fast glance at the charts I said: "Steer 90° and let's get out of here". Mulling over my charts again I mentally projected a track that should intersect the Seine River just to the west of Paris, which would, of course, lead us to the sea. We levelled off at about 8,000 ft and pulled as much boost on the remaining three engines as we roughly calculated fuel and distance would permit. The greatest worry was the windmilling prop, and where it would go if and when the shaft broke. If, on the other hand, the bearings went and the shaft froze, we would be in deeper because of drag, but we could only worry about one thing at a time. We flew serenely along – it was a beautiful day with unlimited visibility, and it would have been a lovely ride if we didn't keep throwing apprehensive glances at the windmilling prop.

'We were making good time when out of nowhere appeared five Focke-Wulf FW.290s. This was a more or less experimental model of the basic FW.190 with an in-line, liquid-cooled engine instead of the radial. (Some Allied references to the FW.190D erroneously described it as the FW.290 with a Daimler Benz 603 in-line engine. Frederic may well have remembered these early silhouettes and expected to see the new type in combat, although it did not enter service until mid 1944 and

was powered by an in-line Junkers Jumo 213). Whatever the powerplant, they spelled
trouble as far as we were concerned. At first glance they seemed more curious than
aggressive, flying in echelon parallel to us at the same altitude. Watching, we saw
four of the fighters chandelle upwards and form a line astern on a heading opposite
to ours and their own original course. The four in line flew about two miles astern,
climbing all the while, and then turned and, still in line, came at our tail in the classic fighter curve. This, of course, gave our tail gunner a beautiful no-deflection shot
as soon as they came within range. On they came, and Joe waited until the lead aircraft was in perfect position, when he cut loose with his two .50s. The lead fighter
virtually disintegrated and the other three scattered in various directions, and in a
trice they had disappeared, along with the aircraft that did not join the attack. In
later conversations we assumed it was an instructor with four students, who thought
we would be easy meat. However, he must have obtained his information from a book.

'We could see Paris distantly, so we started to lose altitude rapidly until we were
a little over tree-top level. We also decided at this time to jettison our bombs. The
bombardier went aft to the bomb bay and unloosed the safety wire for the fuses from
the shackle so that they would not arm when we dropped them. Hopefully some
of the Resistance might get the bombs and be able to use the explosive charge for
their own purposes. However, 500 lb of bomb might prove awkward to handle if one
were trying to stay concealed. We salvoed the load, twelve 500-pounders, and if I
hadn't seen it myself I would have found it hard to believe, for when they hit the
ground they bounced as high as our aircraft, which would have been approximately
100 ft.

'While all this was going on, we were more or less following the terrain contours
without the benefit of terrain-following radar, with which present-day military aircraft are equipped. Ahead of us appeared the Seine which would lead us to the sea.
We had completely overlooked the likelihood of any ground defenses at Le Havre,
of which there turned out to be a plethora. Following the river, we saw it widening
out to the estuary and the great port of Le Havre. Almost home thought I, but it
was not to be so easy. There is a long sea wall running up the river at Le Havre,
and the Germans had positioned a great number of 40 mm guns atop the same. Suddenly, we found ourselves in a practically point-blank gun duel with the German light
flak. By this time we would not have been more than ten feet above the surface of
the water, and jinking madly. There was one group of guns that had our range and
deflection right on the nose, and as I don't believe the Germans had proximity fuses,
they were superb gunners. The only thing that saved us was our constant changes
in altitude and heading. At one point we pulled up sharply and four shells burst
in the water, so close that spray flew in the waist gunners' openings. The next moment,
as we dumped the nose, four shells burst where we had been a millisecond earlier.
All this time we maintained a base course toward the sea. But our troubles were
not yet over, for there, practically dead ahead of us, were two German destroyers
at anchor. We came up on them and passed them before either they or we realized
what was going on. Pulling away from land, we climbed to about 20 ft absolute altitude. I told the skipper to get out of sight of land and then turn due north, so that,
with any luck, we should hit the British south coast about Brighton.

'En route we saw only one other aircraft, a Ju 88 headed on the reciprocal of our
course at about 5,000 ft. We held our breath until he disappeared from sight. Shortly
we could see land appearing I said: "There she is, Blighty!" As soon as we sighted
the coast we started to climb to about 2,000 ft. Wishing to find the quickest way
home, we put out a "Darky" call, identifying ourself and requesting a course to steer
for Bury St Edmunds. (Darky was the code name given to a short-range – 7/10 miles

– emergency r/t network. After calling Darky and establishing your identity, the Darky station revealed its whereabouts, which helped the lost aircraft with an approximate position.) Darky gave us a heading to steer, the track of which, when projected, would have taken us over the Thames estuary east of London and right into East Anglia.

'In all the excitement no one had worried much about fuel, but we realized we must have burned an excessive amount at Le Havre because we were operating our remaining three engines at full boost. About the time we started nervously looking at the gauges and doing mental calculations of distance to run . . . a little red light started blinking on the left side of the pilots' instrument panel, soon to be joined

Looking unhappily fish-tailed, Irwin's gremlin-beset B-17 reposes on Romney Marsh. (Russell J. Zorn.)

by three more. Suddenly, there were four red eyes glaring at us. As we debated whether we were almost empty of fuel or completely empty, the engines just stopped. No fuss, no fury. Complete silence.

'Our co-pilot, Tom Sheedy, who had proved he was a cool hand several times, spotted a sizeable cleared area of what seemed to be meadow. He got on the inter-phone and said: "Everyone to their crash-ditching positions," which meant the radio room, seated with back braced against the forward bulkhead. Anything that wasn't lashed down went out. "We're going in wheels up," he said, "and wait for the second jolt before you try getting on your feet." He then did what in flying school was known as a 360° overhead approach. He circled left over the intended touchdown area, bleeding off altitude and also setting up his final run-in. I believe he dropped about 30° of flaps as he completed his turn and was positioned to touch down. The effect was eerie, as we could feel the aircraft settling with no noise, except that created by this huge bulk pushing through the air. Thump – we hit but we were conscious of continued motion which seemed to be slackening with each second, when suddenly there was an horrendous smash and we halted abruptly. Needless to say, there was no pause for idle conversation as we scurried out of the radio room top hatch. Whether I was trampled on or trampled on someone else, I don't know to this day. First the nervous reaction set in when we found ourselves safe on *terra firma*. Everyone was talking at once, lighting cigarettes and indulging in the senseless chatter usual in such situations. We then turned our attention to poor old Van Man-R for Roger, which had brought us on a long, perilous trip back to England. She was a sad sight . . . we had made our first touchdown on the spongy turf of Romney Marsh, heading on a slight upgrade and leaving a trail of flying sod behind us. As we topped the crest of the grade there, dead ahead, was a herd of grazing sheep through which we plowed like a juggernaut and lo! . . . dead ahead was a semi-dry depression, hole, or whatever you care to call it, into which we pitched nose first. It was a good thing that the bombardier and I had gone aft to the radio room, as the complete nose had been shoved under the flightdeck. The fuselage had snapped at the radio hatch, and both wings were spread out on both sides of the depression but had snapped off outboard of the two outer engines.

'Herein lies the story of how B-17 237820, call sign Van Man-R for Roger, ended up in St Mary's in the Marsh, 30 December 1943.'

Quite what the crew said to the Engineering Officer is not on record, but maybe he felt those gremlins had been at it again.

6: Carol Jane

PRE-DAWN, ANOTHER DAY in the war. January – clear and sharply frosted. Five days into the year 1944, and USAAF strength continues growing. So, too, do the losses.

Long before racing cars hurtled around its track, Snetterton Heath was AAF Station 138, alive with squealing brakes punctuating the chorus of Cyclone engines. Twenty-four Flying Fortresses were jostling into position, the stab of exhaust flames contrasting noisily with the starlit serenity overhead. As each hardstand emptied, some mechanics went for chow, while others slapped arms to keep warm and watched the first B-17 get an Aldis green from control. Today, the heavily-frosted

Carol Jane *and her sisters leave majestic contrails en route to a target.* (G. D. Ward.)

A windswept scene on Snetterton Heath as members of the crew pose by the tail-gunner's twin-fifties. (G. D. Ward.)

Bust and Bombs. Carol Jane's *ground crew pose beneath her nose art.* (G. D. Ward.)

2200-yard northeast to southwest runway was being used, and spectators relaxed slightly as the first B-17 became safely airborne, its sound fading over Larling. It was 6.25 a.m., and 16 250 lb bombs were bound for Bordeaux/Merignac airfield. Succeeding bombers were similarly armed.

Ten minutes and several aircraft later, Lt James H. Marshall with co-pilot Lt Richard Kostal positioned the veteran *Carol Jane* for take off. The lamp signalled green and Marshall steadily advanced all four throttles. Kostal scanned manifold pressure gauges, r.p.m. and other instruments while S/Sgt Alfred J. McKay stood calling off airspeed. Beyond 115 m.p.h. Marshall committed *Carol Jane* to flight. At 500 ft she eased into a right turn then abruptly dived into oblivion.

There was a brilliant flash, followed by the roar of bombs and bomber exploding on Shrub Farm, Larling. As the next B-17 powered skywards, flames flashed and danced, consuming nine airmen and *Carol Jane* on the dark earth below. Firecrews and medical personnel raced to the scene as take-offs continued. Rescuers found that *Carol Jane* had hit the ground, skipped nearly 30 ft and exploded on a rough meadow near the farmhouse itself. The blast severely damaged Shrub Farm, injuring several animals but causing no civilian casualties.

Despite the risk from exploding ammunition and the hazard of unexploded bombs scattered nearby, rescuers searched for survivors. Only one of ten airmen survived the impact and blast: S/Sgt Kelsal C. Close lay grievously injured in the wreckage. Group Surgeon Maj Henry Slessinger and the 339th Squadron surgeon, Capt Thomas Hodges, strived to keep Close alive as he was extricated from the debris. Engineering Chief Warrant Officer John W. Cole assisted the surgeons, along with Sgts Thomas Malloy and Clinton Parcels. These men were later awarded the Soldiers Medal for their heroism, but their courage lost its real reward when Staff Sergeant Close died

A scene of devastation on Shrub farm, Larling. Pieces of Carol Jane *litter the landscape.* (Russell J. Zorn.)

in hospital the following day.

Carol Jane was not the 96th Bomb Group's only casualty that day. Four B-17s were lost to German fighters as the 96th established an unhappy record for suffering the highest loss rate of any Eighth Air Force Group during the period until May 1944.

7: Fate

IN WAR, FATE deals cruelly with some and blesses others with miraculous survival. On 24 January 1944 it played a hand in the lives of two 100th Bombardment Group airmen, both originally members of the same crew. Frank Valesh, captain of that crew, became something of a legend for survival with his irreverently named series of bombers *Hang the Expense*, as one mishap followed another. Frank's adventures have been related elsewhere – our story looks at what happened to two of his original crew: Lt Maurice G. Zetlan, bombardier, and, at the other end of a B-17, Sgt Roy Urich, tail gunner.

That Monday they were not destined to board the same aircraft because Zet had requested a transfer from the Valesh crew for personal reasons. Perhaps he felt he would be luckier elsewhere. It was a fateful decision. Roy Urich continued as the Valesh crew's tail gunner. The cards were being cut and were dealt on the mission to Frankfurt, their thirteenth since November. 'It started like any other scary day when your name was on the roster of crews assigned,' John Johnson, navigator on *Hang the Expense III*, remembers. 'The mission began with our being called in the early dark. You'd hear the caller coming, as you seldom slept well when the group was alerted. Breakfast was the usual greasy bacon and "fresh" eggs of dubious vintage.' Some ate heartily, others retched or chewed stolidly, fearing the day ahead.

Zet was crewed with pilot Arch Drummond on a veteran ship named *Skipper*. As one of the group's more experienced pilots, Arch was to be second element leader in the 351st lead squadron. The 'Bloody Hundredth' were putting up twenty aircraft, and the now-familiar noise from its associated airfield vibrated windows and rattled breakfast cups in nearby Thorpe Abbots village. Runway 28 West took the heavily laden bombers over the A140, a surprisingly straight road testifying to the Roman occupation, when chariots clattered north to the fort at Caistor St Edmund. Now the Forts were overhead, and East Anglians had grown accustomed to an even noisier army. From Horham, Rougham, Knettishall and numerous other bases, B-17s and B24s, gorged on fuel and bombs, heaved wearily off runways and began the laborious process of climbing on carefully prescribed routes. Straying from plan tempted fate, as *Skipper's* crew were about to learn.

As the B-17's main wheels drew slowly into the inboard nacelles, the crew kept an alert watch for other bombers. Below, navigation lights glittered like stars from the darkened landscape. Bombers level and above were more difficult to spot, but self-preservation kept wits sharp as *Skipper* continued climbing straight ahead. At 700 ft Arch and his co-pilot, Lt Claude E. Schindler, were horrified to see the lights of another bomber on a course converging from the south. Flashing *Skipper's* powerful landing lights, Arch warned the interloper out of their airspace, but it kept on course, seemingly oblivious of pending disaster. It was almost on them, and *Skipper* had no choice but give way. Too low and dangerously laden for violent evasive action, Arch shoved *Skipper* into a steep, avoiding dive.

Sitting in the nose, Zet was alarmed as the bomber dropped steeply then banked right. Little airspace remained between the two aircraft as Arch averted one disaster and risked another. Shedding precious height, he was now trying to level out. Had the obstruction been lower or situated elsewhere *Skipper* would have terrified her

Pictured at Thorpe Abbots, the 100th BG's B-17F-45-DL Skipper *bore the 351 Squadron fuselage code EP-N. (R. J. Bowden.)*

Striking the roof of this barn on High London Farm, Shelfanger, Skipper *scattered corrugated sheeting like leaves. Fifty years later the repaired but ramshackle barn is still in use.* (Russell J. Zorn.)

Ten clusters of 500 lb M17 bombs and M50 and M50A incendiary bombs continue smouldering as NFS personnel foam the wreck. (Russell J. Zorn.)

crew and a few cows before climbing safely skywards. Instead, at 7.14 a.m. her port wing struck a dilapidated barn on High London Farm, Shelfanger, some 15 miles from Thorpe Abbots. Scything through the roof, the mainplane chopped beams and spilled corrugated sheeting skywards like kicked leaves. Flames streaked from ruptured fuel tanks, and *Skipper* plunged through a grove of trees, lawnmowering a swathe of five-foot-high stumps. Bursting from the copse, the Fortress smacked heavily into a meadow and slithered wildly onwards, shedding pieces. Somewhere in that bedlam Maurice Zetlan was thrown through the Plexiglass nose and broke his neck. As *Skipper's* battered hulk stopped, surviving crewmembers faced cremation when her load of incendiaries ignited.

The mayhem caused by over 25 tons of bomber did not go unnoticed. First on the scene was farmer David Drummond from Old Beyland Hall, Bressingham, who thought it had crashed on his land. Driving quickly to the scene, he found nine shocked airmen sheltering near the inadequate cover of a straw stack, two small fields from the inferno of their bomber. David Drummond volunteered to help, and asked his badly-shaken namesake if anyone had been left on board. Arch returned to the wreck with the farmer and found Zet, but little could be done and the bombardier died of his injuries. By now, *Skipper* was being consumed by her own bombload, and farmer Drummond took the pilot home to report what had happened. As the badly shaken pilot phoned Thorpe Abbotts, take-offs continued and the farmhouse resonated to the sound of bombers passing overhead.

One of these was *Hang the Expense III*, carrying Roy Urich towards his own destiny. As their B-17 flew over its fallen sister, they recognized the substance of the hideous beacon and guessed who it was when *Skipper* failed to rendezvous.

Nineteenth 100th Group ships managed to formate, but the planned assault force

The crew of Hang The Expense. *Standing, L to R: John Mytko, Roy Urich, Louis Black Jr, Paul Carbone, Herschel Broyles and Ernest Jordan. Kneeling, L to R: Frank Valesh, Maurice Zetlan, John Booth and John Johnson.* (John Johnson.)

of over 850 bombers was seriously handicapped by adverse weather conditions. Eighth Air Force commanders grew increasingly concerned for the safety of their force and finally issued a recall signal at 10.20 a.m.

Leading forces, including the 100th, were already over the German border confronting a ten-tenths undercast without PFF guidance. To add to their troubles, a strong tailwind hastened progress into Germany, and the reverse would apply when they turned for home. The weight of unused bombs and strong headwinds would burn fuel reserves needed for emergency diversions to other airfields, so they looked for a target of opportunity. A break in cloud cover revealed the power station at Zukunft, which became the ungrateful recipient of over 100 tons of high explosives.

Crossing into Belgium, the 100th Group lead ship, *Nine Yanks and a Jerk*, gradually descended – customary procedure to ease the strain on engines and airmen. Routes to and from targets were planned to thread between known anti-aircraft concentrations, but the crew were unsure of their position and a thinning cloud base made the task easier for AA gunners below. On *Hang the Expense III* John Johnson compared his position estimates with the landscape being revealed, and realized they would overfly a well-defended airfield near Ostend. Alarmed, he notified Valesh, who called the lead ship Command Pilot. Their concern was met with a curt order: 'Shut up!' Now at only 12,000 ft, with the headwind reducing groundspeed to about 95 kt, the bombers lumbered majestically into danger. Luckily there were no fighters, but flak had a prize target. Johnson remembers: 'I was looking down at the airfield, trying to see if there was any activity, when I actually saw the flak guns go off. I saw four bright flashes and immediately called 'here it comes' on the intercom. Seconds later there was one hell of a jolt and the aircraft nosed violently upward. Frank immediately called on the intercom to standby to bail out.' John pulled the quick release tabs on his cumbersome flak jacket, buckled on his parachute and joined bombardier Lt Frank C. Gregory, trying to keep his balance by the nose hatch.

In the cockpit, Frank Valesh and co-pilot Lt John E. Booth struggled for control. When it was hit there was an awesome blast and *Hang the Expense III* reared like a cactus-saddled stallion. Pushing forward on the control column drew no response, and both rudder pedals sagged uselessly, signifying major damage. Frank was afraid they would stall and spin, but he still had aileron control and found that rolling gently dipped the bomber's nose. Reacting fast, Frank reached forward and snapped switches which gave them their last chance – the autopilot. Named AFCE (Automatic Flight Control Equipment) the autopilot had subsidiary control systems, and Frank gambled on their continued effectiveness. Thank God! The B-17's nose dropped as the autopilot elevator linkage functioned to level off.

Poised in the nose, John Johnson was understandably relieved when they eased back to normal flight and Valesh came through with a comforting comment to 'Stick around'. At that instant the excited voice of waist-gunner Paul J. Carbone blurted over the intercom; 'Roy's gone!' Indeed, not only had Roy Urich gone, but the burst of 88 mm had blown off the entire tail-gunner's compartment. Damage to the rear of *Hang the Expense III* was unbelievable – guns, ammunition boxes, and even Roy's stool had vanished! There was nothing but air, with loose shreds of aluminium flapping in the slipstream. So violent was the blast that it had thrown right-waist gunner Herschel Broyles some seven feet further up the fuselage. Roy Urich was less fortunate – he had simply disappeared. No blood inside, no sign of a parachute. They mercifully hoped that the explosion had killed him instantly, before he fell. Waist gunner Paul Carbone gave a damage report: little remained of their left elevator, the right one was damaged, and Valesh already knew his rudder was useless. Seemingly, Providence alone held the control cables together, but the prospects of parachuting

Damage to the rear of Hang The Expense III *was unbelievable. Tail-gunner Roy Urich had vanished.* (Russell J. Zorn.)

or ditching offered only minutes of life in icy waters, so they elected to try and reach England. Limping homewards, 'Mayday' was repeatedly transmitted while more discarded USAAF equipment joined the Channel's already considerable inventory. Minutes later two P-47s appeared, their pilots gaping at the well-chewed tail of *Hang the Expense III*. Shepherded by the Thunderbolts, the B-17 made landfall near Sheerness and the escort entreatied the crew to jump. A straw poll revealed a reluctance to trust to silk and confidence in the pilot's abilities. Skilfully, Frank had mastered an unorthodox control system of manual ailerons, no rudder, and AFCE elevators. He was intent on reaching the RAF aerodrome at Eastchurch and, easing earthwards, ordered the crew to crash stations. Reassuringly, the undercarriage came down and locked. Gently, gently, Frank took a long, gradual approach: abrupt manoeuvres might prove disastrous.

Hunched anxiously in the radio room, the crew felt the bomber sinking earthwards. Then came the oh-so-beautiful rumble of wheels on grass as *Hang the Expense III* kissed the ground in 'one of the sweetest landings Frank Valesh ever made'. Clambering out on to the spongy turf, the crew were enthusiastically welcomed by RAF airmen full of admiration for their performance. Graciously accepting the praise, the crew surveyed the ruined tail section and wondered if it would have been smarter to jump. While they were unscathed, fate, it seemed, had dealt cruelly with their comrade – but had it?

As his crewmates enjoyed the RAF's whiskied hospitality, Roy Urich was being less amicably entertained by German hosts. Years later Roy related how he, too, had seen the guns fire. He was leaning forward, about to use his microphone switch, when the world roared about him and consciousness vanished. When he came to, his oxygen and radio lines were still connected but virtually everything of substance had gone and the bomber's attitude signified disaster. Luckily, the 100th required tail gunners to wear back-pack parachutes, so Roy simply unhooked his oxygen and intercom lines before rolling out backwards and pulling the ripcord. Floating gently earthwards, he took stock. There was an ominously warm trickle running down his neck, but a cursory check revealed only a slight scalp wound. Looking at the terrain, Roy began preparing his escape as he dropped into a Flemish farmer's field. Hastily bundling his 'chute, he was approached by the farmer but could not understand what the man said. Unable to communicate, Roy felt his exposed position and inactivity were dangerous so he tossed his parachute into a ditch, jumped in after it and scurried away. A few moments later he clambered out on the opposite side into the arms of a German patrol. Roy was posted as Missing in Action, but was freed sixteen months later. Sadly, fate had placed Maurice Zetlan's name on a grimmer set of statistics.

8: Hurry home boys

AS SHE PUSHED her daughter's pram along Eldon Road, Eastbourne, Mrs Ellen Barrow paused, somewhat worried, and listened intently. From seaward throbbed the sound of aero engines beating through the mist, and her first fears were of a German sneak raider. The engines sounded irregular and the aeroplane very low, but Ellen had heard enough Jerries to know that this aircraft was friendly, though it seemed in trouble. Moments later a huge twin-finned four-engined bomber lumbered wearily over the rooftops, its crew undoubtedly grateful to make landfall. The great machine seemed exhausted, and Ellen thought how eerie it looked, looming from the vapour and flying so slowly. As it passed, she clearly saw an airman standing at one of the waist-gun windows and, as a mother, her heart reached for the unknown flier. 'Hurry home, boys,' she whispered to herself.

Ruth-less on her hardstanding at Shipdham. The diminutive flier pushing back his cap is believed to be the ball-turret gunner, James Wilson, a very young man from South Carolina who died on the Sussex Downs, England. (W. Lundy via S. Adams.)

The young airmen Ellen wished safely home came from the 506th Squadron, 44th Bombardment Group, based at Shipdham, Norfolk. The date was 2 February 1944, and Lt James O. Bolin and crew had only been with the group three weeks. They had no regular aircraft, and had borrowed a veteran B-24 named *Ruth-less*, so called because the wife of its original pilot, Frank Sloush, was named Ruth. Arriving with the group in March 1943, *Ruth-less* had flown on some of the war's toughest missions, including the famous low-level raid on Ploesti. Today, the 67th squadron had lent her to these freshmen for a raid on the V-weapon site at Watten. Before she reached the target *Ruth-less* had engine problems, and turned homewards, presumably jettisoning her bombs in the Channel. There was an emergency strip at Friston, near Eastbourne, and the ailing aircraft was struggling for this haven.

Police Constable Neville Adams also saw the bomber, and noticed how the 'engines were cutting in and out'. Schoolboy Derek Wilkinson was enjoying a break period on the grass outside the clubhouse classroom on Willingdon Golf Course. German hit-and-run attacks and forced evacuation of Bourne Senior Schools pupils to safer accommodation inland. Tucked into the foot of Downs encircling the west of Eastbourne, the clubhouse was sheltered by slopes climbing steeply to a height of over 600 ft. The on-coming drone stilled chatter, then Derek saw the Liberator and real-

The chaos of a crash – only the Liberator's fins are recognisable. (Russell J. Zorn.)

ized with horror that, unless it climbed, it was too low to escape the mist-shrouded heights. Passing overhead, the aircraft seemed to sense danger and its nose lifted, seeking height as it vanished into cloud. Another schoolboy, John Palmer, heard its faltering engines and felt sure that two propellers were stationary when it flew over Eastbourne Grammar School. Housewife Mrs Clark clearly witnessed 'that one engine propeller had stopped – it was twisted . . . I was shouting to myself: "It's going to crash, it's going to crash," and I prayed.'

Closer to the unfolding tragedy was Land Army girl Audrey Armstrong. High in the mist over the golf links, Audrey was rounding up sheep with Ned, the golf-club greenkeeper. So dense was the cloud that the town below was lost from view. Their grey-green world of cloud and grass seemed removed from reality, and the peaceful bleating of sheep remote from war. Then, in growing volume, came the thunder of engines straining for power. Terror-stricken sheep fled as the bomber's huge shape surged from the mist shrouding the hill top. For an instant Audrey saw the pilot's face – she knew they were too low to escape the hill's embrace. So, too, did the doomed aviator. Moments later a violent explosion stunned Audrey, and her own peril was emphasized when a smoking engine cartwheeled past, rolling down the hillside. Despite the danger, she and Ned ran towards the wreck, hoping that someone had survived. Another blast boiled from the clouds ahead, and Ned pushed Audrey down as bullets from exploding cartridges zinged past. Picking themselves up when the risk had diminished, they reached the crash.

Ruth-less was unrecognizable, a scar of burning debris smeared violently across the downs. Another 40 ft would have seen them scrape over towards the safety of Friston. Audrey felt sickened by their misfortune, there seemed no chance of life in the smouldering debris. Other hopeful rescuers raced to the scene. Hearing the crash, her prayer unanswered, Mrs Clark grabbed a big kitchen knife and her neighbour, Mrs Tutt, took an axe, both of them intent on cutting free any survivors.

Official response was also swift. When Fire Officer Albert Green reached the site the main fuselage was still ablaze, and sporadic fires dotted the hillside above Butts Lane. Dousing the flames proved difficult, because the only water available was that carried in their appliance. Amidst this chaos lay ten aircrew, and firemen assisted army personnel in the gruesome task of stretchering the dead down the slippery slopes because ambulances were unable to climb the steep track. One flier showed a flicker of life, and an army officer desperately tried heart massage, but to no avail. Two more were still alive when carried down the hillside but died later in the Princess Alice Memorial Hospital. One corpse lay crushed and burnt beneath the weight of a Pratt & Whitney Twin Wasp engine, and others lay badly mutilated amid the gutted remnants of *Ruth-less*.

The ensuing days saw numerous Eastbourne folk visit the site and leave with lasting impressions of the disaster that befell ten young Americans. Schoolboys were particularly fascinated, and one, Donald Payne, remembers hordes of youngsters gathering souvenirs. Some of them even tried to make a machine gun work, but were blessedly unsuccessful. Finally, police purged local schools to recover trophies. In 1987, however, the authors heard of at least one cigarette lighter fashioned from a brass, fifty-calibre casing. Even now pieces of *Ruth-less* still lie on the overgrown hillside, and one local resident, Arthur King, annually places Remembrance Day poppies to signify the townsfolks' feelings for the boys who never went home.

9: The Dymchurch bomber

SITUATED FACING THE Straits of Dover, the coastal village of Dymchurch was on Britain's 'front line' during World War Two. Residents witnessed ferocious air combats during the Battle of Britain and were frequently attacked by hit-and-run raiders in the years that followed. However, it was not enemy action that caused chaos in the community on Saturday, 5 February 1944, but the unintended arrival of an American heavy bomber.

Airborne from Snetterton Heath that day were 23 Fortresses from the 96th Bombardment Group. Poor visibility prevented an attack on their primary target, an airfield at Romilly-sur-Seine, and they diverted to their secondary objective, another airfield at Villacoublay. En route, Lt Donald O. Kasch and crew found they had their own peculiar problems when their number two propeller ran away, forcing them to leave formation and turn homewards. Minutes later their predicament worsened when an identical malfunction occurred with the number four propeller and, to compound it all, the gasoline supply to number three engine failed. After jettisoning his bombload over open countryside, Kasch ordered the dumping of excess equipment as the bomber descended across the Channel. Kasch and co-pilot Lt Leroy E. Allen struggled for control of the violently-shaking bomber. As they lurched into English airspace it was obvious they could not risk landing, so Kasch gave bale-out instructions and set the B-17 on a seaward heading before being the last to leave. All ten airmen landed without serious mishap, confident that their errant bomber would dump itself in the Channel, but its final movements were disastrously unpredictable.

From his Royal Observer Corps post in the Martello Tower at Dymchurch, Arthur

'Kasch's Kids' – the name the crew intended but never painted on their bomber. Standing, L to R: Boles Masy, Joseph Gerba, Norman Wilcox, John Lawsky, Robert Stott and Guy Wert. Kneeling, L to R: Eugene Shadler, Donald Kasch, Robert Allen and Roger Buhla. (G. Ward.)

Derick Woodland was trapped beneath part of the burning bomber. (D Woodland.)

Police War Reservist Frank ran to help his trapped son. (D. Woodland.)

Gearing saw the B-17 limp in over Rye and turn towards Folkestone. Eight parachutes blossomed before it swung back towards the sea, and the last two airmen emerged at about 3,000 ft. Arthur realized that the entire crew had abandoned their machine, and watched with alarm as it descended on Dymchurch .

Lyndhurst Road typified the village's residential nature, though it bore evidence of the war's intrusion. Several bungalows had been damaged by German raiders, while others were taken as billets by the army. Even so, some aspects of life seemed untroubled by the war – until now. As the bomber dipped into its final dive, children played games in the street. Adult residents continued with life's more mundane chores, and it was nearing 2 p.m. as Mrs Dinah Woodland stood ironing in the kitchen. Her son, Derick, was outside with his cousin, Ian Jones, while her husband, Frank, a Police War Reservist, was preparing for work in the wooden police-hut alongside number 23. Also arriving on duty and carefully parking his car was Police Sergeant Good. Across the road his colleague, Sgt H.W. Wood, was just leaving his bungalow, and paused to note winter's grey overcast and the familiar sound of aircraft.

The abandoned bomber swishing unobserved towards him caused no alarm, and the most prominent sound in those last tranquil seconds was the chopping of wood. Private Joe Hampson was preparing firewood in the front garden of number 25, where Somerset Light Infantry soldiers were billeted. The wartime colloquialism 'getting the chop' was about to assume tragic significance for the 21-year-old private. A few doors away, another serviceman, RAF Corporal Jim Avery, was on leave helping his wife and daughter move from his in-laws at number 11 to number 14, *Sunnyside*, just across the road. Most of their furniture was installed, but the couple still had work to do and Jim was about to carry their wireless set over while his wife Ethell, got baby

Christine ready. Reaching the front door, Ethell realized she had forgotten her toddler's hat, and turned to fetch it. This simple action saved their lives.

In the road outside, eight-year-old Derick Woodland was larking happily with his cousin when they saw a large aeroplane coming towards them. Too young to appreciate the danger, Derick was thrilled, anticipating the excitement as it flew perilously low overhead. Suddenly it dipped and came straight at him. At that instant, his father saw what was happening and yelled for the boys to run. It was too late. The bomber snapped a telegraph pole and veered directly into Lyndhurst Road. Derick saw the B-17 smash through a house and started running, but was then whirled skywards, twig-like, in a hurricane of metal and noise. Somersaulting through the air it felt like bouncing off a trampoline and Derick clearly saw bits of wreckage catapulted skywards with him. As he tumbled to earth a section of fuselage fell on him and his world erupted in a nightmare of flames.

Frank Woodland was racing towards the boys when the tornado of wreckage and noise overwhelmed them all. In number 11 a terrified mother, Ethell Avery, clung to baby Christine as a blazing fuel tank flashed past the window and exploded nearby, shaking the house. Outside, Jim Avery dived for cover beside the house but Joe Hampson, caught in the open, died instantly in a lacerating storm of torn metal. Police

'The bomber's starboard wing sliced through the roof of Sergeant Wood's bungalow . . .' The square 'C' denotes the 96th BG. (Russell J. Zorn.)

Sergeant Good leapt for the flimsy protection of the police hut as his car was obliterated by an engine torn from the disintegrating bomber. The other three engines cartwheeled into buildings, and the Avery's new furniture became blazing matchwood. The bomber's starboard wing sliced through the roof of Sgt Wood's bungalow, causing the whole building to sag drunkenly sidewards in clouds of brickdust. *The Moorings*, a bungalow belonging to the Warren family, had suffered air-raid damage, but the USAAF now achieved what the Luftwaffe failed to do and razed it to the ground. Luckily it was unoccupied, but, by coincidence, George Warren had been rewiring another bungalow in Lyndhurst Road and might have been killed had he not taken a lunch break. Instead of returning as an electrician, George was now one of the NFS firemen called to help rescue Derick Woodland, still trapped in the debris.

Unable to move his legs, Derick lay pinned in a personal hell of flames and exploding ammunition. His right arm was fractured, with bones protruding through the skin, but just then, the pain seemed distant and events unreal. Some yards away his father struggled to free himself from fallen masonry and wreckage, knowing his son was somewhere amid the fire and acrid smothering smoke. Despite a broken leg and back injuries, Frank dragged himself clear as a dazed Ian Jones, bleeding and bruised, stumbled from the devastation. Pluckily thinking of his cousin, Ian called out: 'I'm here – Derick's bleeding,' and motioned towards a section of rear fuselage. Conscious only of his son's need, Frank ignored flames and exploding ammunition, scrabbling at the wreckage until he dragged the boy free. Hoisting Derick over one shoulder, Frank scooped Ian under his other arm and stumbled from the scorching heat.

Such are the vagaries of blast that Dinah Woodland heard only what sounded like a squall followed by tearing and ripping sounds as the B-17 gorged its furrow of destruction. Leaving her kitchen, she stook looking aghast at the devastation. Shrouded in smoke and dust, Lyndhurst Road was a shambles of smashed masonry and fencing, with once-neat gardens now a rubble-strewn wasteland. Apart from the destruction of *The Moorings*, both *Sunnyside* and *Claremont* had been torn open and were now ablaze, and the mutilated body of poor Joe Hampson lay amid the firewood

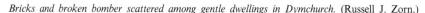

Bricks and broken bomber scattered among gentle dwellings in Dymchurch. (Russell J. Zorn.)

Goodwill letters from Derick's school chums graphically record their impressions. (D. Woodland.)

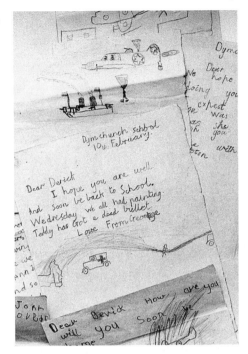

he had been gathering. NFS units from Dymchurch, New Romney and Hythe arrived to support the ARP and save what they could. Rescuers agreed that the loss of life could have been worse, and that Derick Woodland was very lucky to survive. Soon the youngster was in hospital, starting a long process of treatment supported by letters of goodwill from his classmates. Lyndhurst Road eventually returned to its former tranquillity. Nowadays, people passing on their way to the sands might be forgiven for thinking nothing ever happens there, but the Dymchurch bomber is now as much part of village history as its smugglers.

10: Star Dust

IN EARLY 1944 strategic bombers were frequently assigned mysterious tactical targets codenamed as 'no ball' objectives. This was the reference used for 'V' weapon installations, primarily V1 launch sites, which were proliferating in occupied Europe. Allied commanders feared both the physical and political impact of these weapons, especially in view of the pending invasion.

To most airmen such esoteric thinking meant little. They simply knew that 'no ball' missions offered some respite from early morning calls, hours spent assembling, and the long fearful haul into Germany. Instead of unwieldy Combat Wings, Groups might be assigned individual targets or even divide themselves into 'A' and 'B' Groups from the same base, subdivided into squadrons. On 13 February 1944 the 385th launched two 18-ship groups as part of a force attacking V1 sites near Calais. Leading the high squadron of 'B' Group was Lt Leonard C. Swedlund and crew in a B-17 named *Star Dust*. 'Swede' had been an instructor before coming

The crew of Stardust. *Standing, L to R: Charles Day, Grendall Hawes, Ernie Meyer, Charles Thompson, Jack Osborne and Jack Brutenback. Kneeling, L to R: Andrew Minkus, 'Swede' Swedlund, George Guscatt and Fred Berlinger.*

overseas, and his experience, plus their performance on missions since December, led to their early selection as a Lead Crew responsible for squadron bombing accuracy. Because they were comparatively small, 'no ball' targets were bombed from lower altitude, but this also gave German gunners a splendid opportunity to improve their own accuracy, as Swede would soon discover.

Forming at 2,000 ft over Great Ashfield, 'B' Group set course at 1.25 p.m. and climbed steadily South towards the Channel in a somewhat ragged formation. With other units converging on similar targets in the same area, it was important that each unit left England as planned. Finding themselves ahead of schedule, the 385th made a full 360° circle before continuing in a series of gentle 'S' turns, giving time to tighten formation. Departure across the Channel was exactly as planned, one hour after take off.

The near continent was blessed with a faultless blue firmament, and crews dutifully noted their observations: enemy encampments, construction works and airfields were sighted as the B-17s droned towards their objective. Seeing meant being seen and 'Swede' tried to put fear aside as flak fouled the sky ahead. It was not heavy, but it still seemed too personal and far too accurate, dirtying the blue with ugly black smudges. Shrapnel rattled like hail on a tin roof, and Swede knew that shards of metal were cutting into *Star Dust*, but the sturdy bomber seemed impervious to this irritation. In the Plexiglass nose bombardier Fred Berlinger felt very exposed, but concentrated on his bombsight as they began the run-in to target.

Suddenly *Star Dust* convulsed, punched in the belly by three bursts of flak close to starboard. Tail-gunner Grendall Hawes felt the B-17 surge upwards before wallowing back as Swede and co-pilot George H. Guscatt reacted to blast, damage and injuries. Amazingly, there was only one slight wound – waist gunner S/Sgt Charles R. Thompson had been hit in the right leg. Shrapnel had smashed their transmitter, and Swede was unable to hand over lead position in time to release on target. Their number one engine was so badly damaged that Swede shut it down, but the propeller kept unfeathering and drag forced *Star Dust* out of formation. More frightening was the rapidly increasing temperature of number three engine, combined with the stench of aviation fuel leaking from the pierced tanks in the shrapnel-riddled starboard wing.

As *Star Dust* descended across the channel the bombs were jettisoned, followed by an assortment of equipment as the number three Cyclone faded and the B-17 struggled for height. Swede ordered the enlisted men to ditching stations. The crew briefly discussed the merits of baling out or ditching, but survival prospects in February's icy waters seemed worse than the risk of explosion. They voted to go on. *Star Dust* limped towards England, leaking fuel and with ten nervous airmen whose last moments might be in a fireball plummeting seawards. Crossing the coast offered scant relief – they desperately needed an airfield, but the first two seen were incapable of taking a B-17. Altitude and fuel were fast running out when they saw the fighter airfield at RAF Detling, near Maidstone. Unable to make radio contact, *Star Dust* indicated

Star Dust *crunched against a concrete pill-box at RAF Detling.* (Russell J. Zorn.)

her intention by circling gently before beginning the approach.

Gren Hawes braced himself as they settled, but then came that welcome reassuring bump and rumble as wheels settled on grass. It seemed a surprisingly safe homecoming. Relieved, the crew got up from their crash positions just as *Star Dust* lurched abruptly skywards and the crash alarm clattered. Gren tried to reach his crash station again, but it was too late.

In the cockpit, Swede felt happy with the touchdown, cut throttles and trod the brakes. Whether it was flak-damage, wet grass, or a hump in the field Swede never knew, but *Star Dust* suddenly bounced, hit the turf, and skidded left, out of control. Ahead lay a gun emplacement. Unable to stop the aircraft Swede punched the crash alarm and both pilots braced themselves as *Star Dust* slammed into a concrete pill-box.

Those in the radio room were tossed violently into a jumble of bodies, parachutes, ammunition and equipment. Clamouring over the sudden stillness, the alarm stimulated action and six frightened airmen disentangled themselves and leapt for safety from the waist exits. Gren dashed out 50 ft from the wreck before turning to see who else had escaped. *Star Dust*, her nose crunched against the pill-box, had broken her back and, from, the grotesquely tilted cockpit, someone was yelling for help. Smoke streaming from the hot port-inner threatened fire and explosion, but one of the crew needed help. Gren ran back into the wreck.

Surprisingly, both pilots were unhurt, but the engineer, Jackson T. Osborne, had been thrown forward and pinned between the pilot's armoured seats. Also trapped in the cockpit was navigator Lt Rex. M. Cantrell, while poor Fred Berlinger had been thrown through the nose and lay, badly injured, on the roof of the pill-box. By now, Gren had clambered through the bomb bay and squeezed into a position where he could help the pilots prise apart the armour plating and release Jack Osborne. A tangle of wreckage prevented exit aft from the cockpit but, luckily, the left-hand window slid open far enough and Swede helped his crew out before slithering to freedom as RAF personnel doused the smoking engines.

Other than Fred Berlinger, who had a leg amputated, the injuries were remarkably light, and the crew spent that night as guests of the RAF, with a memorable view of a Luftwaffe raid on London. The following day, Col Vandevanter collected them and treated Detling to a superb 'buzz-job' before heading for Great Ashfield. With the exception of Berlinger and Guscatt, the crew completed their missions, while *Star Dust* joined the reprocessing queue. In that inexplicable loyalty that bonded man-to-machine, her crew never forgot the service she gave.

11: Heaven Can Wait

RELENTLESSLY, THROUGH MARCH 1944, the Eighth Air Force continued to hammer targets near and far. On 11 March planners thought that the next day offered weather conditions favourable for a deep penetration, and instructions reached the 2nd Air Division to load their Consolidated B-24 Liberators accordingly. At Shipdham, Norfolk, home of the 44th BG, some 2,700 gal of fuel were pumped into a B-24 named *Heaven Can Wait*. This would be the sixth mission for her crew, commanded by Lt Samuel H. Bowman III.

As the fully-loaded *Heaven Can Wait* thundered down the runway, her crew had the slight satisfaction that weather over Germany had forced a change of target, and

Heaven Can Wait, *B-24 42-7507 of the 68th BS, kept her promise.* (S Adams.)

Young men and a bomber – the crew of Heaven Can Wait. *Standing, L to R: Sam Bowman, James Rossman. William Young and Charles Gordon. Kneeling, L to R: Kenneth Dropek, Tom Curry, Bernard Creedon, Patrick Commisa. Donald Ennis and Michael Tarzia.* (James Rossman.)

their bombs would be making a shorter journey to a V-site neat Siracourt. Conditions over East Anglia were little better, and only three groups, the 44th, 93rd and 392nd, eventually got airborne, struggling through ten-tenths cloud for assembly over a shimmering white cloudscape stretching for unbroken miles over southern England and France. The promised fighter escort failed to appear, but Luftwaffe pilots, facing similar conditions, left 52 Liberators with the sky almost to themselves – apart from the ever-present flak over their unseen target. After the bombs had been released from *Heaven Can Wait*, falling oil pressure on the number two engine suggested that some flak damage had been sustained.

Feathering the recalcitrant motor, Bowman held formation as the B-24s returned to an England, still hidden by cloud. An *en-masse* descent risked collision, so the formation commander ordered the aircraft down individually, cripples going first while the remainder continued to use up surplus fuel and hoped for a break in the clouds. Co-pilot James M. Rossman felt that the loss of an engine qualified for an early departure and wanted to land immediately, but Sam Bowman disagreed. The loss of one engine was not that serious, and he elected to burn off fuel before descending.

For some three hours the Liberators circled southern England, even re-entering the French coast at one stage. Trailing along on three of her Twin Wasps caused higher fuel consumption for *Heaven Can Wait*, and S/Sgt Kenneth S. Dropek grew increasingly concerned as his gauges fell with no lessening of the undercast. Their B-24 may have been leaking fuel and, with reserves becoming critical, Sam Bowman was forced to proceed independently. As they eased into cloud both pilots tensed for any shadow that might indicate high ground, but the Liberator emerged at 600 ft, almost over a grass landing strip. Unknown to them this was RAF Friston and, although it appeared too small for them, Rossman suggested that they orbit until navigator Lt William A. Young had determined their position and could suggest an airfield more

The end of Heaven Can Wait *at RAF Friston.* (Russell J. Zorn.)

suitable or the exact course for Shipdham, fuel permitting. Sam Bowman felt that time and fuel would be wasted just circling, so he headed generally in the direction of Norfolk, asking Young to correct as they proceeded. In poor visibility this task was difficult, and they ended up over the sea with another engine faltering.

Handling a B-24 with two dead engines was tough, but both pilots skilfully swung on to a reciprocal heading, hoping to find the airfield seen earlier. Fighting for every inch of height, they just cleared the cliffs near Beachy Head and were so low that they passed beneath high-tension cables as the last engine spluttered into fuel-starved silence. At that instant Rossman spotted Friston in an almost perfect position for a landing. Banking what was now a most reluctant glider, the pilots had no time to think about landing gear as they lined up. Seconds later the bomber's belly slithered on to turf, with her crew fearful of the disintegration and death that frequently accompanied such escapades in a B-24. Instead, to their amazement, *Heaven Can Wait* slid to a standstill in a faultless example of a wheels-up crash landing.

It was a few moments before they reacted, unable to believe the miracle. Snapping open his seat harness, Rossman released the top hatch and stood with Art Young, heaving crew members out on top of the aircraft. Suddenly they were engulfed in a ball of suffocating smoke, like black cotton-wool. Bernard Creedon, the radio operator, was boosted out with such force that he fell from the fuselage and lost a false front tooth in his second crash-landing of the day. Ross and Young scrambled clear and joined the others, watching while *Heaven Can Wait* created her own funeral pyre.

Years later, her crew cheerfully disagreed over the details of what happened. Dropek insisted that Bowman called for 10° of flap, which ballooned them over the power lines, not underneath as Rossman remembered. On one point, however, they were unanimous: *Heaven Can Wait* had lived up to her name.

12: The milk run

FOR S/SGT FRANK W. 'Bud' Buschmeier, 19 March 1944, started blearily with the noisy arrival of unexpected guests. Returning from operations to find their own airfields weatherbound, RAF and RCAF aircrews landed elsewhere, including Frank's base at Thorpe Abbotts. As they came in chattering to use the ominously large number of spare cots, their 2.30 a.m. arrival was barely appreciated. However, cheerful assertions that such lousy weather would give him a lie-in placated the sleepy American. It seemed that Sunday would be a day of peace, but USAAF commanders deemed otherwise, and Frank returned from church to find that an alert had been called. Two of Frank's four missions had been to Berlin, and vacant barrack beds symbolised losses suffered by the 100th BG. Today's late start precluded long-range targets and briefing officers promised a 'milk run'. Their target, a V-weapon site at Marquise Mimoyecques, meant that only eighteen minutes would be spent over enemy territory.

As Lt John P. Gibbons pre-flighted their B-17 *Miss Irish*, her crew busied themselves checking equipment and ensuring that personal 'lucky' rituals were followed, supporting the shamrock on their bomber's nose. At 3 p.m. *Miss Irish* was airborne with 64 other 3rd Division B-17s, and Bud could be forgiven for wishing that the

John Gibbon's crew during training at Kearny, Nebraska. Standing, L to R: Ira Arnold, John Gibbons, Bob Dykeman, Sterling Blakeman, Max Johnson and Myron Ettus. Kneeling, L to R: Walter Waggoner, Bernard Spragg, Archie Bunting and Frank Buschmeier. (F. W. Buschmeier.)

Twenty-year-old Ed Walker Jr was sucked from a gaping hole in the B-17's fuselage. (The Walker Family via Dr K. Percival-Barker.)

Two views demonstrate the severity of flak damage to Ed Walker's radio compartment on Miss Irish. *(Russell J. Zorn.)*

RAF assurances given twelve hours earlier had been correct. Even a 'milk run' was poor consolation if you got hit. It was six minutes into France when Bud felt the B-17 lurch from the 'whuump' of a shell exploding below the nose. Moments later, another round detonated near the tail. The Fortress flew on unscathed, but Bud was uneasy. Peering anxiously from the left waist window he tensed, every instinct clamouring alarm, as the third shell hurtled towards them at 3,000 ft per second. There was a violent, terrifying roar, and the B-17 was punched more than 100 ft straight up. In those microseconds of bedlam, blast threw Bud backwards as shrapnel and pieces of radio-room equipment peppered his flak suit. Staggering to his feet, he looked in horror to where the torn-off door of the radio compartment exposed a scene forever imprinted on his mind. Ed Walker, the radioman, had been blown on to his work table, and Bud saw that the young flier's legs were torn to shreds. Death must have been instantaneous – or was it? Even if *Miss Irish* was doomed, Bud had to help his comrade. Jerking the quick-release tabs on his flak suit, Bud turned, grabbed his parachute, and started forward, clipping it on as he went. At that moment he was distracted by a piece of the radio-room door whipped off in the slipstream, which was bouncing along the fuselage towards him.

When he looked up, Ed had fallen from the table and, with increasing horror, Bud realised that his crewmate had been sucked through a gaping hole in the fuselage. Ball gunner Bernard L. Spragg watched, sickened and helpless, as Ed's body tumbled past his turret. Falling earthwards, the figure diminished until it was lost from view. Bud, peering into the radio-room, gaped at a hole 'a jeep could be driven through,' and realised the B-17 might break in two at any moment. Bud nervously called Lt Gibbons, and his report drew shocked disbelief from the pilot, who ordered engineer Ira Arnold aft to give an unexaggerated account. Bombs were jettisoned to ease airframe stress, but in his progress over the catwalk Ira discovered more troubles. One of the 500 lb bombs had jammed in its shackles. This was frightening enough, but Ira's face showed real terror when he reached what was left of the radio-room, where loose aluminium shrieked in the slipstream. Handing control to co-pilot Lt Robert Dykeman, John Gibbons came to see for himself, and Bud saw the pilot's eyes widen with disbelief.

To add to the mounting confusion, it was realized that several parachutes had been lost or damaged, and Ira's panic increased when he realized that his was missing. To placate his frightened crewman, John Gibbons courageously unclipped his own parachute and passed it to the engineer before returning to the cockpit.

As armourer, it should have been Bud's task to deal with the hang-up, but access across the radio-room was impossible. Bud tried explaining to Ira how he could trigger the release mechanism manually using a screwdriver, but the badly-shaken engineer failed to comprehend. Finally, the bombardier, Sterling Blakeman, encouraged and helped Ira to release the bomb while *Miss Irish* circled gently over the Channel. Stretching from the narrow catwalk over a wind-screeching abyss demanded courage, and both men were exhausted when the bomb tumbled clear. While they struggled, further misfortune struck when one of the damaged parachutes opened and a stream of silk erupted through the gashed fuselage, threatening to wrench off the weakened tail section. Leaning from the right waist window, Bernie Spragg caught and deflated the writhing nylon by holding it against the fuselage. The structural integrity of their B-17 was now so precarious that Gibbons abandoned thoughts of Thorpe Abbotts and searched for the nearest airfield. Darkness was subduing the landscape when they spotted the 358th Fighter-Group base at Raydon, in Suffolk. The pilot knew that their lives depended on the sweetest of touchdowns: a heavy landing might break the bomber in half with disastrous consequences.

Easing into the final approach, John called for gear down and welcomed the comforting green from the instrument panel as they shed height. Once before, on a Stateside training flight, John had landed a B-17 on one main wheel, and his crew trusted him. However, no one could anticipate what would happen when the bomber's damaged spine suffered landing stresses. Gently, gently, John eased off the final inches and *Miss Irish* came softly in to land. Tyres touched tarmac in gentle puffs of rubber and the bomber settled, her crew scarcely believing they were down as it rolled to a standstill. Within moments the battered B-17 became surrounded by admiring airmen as her crew spilled gratefully on to *terra firma*. Soon, two bottles of Scotch appeared as gifts to celebrate their amazing arrival. Nine weary survivors appreciated something strong to ease the tension of their so-called 'milk-run'.

13: Intruder

FORTUNATELY FOR THE Allies, Hitler was unenthusiastic about Luftwaffe intruder activities over Great Britain. The propaganda benefits of a bomber destroyed over Germany outweighed the effectiveness of attacking aircraft in the vulnerable stages of take-off or landing. Indeed, from October 1941 until August 1943 Allied aerial operations and training activities were unmolested by the *Fernnachtjäger* – long-range night intruders. During the winter of 1943-4 the Luftwaffe reconsidered its policy and reintroduced intruder attacks against Bomber Command. In March 1944 the specialist unit II/KG51 was formed, and began incursions from bases in Holland.

MacGregor's lead crew. Standing, L to R: Howell Thompson, James McLean, Arthur Flint, Paul Morgan and Jesse Graham. Kneeling, L to R: Donald MacGregor, Leslie Hightower, Francis Uihlein, and John Petrowski. (F. P. Uihlein.)

During the night of 11-12 April, ten intruders penetrated British airspace over East Anglia and, at 00.05 a.m, the Flying Fortress flown by Lt Donald M. MacGregor fell victim to a Messerschmitt Me 410 of the 'Edelweiss' unit. That a day bomber was abroad at night resulted from recently introduced Eighth Air Force PFF procedures, when skilled crews were chosen for advanced training on the systems available. Each Division allocated a squadron from one of its groups to create a centre of excellence for training and maintenance. Lead crews would then return to fly PFF ships on missions with their original group.

MacGregor's crew had recently completed this training, initially at Alconbury and then with the 413th Squadron, 96 BG, at Snetterton Heath. Following R & R in London, where they had seen some shows and attended Easter Service at Westminster Abbey, they returned to duty refreshed and eager to demonstrate their new skills leading their own 390 BG from Parham. At 10 p.m. on the 11th they were instructed to take their B-17 GSH, 42-97556, and attend the 390BG's briefing for a planned assault on Leipzig. Somehow, the relaxed confidence felt earlier dissipated in doubt and superstition. Don MacGregor recalls: 'As I look back on the boarding of the plane, there were a number of unusual things that come to mind. The radio operator, Tech Sgt Howell 'Tommy' Thompson, never called me 'Sir' when we were alone, but this night he said 'Good luck, Sir.' I had never put on my parachute harness before, but that night I buckled it up . . .' Lieutenant Francis P. Uihlein, the PFF operator, had similar forebodings: 'That night the crew did everything that was taboo. MacGregor changed his flight hat, Lt Les Hightower (the co-pilot) shaved his moustache, we all made up our bunks, and a black cat walked in front of us on the way to the flight line.'

As they stood by the dark silhouette of their B-17, the atmosphere was subdued even though a crisp starlit night offered no weather problems for the brief flight to Parham. MacGregor recalls: 'The crew checked out the plane to ensure that all guns, ammunition, bombs and flares for the target were properly loaded and that the tanks were filled with 2,800 gal of fuel. As the pilot, I was always last to board, and wished each member of the crew good luck as I progressed to the pilot compartment . . . instrument flight was necessary as England did not exist as far as light from the ground was concerned. Lieutenant Pietrucha gave me the heading for the 390th and, as a back-up, we set up the radio-compass as well.' Twenty-four-year-old Lt George A Pietrucha was their newly-assigned 'dead reckoning' navigator and had flown several, daylight practise missions but, lacking night experience, he became confused and took the bomber off course. Overhearing Pietrucha's corrections, Francis Uihlein became concerned. 'We took off at 0030 hr on a heading of 270°. Our course from Snetterton Heath to Framlingham (Parham) was 135°. Shortly after we were on course, Lt Pietrucha corrected MacGregor to 90° – this didn't make sense, because the wind was from the west. Why correct to the left? I spoke to MacGregor and advised him I'd check the situation. By this time we were approaching the coast. I recognized the area and corrected MacGregor to fly 180°. We intercepted the inlet that pointed to Framlingham. MacGregor acknowledged the landmark and started the approach to the field.'

Donald MacGregor was apprehensive about the landing. In America he had trained on twin-engined Martin B-26 Marauders, and his entire four-engined experience had been in daylight. He had never landed a B-17 at night, let alone one laden with four 500 lb M64 bombs, skymarkers, ten crew and two extra ground personnel, Cpl Nyle Smith and Tech Sgt Emmett L. Matthews. They would not fly the mission, but provided support and security for the PFF equipment while the B-17 was at Parham.

Throughout the flight the crew were vigilant for intruders, but spotting the stealthy approach of such an assailant was difficult and, in truth, it was already too late. Homing like a shark on blood, the sleek shape of an Me 410 remained submerged in shadow as it closed in. Tommy Thompson contacted Parham and the airfield lights came on. Those on duty in the control tower saw the B-17 approaching the 'two red lights plus others clearly showing'. Close to the airfield's number one hangar, Maj Price watched the B-17 fly over, followed by a darkened, twin-engine machine he did not recognise. In the tower, they assumed the stranger was a British night-fighter 'checking-up' on the pathfinder. Even when the interloper suspiciously gunned engines and closed in on the B-17, no alarm was given. Following the Fortress downwind, the intruder banked behind and below, trailing the American on his base-leg approach. MacGregor throttled back, little realizing what a beautiful target his four glowing exhausts made for the enemy pilot.

So low was the intruder that the flash of his cannon illuminated the ground. A vicious burst snapped towards the B-17. Some hit, others scorched past. A momentary correction, then a withering enfilade ripped along a target already ablaze and going down. Donald MacGregor relates: 'My first thought was that the English were shooting at us from the ground, by the look of the tracers coming from six o'clock. I immediately gave full throttle to all four engines, but numbers 3 and 4 were out, and asked for the landing gear to be retracted. Needless to say, any multi-engine plane tends to rotate towards the dead side when power is applied only on one side.' As the bomber rolled over uncontrollably, its pilots faced a desperate situation because part of the right wing had been blown off, destroying their aileron controls. Fighting to regain control, MacGregor pushed full left rudder and then throttled back because power was useless in the bomber's steep, sliding bank into the ground. A crash was inevitable, and Hightower cut the ignition switches to reduce fire risk, but their assailant had not finished. Another burst of cannon fire blew a gaping hole in the left side of the cockpit and tore off the windshield. An icy blast of night air surged in on two pilots striving to lift the right wing before they cartwheeled and exploded. MacGregor remembers those final seconds: 'Many times I have been told that people relive their lives when death approaches. From the attitude of the plane, I knew we would cartwheel and the end was near. My only concern was for the safety of my crew, and I prayed that the Lord would allow me to straighten up the plane and save the lives of the men on board. Just before we hit the ground I remember thinking, 'This is it'.' Perhaps Providence intervened. Just as cartwheeling seemed inevitable, the port wing clipped some tall trees, slewing the bomber into a violent but level crash-landing.

From his waist-gun position, S/Sgt James McLean saw how: 'A direct burst in the waist and tail was followed by a pause, and then a continuous stream of fire into the radio room and towards the nose. Lieutenant John J. Petrowski (bombardier) jumped up and said "What the hell is this?", then he pitched over on his face. He was killed by a direct hit. Tracers continued to rake the ship from the nose to the waist ... Next we hit the ground and bounced once before we stopped. I started to get up, but a machine-gun had fallen on my back and pinned me down. I lifted the gun off and got up, then pulled out a flashlight and shone it around the plane. I saw a body with an ammunition box on the face. As I reached down to pick it up, my foot gave way and I realized I had a broken leg. I crawled out of the ship.'

Francis Uihlein recalls: 'As we approached the base I turned to Lt Pietrucha and suggested we get to a better position, as night landings are usually rather rough. We went forward to the pilot's compartment and seated ourselves between the pilot and co-pilot. A sound like the engineer firing flares was heard, and I turned round to bawl him out for being careless. Suddenly the ship went into an odd position. It seemed to be rocking from one side to another. From then until we hit the ground and stopped, I only remember the sound of shattering glass.'

Of the impact MacGregor remembers nothing: 'My next awareness was being out near the wing with the plane behind me and trying to get up . . . to save my crew.' Equally dazed, Uihlein's returning senses only sharpened agonizing spinal pains, yet his thoughts were also for his comrades. Painfully pulling himself up, he searched for other survivors and found MacGregor near the burning right wing. The pilot was struggling to raise himself on elbows and knees in a courageous but futile effort to reach his crew. MacGregor had compound fractures of his left leg, a broken arm, and multiple lacerations. Grabbing MacGregor's harness, Uihlein dragged him away from the spread of burning fuel. Thinking that co-pilot Hightower might be injured and lying nearby, Uihlein struggled back into the smoke. Just then he heard the tail-gunner, S/Sgt Jesse L. Graham, yelling for help, and turned towards the sound.

After the crash, Graham had disentangled himself from his parachute harness and clambered forwards searching for others who might be trapped in the burning hulk. Near the ball turret he found waist-gunner S/Sgt Arthur L. Flint, his left leg broken and almost buried under a pile of ammunition. Realising that the bombs might detonate at any moment, and ignoring the searing heat, Graham tore at the tangle of flexible-feed with his bare hands and, when Uihlein arrived, they broke enough linkages to release Flint. In graphic understatement, the wounded waist gunner kept repeating: 'We need to get outta here.'

Similarly stimulated by burning fuel, exploding ammunition and thoughts about bombs, McLean dragged himself from the debris, but progress was slow and painful. In the glare he saw Uihlein using MacGregor's parachute harness to haul the pilot away from the flames. Seeing McLean in trouble and still too near the wreck, Uihlein released MacGregor and ran to the wounded gunner. Supported by Uihlein, McLean stood up and, although his weight was excruciating for the navigator, Uihlein helped him hobble from the conflagration consuming their B-17. Unable to manage both his comrades, Uihlein shouted for help, and his cries brought Lt Hightower stumbling through the smoke. The co-pilot had regained consciousness sitting near an orchestra of flames. Convinced the others had perished, he struggled from the wreck and ran about twenty yards before flopping to the ground, shocked and frightened but thankful to be away from the heat. Spurred by his proximity to the bombs, Hightower had started away from the inevitable blast when he heard someone shouting. Disregarding his own safety, he turned back into the asphyxiating smoke.

Between them, Uihlein, Hightower and Graham helped MacGregor, McLean and Flint towards the shelter of a brick wall. The two ground personnel, Smith and Matthews, were less seriously injured and escaped unaided. Pietrucha and Petrowski had been killed in the attack, which left Tommy Thompson and Tech Sgt Paul Morgan, the top-turret gunner, still missing. Again risking his own life, Uihlein disappeared into the smoke, and emerged a short time later behind Paul Morgan, who was clad only in his shorts. Somewhere in the wreckage lay Tommy, and the exhausted navigator would undoubtedly have tried to find him had help not arrived. British soldiers billeted nearby heard the crash and hurried to assist. Realizing that not all of the airmen were accounted for, several soldiers dashed into the wreck while others comforted the injured. Donald MacGregor had passed out from intense pain when Hightower used his pilot's harness and hauled him bodily over the wall for shelter. Coming to, MacGregor warned the soldiers, but was grateful for their courage as they searched amidst flames and exploding ammunition to find the missing flier. Sadly, only the bodies of Pietrucha and Petrowski were found before intense heat and the risk of explosion drove the rescuers back.

Brick-wall rubble and wreckage lay in the foreground, and tile and blast damage can be discerned on property belonging to the Earl of Cranbrook. (Russell J. Zorn.)

Although MacGregor lay on the freezing ground, no-one would risk increasing his injuries by further movement until the medics arrived. Soldiers comforted the wounded as best they could, and MacGregor remembers feeling almost crushed by the weight of sympathetically-placed great-coats. Cigarettes shook in trembling fingers as surviving fliers and rescuers waited for the bombs to explode. Those airmen able to walk were helped to nearby homes, and an exhausted Francis Uihlein, still unaware that his back was actually broken, had gone to Granny Johnson's cottage. Learning that the bombs might explode, the old woman insisted he lie under the kitchen table while she fetched blankets. Uihlein's pain was intense, but he still appreciated Granny's care as she lay alongside, waiting for the bombs to detonate.

Other houses were being evacuated. The B-17 had crashed in the grounds of Glemham House, on the Earl of Cranbrook's estate, demolishing a section of boundary wall but missing dwellings and the church. So far there had been no civilian casualties, but some 32 people were now being urged from their beds to seek safety away from the threatening blast. At 1.10 a.m. there was a dull explosion and a blossoming of fire, probably caused by the skymarkers. Ten minutes later came an enormous double-blast. Two 500 lb bombs detonated, sending a pillar of flame flashing 300 ft into the night sky. Windows shattered and blazing debris showered to earth, but action by the NFS from Framlingham prevented the flames from taking hold and, other than fright, there were no injuries.

As ambulances conveyed survivors to hospital, personnel at Parham searched for anti-personnel bombs thought to have been dropped by the intruder. Several explosions had occurred near the control tower and number one hardstand, but these turned

Viewed from the other direction, wreckage of the intruder victim is scattered across the estate. In 1989 Don MacGregor attended the informal dedication of a memorial made from a propeller blade, which now stands near the crash site. (Russell J. Zorn.)

out to be from cannon-shells which missed MacGregor's B-17. No bombs were found, and loading for the day's mission restarted after some delay.

That night, the intruder's effectiveness was amply demonstrated. In addition to Mac-Gregor's B-17, the RAF lost three aircraft and the USAAF base at Seething was bombed. As we shall see, even worse would follow.

14: Thunder cloud

ALL COMBAT FLIERS face more than human adversaries when taking to the skies. For Americans the European climate became a test of endurance in itself, especially when dealing with the renowned British weather. Sometimes it graciously 'socked in' their bases, giving tired airmen some respite and another day to live. More often, it deceived and double-crossed the met man's predictions and, on occasions such as that on 21 April, 1944, it suppressed even the might of the Eighth Air Force.

To tail-gunner Ken Seibert, it seemed certain that operations would be cancelled. Waiting on the apron with other members of Lt Dixon I. Wands' crew, he saw ugly masses of cumulus clouds drifting eastwards over Deopham Green. Thicken-

The men who rode thunder. Standing, L to R: Leroy George, David Boyd, Warren Hickey, Charles Anderson, Ralph Goschey and Kenneth Seibert. Kneeling, L to R: Dixon Wands, John Gattrell, Charles Lovelwell and William Wroblewski. Only four survived. (Charles Anderson.)

ing layers, topped by massive anvil-headed cumulo-nimbus, portended powerful forces at work in the approaching front. Apprehensively, aircrews of the 452nd BG waited, but no cancellation came through. Soon, bombers were boarded, kit stowed and pre-flight checks proceeded, still without the anticipated signal stopping what seemed like madness.

Wands, piloting *Little Chum*, had 447 hours experience on B-17s but even his skills would soon be disastrously overwhelmed by the elements. Manning the left waist gun was S/Sgt Charles E. Anderson, who was equally convinced of the insanity of operations and wore his chest-pack parachute from the moment of take-off. Swinging into a climbing orbit over the Norfolk countryside, Wands eased *Little Chum* towards the unwelcoming cloud base. Surely there would be a recall? At 4,500 ft wisps of cloud flickered past Anderson's waist hatch. The gloom on board thickened, literally and figuratively, as the B-17 lost visual contact with the world. Looking across, Anderson saw the concern of the other waist-gunner, S/Sgt Ralph Goschey. *Little Chum* had been named after Goschey because of the affection the crew had for the young flier. Anderson tried covering his own anxiety by encouraging the lad, but every lurch or sudden drop only added to his fear. So dense was the cloud that the bomber's wing-tips were scarcely visible, and the sound of straining Cyclones chorused their unhappy ascent.

Convinced of an imminent recall, Anderson and Goschey broke their custom of pulling the bomb arming pins before going on oxygen at 10,000 ft. Above that they required portable bottles to perform this task on the 38 100 lb M30 bombs nestling in the bomb-bay. As the altimeter edged past 14,000 ft all of the crew had taken their positions except for S/Sgt Warren H. Hickey, the ball gunner, who understandably did not relish the prospect of riding a cramped turret in a bomber bouncing on shafts of air surging amidst the cloud. Hanging on for balance, Hickey joined the radio operator, Tech Sgt David W. Boyd, who was listening intently for a recall. There was nothing, but static crackle and the hiss of atmospherics.

The waist gunners found standing increasingly difficult as the bomber's fuselage swayed and dropped in sickening gyrations. On previous occasions they had been thumped by propwash, and this sensation was similar but more constant. Then, like a fairground ride gone mad, the B-17 bucked and began rocking violently as if suffering serious control problems. Abruptly, the intercom went dead. Thoroughly alarmed, the waist gunners headed for the rear-fuselage exit. Nearing the door, Anderson hesitated and turned to see what was happening forwards. His own fears were confirmed when Boyd appeared at the radio-room door, obviously preparing to come aft and bale out. At that instant the Fortress rolled over and went nose down, inverted, falling from control in a nightmare of flying bodies and equipment. Anderson and Goschey were tossed the length of the fuselage like discarded dolls, ending up by the ball turret. Their terror was heightened by the unrelenting scream of engines now powering downwards. As he bowled down the fuselage, Anderson was hit in the face by an empty ammunition box. Apparatus and airmen whirled brutally, and then the terrified gunner found himself glued harshly to the fuselage ribbing, his arms made leaden by centrifugal reaction. He tried desperately to move, but his body failed to respond until, with utmost effort, he grabbed the nearest fuselage stiffener and, rib by rib, crawled upwards towards the waist door. Hauling himself along, he noticed the slackness of cables leading to the rudder and elevators – the B-17 would never recover!

Close to Anderson, Goschey also gripped the circumferential stiffeners, which provided a ladder to life if they could reach the door. Tragically, Dave Boyd had fallen back into the radio-room, and only a miracle would save him now. Reaching the waist door, Anderson tugged the emergency release. Nothing happened – a jammed hatch taunted him! The dying bomber screeched mockingly as the gunner, hanging on with one hand, pounded in futile frustration on the door to freedom and life. Angrily he smashed at the aluminium. Suddenly, it vanished into the grey nothingness – pray God they had time.

As he pulled himself into the doorway, Anderson's mind raced over the jumping procedure. Four weeks earlier, he had calmly taken instructions for just such a predicament. Mind the horizontal stabilizer. Dive low. He did, headfirst into the slipstream, with thoughts rushing one-to-ten as he pulled firmly on the rip-cord. In an instant his parachute snapped open; it was like 'coming out of hell'. The cacophony of terror became a fading scream, and his mind seemed empty of sound as he descended from the overcast. Wincing with inward tears, he watched his bomber's final moments. Spinning crazily, the B-17 had broken in half near the radio room. Part of the nose section was torn off. At each revolution she shed more pieces. How many men were out? Charles saw a figure detach itself from the doomed bomber. A parachute streamed but sickeningly failed to deploy. Stricken with anguish, the gunner prayed and prayed for the 'chute to open, but the unfortunate airmen vanished into the landscape. He learned later that the victim was S/Sgt Leroy H. George, their engineer and top-turret gunner. The B-17 exploded on impact, and Anderson landed heavily on farmland about three-quarters of a mile away. Looking towards the pall of smoke, he shuddered as he realised how close it had come to being his own funeral pyre. As it was, he had been trapped in the B-17

Little Chum crunched into a meadow near the Suffolk village of Hoxne. The damage to the tail section makes it plain that Ken Seibert's chances of survival would have been small if he had ridden it down. (Russell J. Zorn.)

for 13,000 ft of its plunge to oblivion, and was lucky to escape with minor head injuries and cut knees. Another parachute floated from the cloud base. Someone else had survived – Anderson wondered who it was.

Ken Siebert, the tail-gunner, was equally lucky to be alive. Frightened by the B-17 shuddering from side to side, Ken thought seriously about bailing out, but there was no alarm bell. When the bomber flicked on to its back his mind was made up, bell or no bell. Yanking the emergency release on his escape hatch yielded only one hinge-pin. Both were supposed to eject and jettison the exit panel. Instead, it hung stubbornly on the one hinge, resisting Ken's frantic efforts to knock it free. In despair he lay down, gripping the catwalk, hoping that the tail would break away and he might survive the impact. Then, to his horror, he sniffed the early symptoms of an electrical fire and sheer terror drove him to squeeze through the escape hatch, even with its partially released door. Emerging into the overcast, he thought rapidly about the prospects of an unseen parachutist being hit by a plane in cloud. On the other hand, if the cloud extended to ground level, he might delay too long.

He popped his parachute and hurtled into clear air just as it opened. Seconds later a B-24 thundered by beneath him, only 200 ft away. On the ground, a blazing scar marked the end of *Little Chum*. Below, he saw only one other parachute. Still clutching the 'D' ring, he thumped into a freshly-tilled field, close to a man he assumed was the farmer. Gathering his parachute, Ken apologised for disturbing the soil and gratefully accepted directions to an ambulance that somehow seemed to have expected him. His only injury was a wrenched back, but he would appreciate the lift.

As Ken headed for the rescue vehicle he was horrified to hear the sound of another distressed bomber. Seconds later, a tailless B-17 lunged from the clouds and exploded several fields away. Hurrying into the ambulance, Ken hung on as it raced to the new incident. Before it got there, yet another Fortress spun viciously from death-ridden clouds. Sickened and disheartened, Ken felt some relief when they collected Anderson, then Goschey and, finally, the last survivor from *Little Chum*, Lt William H. Wroblewski, the navigator. They found no survivors from the other aircraft.

After the war, the three gunners kept in touch. Sadly, fate caught up with Wroblewski, who died in another flying incident. Fifty years on, Seibert still remembered his intention of riding the tail section down, and the thought 'scared the hell' out of the veteran. He was lucky. At least 22 American airmen died that day, most falling victim to the overpowering strength of cumulo-nimbus, the thunder cloud.

15: Fragments of history

FARMER RAY DEBENHAM picked his way carefully along the line of crops. Pausing, he stooped and then handed me a piece of scorched Perspex. Nearby lay a machine gun bullet. Examining the heat-baked land, I realised it was littered with fragments of Flying Fortress. Picking up a small scrap of aluminium, I pondered on the story that lay behind it, remembering how tail gunner John Cooney had described those last, desperate seconds on board the doomed bomber.

'A Lt Webb was assigned as an instructor pilot with us. Two passengers, ground personnel, went along that day for the ride. There was a total of eleven men aboard, and only two survived. The aircraft was a brand new model G, and I believe had flown only one combat mission the day before. I and other members of the crew had flown our first combat mission to Hamm, Germany, the previous day, 22 April 1944, assigned to various experienced crews. The experience was a harrowing one, especially the sight of a B-17 exploding in mid-air over the target and the reality of several B-17s going down. The flak was thick when we were over the target, but the Groups following us ran into even more – or so it seemed. The target had been the marshalling yards, and I was told that the results of the bombing were good.

'On the evening of 22 April an ME (maximum effort) was called down to our Group. Our crew was alerted, but it was to be another 'Buddy Ride'. We were awakened at 2.30 a.m., and after a quick breakfast and briefing we sat on the revetment waiting to start engines. The weather went bad over the continent and the mission was scrubbed after three hours. The crew that I was assigned to fly with seemed relieved, since I believe the target was to be Berlin.

'The sun was up and warm when we left the field and, since it was Sunday, Harry and I went to church services. Around 11 a.m., our pilot Pete Skinner, stopped by our Nissen hut to tell us that a practice mission was scheduled for that afternoon. Briefing was set for 2.00 p.m. The purpose of the mission was to gain

Left: *Ray Debenham with a tin of B-17 fragments ploughed from his field at Page Corner, Lawshall, Suffolk.* (Ian McLachlan.) *And (right) tail gunner John Cooney described what happened on the doomed bomber.* (John Cooney.)

experience in formation flying, instrument procedures for the pilots, and in our case to gain some co-ordination as a newly arrived crew. We took off around 3.00 p.m. (although it could have been a little earlier) for what was to be a three-hour flight. The take-off proved to be the first of a series of hairy incidents that day. As we hurtled down the runway the aircraft began to veer towards the edge of the tarmac, and the pilot's corrections caused the aircraft to vibrate and make the damnedest noise. When there was only about a third of the runway left the pilot corrected and we got off the ground. We had made our way to the radio room when it became apparent that the weight was needed up forward to assist take-off.

'We climbed to about 6,000 ft and assembled as a group. I believe we were supposed to fly the wing position of the low Squadron, but the pilot was having great difficulty in trying to hold position. In fact there were times when I thought that we were filling in the diamond. The aircraft slipped and veered – almost skidded at times – and the roughness of the ride was beginning to wear on the nerves. It was about two hours into the mission when the bail-out bell sounded. My reaction was to snap my A-2 chute to my harness and to go forward from my tail position

The modern warrior. Posing self-consciously during training in the States. Sam Tudisco models an Eighth Air Force gunner's apparel – including the parachute which, sadly, Sam never used. (John Cooney.)

Another snapshot during training. Standing, L to R: Francis Tanski (replaced on the crew), Sam Tudisco and Benny Leone. Sitting, L to R: John Cooney, Joe Brownlee and Jackie Copeland. Why the smiling Joe Brownlee refused to leave will never be known. (John Cooney.)

to the waist. I didn't want to jump if the bell proved to be a false alarm. Since everything also seemed to be going awry, I thought that someone had inadvertently set off the alarm.

'Arriving in the waist, I smelt the acrid odour of burning hydraulic fluid – the same odour given off by an aircraft's brakes when landing – and saw a curl of yellowish smoke coming from the forward part of the plane. At about the same time I saw the co-pilot, Kenny Storey, come into the waist, searching for a fire extinguisher. He was told that there were none aboard. They had been removed the day before (being high pressure, the extinguishers were removed to preclude bursting within the aircraft if struck by flak), and he turned and went back to the cockpit.

'Benny Leone and Jackie Copeland were attempting without success to release the waist door. Something had jammed it, and the anxiety and frustration had produced a heated argument. Joe Brownlee was leaning against the left waist wall and smiling at the exertions of Benny and Jackie. The passengers were in a panic, one was crying, and the other fellow looked ashen and terrified. I had instructed both men in how to use their parachutes in response to a query as to what to do if it were necessary to jump.

'From the time that the aircraft left the formation and the bell had sounded the pilot was trying to lose altitude as rapidly as possible, and he spiralled the aircraft down. I can only assume that the fire was out of control when we were at 4,000 ft, since the spiral grew tighter and it seemed the plane was flying itself.

'I was inclined to stay in the waist and jump with the rest of the crew, but Benny Leone spotted me and shouted for me to go back to the tail. As I turned to leave, Harry Sonnet went by me clutching his partially spilled chute to his chest pack. He had grabbed it by the rip-cord instead of the canvas carrying handle when he heard the bell. I followed him to the rear hatch. Harry sat reading the instructions on the hatch before pulling the release. The door did not release, but took several sharp blows with our fists before it blew away. Harry perched in the hatchway and asked if I thought he should jump. I started to say something, but before I finished he had jumped. I literally jumped into the hatchway with my hands and feet at the four corners. I glanced back at the waist – the scene was one of chaos and hysteria. Except for Joe Brownlee, who maintained his position leaning against the wall and still had an amused smile, panic reigned. I caught Joe's eye as I was about to jump and motioned for him to come back, but he still smiled and shook his head in the negative.

'The aircraft was in a climbing stall when I finally pushed myself through the hatch. The slipstream grabbed my chute pack and helped pull me out. I don't remember having pulled the ripcord, but the 'chute's opening pulled me up short. I remem-

The scene at Page Corner, Coopers Farm, Lawshall, on 23 April 1944. Doors ajar, a 'meat wagon' waits. (Russell J. Zorn.)

Page Corner, 1989, L to R: Mick Tipple, Paul Thrower and Michael Nice search for fragments of history. (Ian McLachlan.)

ber looking for Harry's 'chute and not seeing it. I could hear the aircraft, but didn't see it until it swung into view almost at a level with me, but then it dropped down, continuing in a spiral. I thought that perhaps the pilot had regained control, and I couldn't see any smoke. I believe that I bailed out at between two or three thousand feet. I hung in my 'chute and watched helplessly as the aircraft went down in a tight spiral. At about 2,000 ft it went into a flat spin, and at 1,000 ft the tail disintegrated. I remember thinking at the time that were I in the tail at the time it was possible that I would have been thrown clear with enough time to deploy my 'chute.

The quarter, dated 1941, is a reminder of liberty under threat, and the watch of timeless courage. (Ian McLachlan.)

'For that instant of time when the aircraft touched the earth in crashing, and the time it took to melt into the landscape, I thought that through some miracle the plane had landed. The roar of the explosion of the impact reached me after I saw the smoke, and I knew that it was all over.

'Harry landed some 100 ft or so from me, after I reached the ground. Though I had jumped after him I was at a lower altitude when I bailed out.'

As I slid the aluminium fragment into my pocket, I felt a tremendous sadness. Here, nearly 50 years ago, nine men perished in the awful ferocity of a bomber burning to ashes. The gentle balm of a peacetime summer made it seem so distant, yet this field on Cooper's Farm, Lawshall, in the County of Suffolk, would always be scarred by war. Crops grew more thinly, and the plough's annual travel turned up some pieces and buried others. With this in mind. I sought Ray's consent to search for pieces worthy of a museum display as a reminder of those unfortunate souls.

Later that year a small team of enthusiasts unearthed several sacks of debris, mostly bullets and corroded ammunition. However, in an area registering the strongest detector signals they located two coins – American quarters – some parachute buckles, and the remains of a USAAF-issue Bulova watch. Time had ceased for its owner, but the courage it represents is timeless.

16: Borrowed time

MRS McCALLUM SAT bolt upright in bed, startling her husband. 'Frank,' she said, 'something's happened to John'. It was 3.00 a.m. in South Carolina. Three thousand miles away, in the sky over England, something had indeed happened to her son.

Sergeant John Frank McCallum Jr was serving with the 730 BS, 452 BG, and had flown nine missions as ball-turret gunner on Lt William C. Gaither's crew. Their tenth, on 19 May 1944, was another long haul to Berlin, a group 'maximum effort' as part of a force comprising nearly 600 Flying Fortresses. Five 1,000 lb bombs had been loaded by Deopham Green's armourers, and the olive-drab B-17 laboured under their weight as Gaither and co-pilot Ernest M. Demaray watched for a space in the formation. They were flying as a 'spare', which meant slotting in should another ship abort. At briefing, both pilots learnt that the 452nd would fly below the 388th and 96th in a three-group Combat Wing. Blackboard bombers did not bounce — formating was handicapped by turbulence and six-tenths alto-cumulus cloud. Sliding three groups, over 100 bombers, into a Combat Wing was more easily briefed than practised. Assembly was now at the hazardous phase of manoeuvring groups into position, where misjudgment could end men's lives faster than wiping the blackboard.

Blessed with youthful exuberance and self-assurance, 'Mac' McCallum relaxed, sitting on the floor of the radio room and resting his back against the bulkhead.

Some of Bill Gaither's crew involved in the mishap over New Buckenham. Standing, L to R: Bob Sell-strom, George Williams, Nick Harlivitch (not flying that day), John McCallum and Joe Lovett. Kneeling, L to R: Bill Gaither and Roger Soth.(J McCallum.)

Mac usually passed the time with Nick Harlivitch, the radio operator. However, Nick was not flying today, and Mac barely knew his replacement, Tech Sgt Ed Sullivan, who had joined them for this mission. Rather than face the discomfort of oxygen, crewmen not needed during assembly would delay clipping on the uncomfortable green rubber masks. Risking anoxia, they sometimes reached 20,000 ft before using the oxygen demand system. The even thrum of four labouring Cyclones and the lack of oxygen induced a pleasant drowsiness, often enhanced by a cigarette. Conversation was tiring, so Mac and Ed said little, even about the radio operator's recent fatherhood. Contrasting incongruously with the apparatus of war, a pair of white baby shoes hung from Ed's radio, and Mac noticed them swinging gently to and fro with the bomber's motion. Ed was resting, head in arms, on the radio table, trying to sleep. His eyes were bloodshot, perhaps from last night's celebration of the baby, maybe from lack of oxygen. The shoes had arrived in yesterday's mail, and each was now a charm against the misfortunes of war.

Glancing upwards through the radio hatch, Mac saw another B-17 about 500 ft overhead. In its Plexiglas nose the navigator and bombardier had spread maps, and Mac wondered whether they were already arguing their position. His own bombardier, Lt Roger M. Soth, sometimes disagreed with the navigator, Lt John W. Stull, and Mac thought the officers overhead were in a similar dispute. Knowing how close their defensive formation had to be, Mac was unperturbed by the other bomber and thought no more about it as Gaither continued climbing. A few seconds later there came a terrible vibration as though the aircraft had hit severe propeller wash. As he stared upwards, Mac's intended warning choked in speechless terror — it was already too late. With screeching malevolence, the port-side propellers on the ship overhead slashed into the fuselage of Mac's B-17 just forward of the tail.

Leaping to his feet, Mac shook Sullivan from his dreams into the nightmare of reality. Their Fortress was already mushing, sinking like a dazed drunk as Mac lunged for his parachute, stowed by the ball turret. Further aft, waist-gunners George Mondell and Joe Lovett had vanished, and so had the entire tail section with eighteen-year-old Sgt Robert Sellstrom.

Mac's own survival seemed remote as gravitational forces reduced every moment to slow motion when the B-17 entered an uncontrollable loop. In seconds it would hammerhead-stall and spin, trapping him on board. From the severed fuselage, loose control cables flailed wildly as electrical wiring, nerve-ends of the dying bomber, twitched showers of sparks noisily around the crumpled stump. Fighting his way to the rear exit, Mac tugged the emergency release. Nothing happened. Damaged and distorted, it was jammed. Frantically, Mac backed off and then, in desperation, threw himself headfirst at the hatch. Striking it, he blacked out, coming to only when the rush of cold air brought him round. How far had he fallen? Still dazed, he heard another noise, the rush of unfurling silk. Thump! His parachute snapped open, snatching off both flying boots as he clicked into full awareness. Had he pulled the ripcord? Mac had no recollection of doing so: perhaps God had answered the prayers of one frightened mother.

Taking stock, Mac searched for other parachutes. The B-17 was in its death throes. For a moment, Mac thought that another parachute had emerged, but then, in fascinated horror, he realised it had been snared by the B-17. One of his crew was being dragged to oblivion. Sergeant George C. Williams, their engineer and, at forty, the eldest man in the crew, had been a sky-diver with one of the pre-war barnstorming circuses. This time George had made the fatal error of opening his parachute too soon. Averting his eyes, Mac became frightened when he realised that debris still tumbling past might tear his own parachute.

Russ Zorn's jeep could proceed no further along Harlan Lane, New Buckenham, which was blocked by a crater and bits of a B-17 which had been blown to pieces. (Russell J. Zorn.)

Higher on his left, Mac saw another survivor and instantly recognised Bob Sell-strom's lanky form. When the collision occurred, Bob had been caught in embar-rassing circumstances. The confines of his tail-gunner's position meant that the call of nature had to be answered by laying on his side and urinating in a tin reserved for the purpose. This procedure was being conducted with grateful relief when he was rudely interrupted by whirling propellers trying to alter his anatomy. Despite kidding from the crew, Bob always wore his parachute. This time the precaution paid off. As his B-17 disintegrated, Bob's egress was effected when some wreckage snagged his rip-cord, his parachute popped, and the startled flier found himself exposed high over the Norfolk countryside. Grinning, he responded to Mac's yell, and each inquired after the other's health as they floated serenely towards the vil-lage of Old Buckenham.

In horrific contrast, Ed Sullivan perished. Perhaps anoxia dulled his responses, but the baby shoe charms failed and the young father was found with his parachute unopened.

Ernest Demaray was also disillusioned with parachutes. Instead of rippling into a life-giving, pure white blossom, his pack opened like a miser's purse and nothing emerged. Falling on his back, he thrust handfuls of silk at the sky. His parachute streamed but remained unspread, and the co-pilot's journey to earth looked like being his last. Then, reluctantly, it gradually opened, but Demaray's troubles were not over. Looking down between his feet, he realised with increasing alarm that his descent took him into the heart of the conflagration that had once been his bomber. Cold terror clutched his chest as he tugged desperately at still twisted risers, trying to slip the 'chute away from the flames and heat. Hot air simmering heaven-wards may have deflected him, and he drifted beyond the fire to land, totally unpre-pared, a short distance from the wreckage. Hitting his parachute release box, he dumped the canopy in disgust and hastily put distance between himself and over-heating bombs. As he ran towards a jeep which had halted nearby, two bombs in the wreck detonated, sending debris showering into the countryside around him. Three bombs which had separated from the crashing bomber had already exploded near New Buckenham, injuring two civilians and damaging some property.

After clambering into the jeep, Ernest was driven back to Deopham Green, en route they came across local inhabitants investigating his bomber's severed tail, which lay on the edge of a cemetery in Folly Road, New Buckenham.

Bob and Mac landed close to one another. Mac anticipated a gentle landing on pasture land, even if it startled the grazing horses. Unfortunately he landed on the lip of a depression, indistinguishable from the meadow until it was too late to avoid. The tumble into the hole smacked the breath from him and painfully contorted his back. Ponies, stampeded by his startling arrival, bolted in all directions, terri-fied by his settling parachute, and Mac himself winded and shaken, was frightened of being trampled. His vision cleared as people from nearby houses came to help. Moments later a jeep bounced across the meadow and Mac was bundled unceremoni-ously in and whisked back to Deopham Green.

Congregating in the squadron office, survivors welcomed each other, exchanged stories, and wondered who was on the other bomber and what happened to them. Knettishall's 388th BG records provide the answer. 'On 19 May, 1944, 2nd Lt Donald G. Salles, piloting B-17G airplane number 42-31242, departed this station on an operational mission. After taking his position in the Group formation as lead ship of the second element, low squadron, the group climbed to 18,000 ft and was on course for the point of departure from the English Coast. At 11.11, while the 388th Group and the 452 Group were manoeuvring for position, the two Groups

Damage to the number one propeller of Lt Donald Salles' B-17 after the emergency landing at RAF Watton. (Russell J. Zorn.)

converged and several aircraft passed close to each other. The aircraft that struck No. 242 came up from underneath, the first impact breaking off the entire tail assembly of the other aircraft, and the second impact came as a result of the first. The right wing of the other aircraft coming up and striking the left wing of No. 242, knocking out the No. 1 engine. The other aircraft fell off in a spin and crashed. Aircraft No. 242 made an emergency landing at another field.'

Sergeant Norman F Powell was ball-turret gunner on Salles' crew. He had armed their bombs and entered his turret shortly before the collision which, strangely, he did not see. It happened so quickly and he was looking elsewhere when the B-17 shuddered from impact with the 452nd aircraft. A voice on the intercom screamed: 'Prepare for bail out!' as the Fortress slewed and twisted downwards. Knees bunched in his cramped sphere, Norman had no room for a parachute and stowed it in the fuselage within easy reach of the turret door. At least, that is where it should have been.

Disconnecting himself from the turret oxygen supply and r/t, Norm opened the door and emerged to a scene of 'complete pandemonium'. The waist door had been jettisoned, the crew were queuing to jump and Norm was in trouble. The B-17's sharp, spiral descent swirled all loose equipment around the fuselage, and his parachute was in this whirlwind! Without oxygen Norm would quickly lose consciousness, and he gesticulated to the crew for help. Someone caught his parachute, and a portable oxygen bottle was thrust into his hands. Without intercom Norm could not follow events, but the crew were yelling: 'Don't jump, don't jump — he's going to bring it down.'

Salles and his co-pilot, 2nd Lt Homer Andrews Jr, had regained control and were making for the nearest airfield, at Watton. The stationary, chipped blades of their

Still borrowing – John F. McCallum proudly holds his Caterpillar Club certificate in May 1990. (J. McCallum.)

number one engine were visible scars, but there might be serious structural damage which could cause wing failure at any moment. Crossing Watton's boundary, Salles created havoc with routine flying activities, scattering resident aircraft like startled starlings. Touching the ground was a tremendous relief but, taking no chances, they speedily evacuated the B-17. Norm had no wish to approach it again but, as armourer, he had to re-pin the bombs. Accompanied by a British officer, he reboarded the damaged B-17. To their amazement the bomber's interior was dressed with a thick, brilliant frost, presumably caused by rapid, atmospheric changes. After scraping ice from the bombs, the load was soon secured and Norm rejoined his crew. Ahead lay the remainder of their 35 missions, including four crash landings caused by enemy action, but the assembly mishap ranked high in recollected mishaps.

At his home in South Carolina, John F. McCallum also reflects on 35 missions. The drama over Norfolk was 'just one of them.' To celebrate their good fortune, surviving crew members named their next B-17 *Borrowed Time*. Forty-six years later, Mac was still borrowing.

17: One misty morning

LYING IN AN individual hell, his clothing scorched, Bill Jeffries roasted, unable to move from the inferno. This horror could not be happening, yet burns and agonising spinal pains stabbed home the reality. Bill's senses were further assaulted by exploding ammunition and the terrifying fury of flames gorging on fuel and oxygen. He tried to move, but only his arms responded. Both legs were paralysed. Cremation would mark his end unless bomb-blast spared his torment. Then instinct spurred a defiance which swelled from the core of his being. He would NOT die like this, he WOULD get out.

Minutes earlier, S/Sgt William Jeffries had as much future as any other flier with 837 Squadron, 487 BG. Heavy mists haunting the beautiful, west Suffolk countryside shrouded the Liberators as they jostled from hardstands, brakes squealing, on the taxiway. Amplified by the morning's chill vapours, Pratt & Whitney engines sung a strident war-song that echoed towards the historic wool-town of Lavenham, some $2\frac{1}{2}$ miles distant. Army Air Force Station 137 had only recently become operational, but residents in Lavenham's timber-framed houses quickly became accustomed to their ancient dwellings being rattled by bombers going to war. On arrival, their American neighbours had been distinctly unimpressed with Lavenham, and felt a good wind might flatten it, let alone a group of B-24s thundering over its roof-tops. Such brashness subsided when they realised that these homes were older than America itself, and incidents like the one about to happen created an affection between fliers and local people.

Neither civilians nor aircrew knew the invasion date, but the gathering pace of activities became apparent when bombers sought to marshall in such poor conditions. Not only was the weather bad, but aircrew faced a demoralising outbreak of diarrhoea, debilitating fliers whose judgement might be impaired by an illness cynically called the 'GI's'. Fog or no fog, GI's or no GI's, the mission of 20 May 1944 remained on. Thirty-six Liberators intended taking their GI inducing bombs to the marshalling yards in Liege.

From the discomfort of his rear turret Bill Jeffries cursed the vapoury blindness. Using de-icing fluid, he had at least removed the frost from his turret windows but, like all fliers, he feared the persistent fog, about which he could do nothing. As the bomber taxied out Bill watched rivulets of water gathering on his turret. Shaken by vibration, some of them merged before running erratically down the Perspex.

Gunning the engines, his pilot, Lt Everett F. Goethe, swung the Liberator on to the runway, boosted for a few yards to straighten the nosewheel and then, hold-

Everett Goethe's crew relax by their Liberator. Standing, L to R: Ernest Carmen, Everett Goethe, Louis Moentenich and James Hartley. Kneeling, L to R: Ned Vukemanevich, James Shackleford, Joe Puglia, Stan Allen, Bill Jeffries and Darrell Dustman. (W. Jeffries.)

ing on the brakes, he increased power. Shaken by the engines' rising howl, Bill felt the increasing tempo of airframe tremors and fought back the worry this aircraft always gave him. Liberator 42-52743 was supposed to behave like any other B-24, but always seemed to lack power when loaded. Investigations by the ground crew had found nothing wrong – were the cockpit checks all right this time? As if in answer to his question, the B-24 shrugged forwards, building speed on rising r.p.m. as Bill's anxiety grew. Tyre-scuffs on the concrete sped by – 80 m.p.h. . . . 90 m.p.h. . . . 100 m.p.h. . . . at 130 m.p.h. the B-24 eased skywards, climbing into a domain of turbid greyness. Take-off at 06.30 a.m. was to be followed by assembly over Lavenham. Bill could not see, but the bomber's attitude and power appeared normal.

As the Liberator climbed steadily his tension eased. Then in an instant renewed fear clutched his heart. They were falling. Momentarily, Bill imagined they were doing a crazy buzz job. Then, screaming over the intercom, came the navigator's last frantic words: 'Pull her up! PULL HER UP!' Bill did not know it, but their number two engine had failed, and the pilots were trying to return to base when they apparently lost control. Goethe tried pulling out. Bill felt the B-24 shake violently and then, it seemed to him, the reaction of such a desperate recovery literally tore it apart. At that instant they smashed into some trees and fuel from lacerated tanks engulfed the aircraft in flames as it disintegrated. Stout branches ripped away

Bill Jeffries was thrown through his turret doors into what was left of the Liberator's rear fuselage, seen here with the 837th BS code, 4F, clearly visible. (Russell J. Zorn.)

Part of the B-24's main undercarriage system – scrap in a Suffolk wood. (Russell J. Zorn.)

the entire tail section, which hit the ground with such force that Bill was thrown through the turret doors into what was left of the rear fuselage.

He WOULD get out. Bill surmised that his back was broken but, if it was, his spirit grew resolute. Stretching his hands down, he pulled on both legs and, somehow, the circuitry reconnected and they responded. Hauling himself upright. Bill staggered from the torn fuselage. Using his hands to help propel each leg, he stumped robotically from the blaze. Shock had set his mind adrift. Ahead, he saw a river offering coolness and tranquility, but this peaceful mirage faded into fog-enveloped trees. Perhaps he was dead. Exhausted, Bill slumped behind a large trunk and took out the small testament given by his sister when he came overseas. Dead or alive, it helped. So, too, did the tree when the first bomb detonated. An ordnance report refers to one 'high-order' explosion and several lower-level blasts, but Bill was only vaguely aware of events. The fact that he really was alive reached Bill Jeffries when he felt strong hands helping him. It was not God. Looking up, he saw the kindly face of a British Bobby.

Police Sergeant Ronald Ernest Saunders had not yet dressed when he heard the crash. Throwing on his uniform, he leapt into his car and sped towards the explosions, soon reaching woodland at Kentwell Hall on the outskirts of Long Melford. Evidently, at least one bomb had already detonated, but he knew there must be

In risking his life to help injured airmen, Police Sergeant Ronald Saunders demonstrated not only personal courage but continuity of a proud tradition. (J. E. Saunders.)

more in the wreckage. Dashing past, he warned a small group of civilians to stay clear. Fog, swirling amidst the trees, set an eery scene as the Police Sergeant penetrated the undergrowth. Ahead, the pulsating glow and angry crackle of flames were punctuated by the viciousness of cartridges exploding. Bullets zipped wildly through the woodland, but Sgt Saunders bravely disregarded the danger.

Near the blazing hulk, he found one flier lying in the leaf-mould, his clothing and body alight. Calling for support, Saunders was joined by Special Constable James Thompson, who lived on the estate in the gamekeeper's cottage. Farmer Robert Colson also responded. When the crash occurred he ran to help, but was blown off his feet by the first bomb. Together, they cut off the man's burning clothes, and as the others carried the badly burnt airman to safety Sgt Saunders continued searching for survivors. Despite the fire's intensity and the constant threat from ammunition and bombs, he skirted close to the wreckage and located another airman who was also carried clear. Further away Saunders came upon a bewildered Bill Jeffries and gently led him from the scene. When other rescue services arrived the policeman took them to the crash, and impressed USAAF doctors with his calmness.

Quiet and self-effacing, Ronald Saunders said little to his family about the events that morning, but his courage and that shown by Robert Colson and James Thompson was recognised. The farmer and Special Constable received commendations from King George VI, while the Home Secretary, the Right Honourable Herbert

Morrison, endorsed a recommendation for Sgt Saunders to receive the British Empire Medal. This was granted by the King, and fostered the admiration, respect and friendship which had developed between the residents of East Anglia and the fliers who daily faced death on their behalf. Many like Bill Jeffries, inherited life-long physical and emotional scars. Six of his crew died. Bill's back was injured but unbroken, and he recovered to fly his 35 missions. Years later the legacy of his injuries grew with the advancing years, and Bill became an ageing warrior who felt that his suffering lacked recognition by the post-war authorities. Sergeant Saunders, BEM, retired from the constabulary in 1959 and worked in civilian occupations until his death 16 years later.

In 1963 the British Ministry of Defence, still concerned about the threat of ordnance on the crash site, refused a licence to recover remains of the bomber for museum display. Ammunition and fragments still reside in the woodland, reminders of events one misty morning a long time ago.

18: Lizzy Belle

FLYING ONE'S FIRST mission created enough fear, but doing it on D-Day sharpened the tension unbearably. Survival meant a proud tale for your grandchildren, but thoughts of any future seemed optimistic to S/Sgt Robert G. Murphy, a flight engineer with Lt Harry G Holland's crew on the B-24 *Lizzy Belle*.

Lizzy Belle displays features far removed from more typical Eighth Air Force lovelies as she provides a background for her crew. Standing, L to R: Paul Schmitt, Thomas McMahon, Wilbur Brotherton (replaced by Joe Viskell that day), Charles Baffo, Harry Holland and Robert Murphy. Kneeling, L to R: Marvin Tobin. Ernest Minter. Thomas Spurgetis and George Gaydos. (Paul Schmitt.)

Spattered with foam, Lizzy Belle *looks very bedraggled after her D-Day adventures.* (Russell J. Zorn.)

More than 2,500 Eighth Air Force bomber sorties were launched that day, but bad weather neutralised much Allied air-power and Bob's crew found themselves returning to the 490th base at Eye with twelve 500 lb bombs still on board.

Their target, a specific road junction, remained concealed by cloud and was too small for PFF techniques. An evening cruise over France with bombs on safety frustrated the crew, even if it was a fighter and flak-free milk-run. Fate, however, had other ways of tormenting the tiro.

As *Lizzy Belle* prepared to land, Bob busied himself with normal but essential checks, especially ensuring that the cockpit lights for undercarriage down and locked were visually confirmed. This task complete, Bob went forward and stood between Holland and the co-pilot, Lt Charles Baffo. This was the first time they had landed so heavily laden, and Bob's rôle in calling off diminishing airspeed enabled the pilots to concentrate on touchdown. Additional problems were a rain-soaked runway and a strong-right-angled crosswind from starboard. Compensating for this, Holland applied rudder and slightly dipped their right wing so the B-24 crabbed in on final approach. The skill was to straighten out at touchdown and avoid any sideways stress on the main gear. Crossing the threshold, *Lizzy Belle* landed as Bob called 120 m.p.h. and Harry cut the throttles. Spuming water from both main wheels, Harry held the nose up until momentum slackened slightly and it dipped naturally. Still travelling at nearly 80 m.p.h. the nosewheel touched and he applied the brakes. Nothing seemed to happen, and *Lizzy Belle* skimmed on relentlessly.

Further aft, radio-operator Paul J. Schmitt saw the wheels stop rotating, but felt no speed reduction – they were aquaplaning in 25 tons of runaway bomber! Even worse, *Lizzy Belle* was drifting left, off the runway. Harry's reaction was to apply port throttle, using power to offset the sidewind, but *Lizzy Belle* slid off the runway before he had a chance. Skidding on to soft, sodden grass proved too much for the undercarriage, and the right gear collapsed, dropping the starboard wing. For an instant the number four propeller chewed turf, then ripped completely away from the engine and spun crazily over the wing. More frightening was the crimson flash and burgeoning flame from number three cowling.

Instinctively, Bob released the top escape hatch and was out before *Lizzy Belle* ceased sliding. The lethal combination of fire, fuel and bombs encouraged a swift departure. As he leapt off the wing Bob's feet were going before he hit the ground, and he scurried away from the smouldering bomber. Similar alacrity demonstrated by the others put them at a safe distance while *Lizzy Belle* was doused with foam.

Matters might have been worse, and 34 missions lay ahead. However, good fortune prevailed and, looking back, Bob Murphy still finds such luck unbelievable. *Lizzy Belle* has long since been smelted down, but her adventure adds a morsel to the banquet of history which happened on D-Day, 6 June 1944.

19: Intruders again

'RED ALERT – RED ALERT – RED ALERT'. Tannoying loudly across Mendelsham air base in Suffolk, the alarm warned of enemy aircraft in the vicinity. Staff Sergeant Floyd R. Merkley, Operations Inspector for the 34 Bombardment Group, picked up his carbine and hastened out of the Air Inspector's Office. Working with him that night were Master Sergeants Stephen G. Arsulich and Peter J. Ward, respectively the engineering and armament inspectors. Technical Sergeant Edward P. Ryan, the Communications Inspector, was also waiting with them for the bombers' return. Uncertain what methods the Germans might employ in response

Staff Sergeant Floyd R. Merkley, Operations Inspector, 34th BG. (F. Merkley.)

The welcome throb of Liberator engines overhead said the boys were back. 34th BG Liberators over Suffolk.

to yesterday's invasion, base personnel had been issued with carbines in case paratroopers attacked the airfield.

The welcome throb of Liberator engines overhead announced the boys' return, but a simultaneous alert was worrying. On 22 April 1944 intruders created havoc with 2nd Air Division B-24's based near Norwich, and destroyed 14 in as many minutes. Studying the late evening sky, Floyd anticipated a 'Crash Alert' at any moment. This meant enemy aircraft overhead with attack imminent, yet such hostility contrasted starkly with the beauty of the evening. Even at 11.25 p.m. British Double Summer Time meant that residual light from the setting sun created a sapphire western sky, darkening to a star-clustered cobalt in the east. If intruders were coming, it would be from this cloak of darkness.

Floyd saw several Liberators silhouetted in the sky, navigation lights on, and then he spotted a smaller, twin-engined aeroplane closing in. Like a mute witnessing murder, he watched, helpless, as the intruder pressed closer, selected a kill, and fired a series of short bursts. Almost immediately the bomber nosed down. Seconds later there was a flash of fire as it hit the ground. Banking towards another target, the Messerschmitt Me 410 fired repeatedly before diving beneath its victim and speeding away so low that Floyd saw the pilot's silhouette beneath his cockpit canopy.

Emitting a burst of smoke, the second B-24 nosed up slightly before dipping into a shallow dive straight towards Mendlesham. Transfixed, Floyd saw a figure fall from the bomber streaming a partially-opened parachute, and then, with mounting panic, he realised that the stricken bomber seemed to be heading straight for him. The expressions of fear on the others confirmed it, and all four started running towards the bomber, hoping it would pass over and crash beyond them. Seconds later its steepening dive convinced them that this was folly – their only chance lay in fleeing from its path. As they scattered Floyd saw the others dive for cover through the open window of a partially-constructed building. It was too distant for him. A rabbit beneath the swooping eagle, he fled towards the Inspector's office and then, instinctively, changed direction as the B-24 thundered only 20 ft overhead and slammed into his own office. In the next instant Floyd was bowled backwards when the bomber's fuel tanks exploded. Scrambling to his feet, he grabbed his carbine and ran 'under a rolling cloud of fire'. The sky was alight with waves of blazing fuel shedding fiery rain-drops as it boiled over head. Some spattered on to Floyd's right shoulder, burning his face as he raced from the deluge of burning fuel splashing behind him. Thankfully he out-ran the flames and was able to beat out his smouldering uniform, suffering only slight burns. Reaching an open area, Floyd crouched, carbine cocked, 'scared but alert' for enemy paratroopers.

Luckily, the only parachutists descending that night were bewildered Americans fortunate to escape from bombers attacked by KG 51. One of these was flown by Lt Wilmer J. Dresher, with S/Sgt Jack Blackham as engineer and top-turret gunner. Their ship, *Sweet Sioux*, an olive-drab B-24, was supposed to have a scantily-clad squaw on its nose, but the draft design still lay under a box containing American soil on top of the radio. *Sweet Sioux* had not been stationary long enough to gain her promised nose-art; this was their eighth mission since 23 May.

Once again, cloud conditions had hindered their attack on tactical targets. Heavy flak had been encountered at Tours, west of Nantes and from the island of Guernsey, but there was no fighter opposition. Even so, the gunners remained vigilant on the journey home and continued manning their positions as the force neared Mendlesham. Swivelling his turret, Jack watched the brilliance of navigation and formation lights increase as the daylight diminished. Darkness was a hostile environment for most Eighth Air Force fliers, and their formation slot made matters worse. *Sweet Sioux* was with the low squadron. Above and staggered to their right, the

An eyewitness drawing of the drama at Mendlesham, copied from a sketch on 34th BG microfilm records.

lead and high squadrons were afforded protection by the low squadron because any intruder risked being seen as it climbed. The aircraft in the low slot were more vulnerable, especially because their ball-turrets had to be retracted for landing and would be unmanned during that critical phase. *Sweet Sioux* relied for her tail protection upon Sgt Robert D. Erisch, the waist guns were operated by Sgt William Reschke, and Sergeant J. Golden manned the nose turret. The sonorous beat of the four Twin Wasp engines was deceptively normal.

When the first assault came, Jack was startled by the rattle of gunfire and saw holes the size of saucers suddenly appearing in the wing. Fragments of aluminium, twirled into the darkness but the B-24 continued, seemingly unscathed. Over the intercom Bill Reschke queried what was happening, and Jack surmised that British anti-aircraft guns had mistaken them for Germans. Spinning his turret again, Jack continued searching just in case it was a Jerry nightfighter. With pain in his voice, Bill came on the intercom again and confessed he had been wounded. Worried, Jack asked how bad it was, and Bill replied: 'Pretty bad – it hurts like hell'. Fearing a renewed attack, Jack suggested that his friend should bale out, and Bill jumped a few moments later.

Reaching down, Jack tugged the release which dropped one side of his swing-type turret seat and lowered himself to the flightdeck. Cupping his hands, he yelled into Dresher's ear: 'What the hell's happening?' Before the pilot replied, Jack was tapped on the shoulder by the radio operator, S/Sgt Carrol E. Forister, who handed over a radio message: 'Bandits in the formation. Turn out your lights and head west'. To emphasize the point, another stream of bullets tore through the fuselage.

Realising that they might need to bale out, Jack shouted that he would open the bomb doors and went through the bulkhead exit into the bomb bay. Slipping on the catwalk, Jack smelt the aroma of hydraulic fluid and knew why he had lost his balance. Spilling from severed pipes, the fluid was sloshing around the bomb bay and might ignite at any moment. Groping for the emergency valve under the flightdeck, Jack held it in the open position and was relieved when the doors cranked apart, allowing the blast of night air to clear the fumes.

Just then someone pushed by and leapt out. Unfortunately, the man's parachute harness caught on a bomb-rack, leaving him dangling half out of the bomb bay. Jack had not yet clipped on his own parachute but, leaning from the catwalk over the open doors, he grasped the figure, unsnagged his harness, and dropped him into the night. From the flightdeck someone yelled that Golden was trapped in the nose turret. Continuing to disregard his own safety, Jack dropped on all fours and crawled through the tunnel which led beneath the flightdeck, past the nosewheel, and emerged in the nose compartment. He had just reached the turret when a third storm of bullets savaged *Sweet Sioux*.

Jack froze as enemy fire pulverised the B-24. It was a life-time's terror, five seconds and countless rounds long. Miraculously, the only harm he suffered, apart from fright, was one bullet tearing through his trouser leg. Others were less fortunate. Lieutenant Antoni H. Grabowski, the navigator, was killed outright. 'Red' Erisch had perished in his rear turret and Willard Johnson, the ball-turret gunner, lay dead in the fuselage. Sliding open the nose-turret doors, Jack found Golden unharmed and hauled him backwards into the aircraft. They had precious little time to escape – the port wing was on fire and their dive was steepening. The last altitude Jack had noted was 6,000 ft during their descent so, whatever height remained, it would not be much.

Crawling back to the flightdeck, Jack grabbed his parachute, noting the absence of both pilots. Clipping the 'chute to his chest harness, he stepped on to a catwalk

The burnt-out remains of Sweet Sioux *at Wetheringsett. A main-wheel undercarriage leg lies in the foreground, with a blackened and broken Twin Wasp engine immediately behind.* (Russell J. Zorn.)

illuminated by burning fuel streaming along the wing's trailing edge into the bomb bay itself. Stooping forwards, Jack rolled into the night sky and tugged his 'D' ring. The pack popped, but no parachute emerged until he encouraged it by throwing out a handful of silk. Pendulating in the night's chill air, Jack saw *Sweet Sioux* trail a fiery banner in a steep, diving turn to port. For a moment he feared that the bomber was coming towards him, but it hit the ground seconds before he did, and erupted in a display of pyrotechnics and exploding cartridges.

Unknown to him, the blazing B-24 destroyed three thatched cottages on Joe's Road, Wetheringsett. None of the occupants was hurt but, at neighbouring Meadow Farm, Will Steward was seriously wounded when a piece of exploding bomber tore off both of his buttocks. Will was rushed to Mendlesham base hospital and then to Ipswich. The thatched farmhouse was saved by his brother, Jack, who clambered up a thatching ladder and doused flames threatening to take hold. A horse belonging to the Steward's was killed when hit by blast which tossed wreckage for several hundred yards from the point of impact.

Thumping heavily into what looked like someone's yard left Jack winded but thankful to find that his only injuries were a sprained right knee and sore back.

At that moment Jack Blackham might have been forgiven for thinking his troubles were over. They certainly were not.

Bundling his parachute, Jack felt the need of a nerve-settling cigarette, but discovered he had no matches. Not knowing his whereabouts, he guessed a direction and set off. Clambering over a fence, he dropped on to a country lane and was able to discern the outline of a small house about 35 yards away. His knock on the door of *Yew Tree Cottage* was answered by Mr and Mrs Sam Rose, an elderly couple who did not seem to understand his explanation. Perplexed, Jack tried again. Still there was no comprehension, but after some gesticulation Jack realised they were both deaf mutes.

Trudging back to his parachute, Jack heard noises, and two figures arose from behind a hedge. For an instant, the moonlight glinted on metal – a gun was pointed towards him. 'I'M A YANK!' Jack's yell brought a cautious lowering of the weapon, but further dialogue drew a warmer response. 'Oh, you're a yank. Well, come on in and have a spot of tea.' Jack explained that the pulsating glow came from his shot-down bomber, and was told that he had descended into Walter Pooley's garden at Blacksmith's Meadow. A few minutes later the tired gunner was relaxing in Walter's lamp-lit living room with that British panacea, tea, and a good American cigarette. While contact was made with Mendlesham, word of his presence spread and the flier found himself the centre of attraction as curious neighbours came to wish him well. Presently, he heard a siren and the sound of a vehicle pulling up sharply. The knot of locals parted and a GI came in; he was gathering downed aviators.

Thanking the Pooleys, Jack tossed his parachute into the Jeep and clambered on board. They had travelled barely a quarter of a mile when an ambulance surged from the darkness, hit the Jeep broadside on and almost rolled it over. Then an

B-24 42-52738, flown by Lt Hazen D. Eastman, crashed into buildings on Mendlesham's Technical Site. (Russell J. Zorn.)

altercation began between the ambulance crew and Jack's GI about who should possess the body – his body! Jack got out and said he felt safer walking than with either of them but, after promises of greater care, he was persuaded into the Jeep again. Setting a more sedate pace, they reached Mendlesham and drove in through the northern access road. Suddenly a shot rang out, and Jack was thrown forward as his driver braked hard, shouting 'Malted milk' into the darkness. This password placated trigger-sensitive sentries, and they were allowed to pass.

As the Jeep trundled across the airfield, Jack sat in stunned silence, appalled by the devastation. The B-24 flown by Lt Hazen D. Eastman had been shot down on the base, killing all but one of its crew. Five buildings, including the Air Inspector's office and Flying Equipment Store on the Technical Site near number one hangar were still ablaze as a result of the crash. The base fire service, supported by the British National Fire Service, fought hard to control the conflagration. Another B-24 had been shot down near Ipswich, killing several crewmen, and a fourth ship had crash-landed at Eye. Only one ship had landed at Mendlesham when the tower warned the group to douse lights and divert west as the Crash Alarm signal was given. This resulted in the 34th being scattered over 13 different American and British airfields.

Trying to account for casualties amid such confusion was difficult, and Jack reported to Maj Joe Eaton, the Operations Officer, who stood out on the airfield surveying the destruction with other officers. Major Eaton asked if Jack was wounded, took his parachute, and told him to get some food if he felt well enough and then report to the hospital. Tired, hungry and anxious about his crew, Jack went to the mess hall, grabbed a bite to eat and set off for the hospital. To his relief Bill Reschke lay among the wounded, bandaged and still in pain but at least well enough to grumble about it. Pleased to find Bill, Jack then caught up with

A jumble of engines and smashed aluminium. Eastman's Liberator is cleared away for scrap. (Russell J. Zorn.)

Carrol Forister in their crew hut and the two airmen related their adventures. Still troubled by his injuries, Jack reported to Doc Morgan, who kept him in hospital for observation during what little remained of that eventful night.

The medics were having a busy time as dead and wounded were retrieved from the base and surrounding countryside. When Floyd Merkley came off the airfield he discovered that his was one of the bodies for which they were searching. From the last thing his buddies had seen of him, they concluded he had been killed. Looking at the limbless, burnt and decapitated torso of one flier, Floyd shuddered as he realised that the corpse could have been his. At least 13 airmen perished that night, when KG 51 again demonstrated the effectiveness of intruder attacks. Strangely, the four Liberators destroyed were the only 34th BG aircraft lost to enemy fighters.

Throughout 1944 Allied air superiority so eroded the German fighter force that some Eighth Air Force Bomber crews never even saw an enemy fighter. Jack Blackham was delighted about that – he had experienced his fair share. After some days recuperating, he resumed flying on 20 June with a new pilot and replacement aircrew. This time his new ship, *Piccadilly Filly*, did get her nose-art. In November 1944 Jack returned home, having completed 30 missions and with the dubious distinction of being shot at by both sides. After the events of 7 June, 1944 USAAF operations were never again seriously troubled by intruders.

Jack Blackham with his new pilot and replacement crew. Rear, L to R: Kenneth Humphreys, ? Bilas, Carrol Forister, Francis Rowley and Robert Bice. Front, L to R: Jack Blackham and ? Woelfel. (J. Blackham.)

20: Mission Mistress

BY JUNE 1944 the 94th Bombardment Group's *Mission Mistress* was already a veteran of 19 bombing raids, but the mission of 25 June would be something special.

Attached to Field Order 289, transmitted to 3rd Bombardment Division Groups on 24 June, was the following 'Intelligence Annex': All Targets.

'The French Maquis (Partisans) in southern France have been rendering far more assistance to the Allied invasion than was ever thought possible. Not only did their activities delay for several days the movement of the 2nd SS Panzer Division from Toulouse to Normandy, but it now appears likely that both the 9th and the 11th Panzer Divisions will be pinned down in southern France in an attempt to restore the situation for the Germans. In addition to the enemy armour, the Maquis are also tying up substantial numbers of German Infantry Troops.

To cope with the situation the Germans have recently launched a large-scale offensive against the Maquis. Several of the areas controlled by the French have already been lost to the enemy, necessitating several changes in plans for this operation. On June 20th this message was received: 'We are being attacked by two divisions coming on all roads . . . we ask urgently for assistance . . .' Unless weapons and ammunition reach them soon, thousands of these allies of ours will be slaughtered and this diversion of German strength will be ended.

Crews will be briefed that all details concerning this mission will be treated with the utmost secrecy. The purpose of the mission, the type of 'bomb load' carried, route, target areas, and all similar details will remain secret after the mission has been completed, and crews will not discuss the mission even on their own bases. Public Relations Officers will be instructed that this mission is to be given no publicity whatsoever.

Note: it is desired that all containers hit within 1,000 yards of Aiming Point . . . Any containers that drop outside of this controlled area very probably will fall into enemy hands.'

Aircrew slept, if they could, completely unaware of what the morrow held in store. One pilot restlessly squirming in the discomfort of his bunk at Rougham was Lt Raymond J. Graves, who takes up the story of his 20th mission:

'Everything is the same. You lie there half asleep, half awake, expecting it to happen but hoping it will not. Then it happens, the crunch of footsteps in the gravel coming closer and closer, the door of the quanset opens, a voice calls out "Graves", and you know you're on for today's mission.

'Rise and shine at 0100 hours and go through the routine of shower, shave, dress. Trying not to think too much of what the day might hold for you. Emerge into the dark English morning and continue the routine. A quick visit to the "Sky Pilot", breakfast of powdered eggs "Continental", and on to briefing.

'The scene in the briefing room this morning is the same as many others, A lot of nervous small talk and private thinking. A call to attention and things start moving. Immediately we are made aware that this one is different. No bombs today. Today we are flying supplies and munitions to the Free French in southern France. A mission of mercy instead of destruction. A "piece of cake", since the invasion was already in progress, having been launched 20 days ago, and part of the mission will be over occupied territory. Our own 94th Bomb Group with 36 aircraft assigned is leading the 4th Combat Wing. We are flying aircraft No. 42-97082, *Mission Mistress*.

'Briefing over, watches synchronized, equipment checked out, and a short Jeep trip to the hard stand, where the mighty B-17 Flying Fortress stands at the ready, thanks to the ground crew having spent much of yesterday and most of the night healing her wounds and coaxing her back to good health after yesterday's mission into Germany.

'Preflight check, equipment check, and all aboard, with no mention of the fact that Bombardier Silva has managed to scrounge a few extra flak suits with which to line the nose of the big bird. The crew, besides myself as pilot, includes Vern Kreger, co-pilot, Al 'Salvo' Silva, bombardier; and Wally Parke, navigator; Ray Cabel, crew chief and top turret gunner; Henry Lence, radio man; Roland Attaway, ball turret; Cliff Eby, and Norm Ratliff, waist gunners; and Manny Grant, tail gunner. Ratliff is flying his first mission.

'Take off at 0345 hours into the first light of dawn over the English countryside. Form into a flight of three, meld into position with three other flights to form a squadron, always in a gradual climb to altitude, and in time join forces with two other squadrons to complete the group. Other groups, having formed in like manner, will follow at intervals to complete the Wing. This operation must rate high on the list of well orchestrated, finely co-ordinated mass efforts of all times, and it happened at the 94th almost daily, weather permitting, for just under two years.

'As we leave the south coast of England and head out over water, the signal is given to test fire the guns, after which we settle down to staying in position in the formation, and keeping all eyes on the sky for "Bandits".

'We cross the French coast at 0723 hours. Beyond Caen, and the relative safety of being over Allied occupied territory, the group is hit by German fighters, one of which seems to have a fascination for our position in the formation. It is hypnotic to watch a plane closing in on you with its guns winking at you as it comes closer and closer. You are drawn to it, but you must ignore it. Stay in formation. Let the gunners worry about that. Suddenly the plane is rocked by the force of an explosion. A shell has detonated between Nos. 1 and 2 engines, putting them both out of commission – a split second difference and the wing could have been gone.

'The procedure is well known. Feather the propellers to reduce drag, increase power on the good engines to compensate for loss of half of your power, stabilise the 'plane, drop out of formation, and call for a crew check to assess damage to crew and 'plane. With the realisation that we are still flyable comes the decision to chuck anything we can spare to reduce weight and help maintain altitude. This is done in record time and includes unbolting the ball turret and dropping it on the French landscape.

'Heading back to the coast, we are treated to a few more bursts of flak in the area of Caen and sustain the only injury of our tour. Tail gunner Manny Grant takes a piece of flak in his own tail section. Only superficial, thank God.

'We have no bombs, but we do have munitions and supplies which we don't want falling into the wrong hands. The decision is made to fly back over water, cut the canisters free from their parachutes and drop them in the channel. This we do, praying that one of our good Allies below will not misinterpret what we are doing and fire on us.

'Freed of this weight, and having decided we would not try the long trip back to base over water, we head back in search of a fighter strip we can land on. Before

Mission Mistress *at rest in a French pasture. Note both port engines feathered, the absence of the ball turret and the jettisoned tail gunner's escape hatch.* (Russell J. Zorn.)

this time, the only option you had was to try to make it home, and, if you couldn't, to ditch and hope that your signals had been picked up.

'After some searching, a landing strip is spotted and we start our landing procedure. All goes well until we are on final approach and committed to a landing, when we observe flares at the far end of the runway; an obvious invitation for us to go away. We learn later that it was an American fighter strip and that they were under attack at the time.

'Pulling up from a landing approach with two dead engines on one side isn't a pilot's favourite manoeuvre. Practice and training pay off, however, and with the help of engineer Cabel, watching the instruments, and much right rudder pressure by co-pilot Kreger, and myself, we are able to gain altitude and once again start our search.

'Our second attempt is successful, and we set down on a Canadian Spitfire strip with no further problems. Not being sure what to expect, bombardier Silva had his .45 at the ready to destroy the Norden bombsight if necessary.

'We are treated royally by the Canadians and, after some paperwork, souvenir bartering, and a delicious meal, we are taken to Bernier-Sur-Mer, where we are processed for our trip back to England. From here we are taken to Graye-Sur-Mer, where we arrive at a British-held beach in time for afternoon tea, a time honoured ritual with our Allies and a welcome bit of sanity amid all that chaos.

'An American LST, No. 288, is standing by with wounded and prisoners and we are taken aboard for the trip back to England. The night is spent aboard ship with departure set for 0800 the following morning. As the engines are revved up for departure a mine is detonated about 200 ft off our port side. One wonders how

Home from their jaunt on the continent, the crew of Mission Mistress *show off their souvenirs. Standing, L to R: Clifford Eby, Vernon Kreger, Ray Graves, C Walder Parke and Roland Attaway. Kneeling, L to R: Henry Lence, Al Silva, Ray Cable, Manuel Grant and Norman Ratliff.* (R. Graves.)

it had been avoided for the 20 days since the invasion. Our trip back is uneventful, and we dock at Southampton that evening and spend another night on board.

'In the morning we are on our own again as a crew, and we start our journey back to base via the British railway system. We board the train at 1220 hours and cause quite a stir in our less-than-regulation attire. At one point, while passing through London, Cabel gets separated from the crew and is picked up by the Military Police for being out of uniform. This is taken care of and we proceed. We arrive back at the base the evening of the 27th at 1800 hours.

'The mood back at the 94th Bomb Group, Rougham, England, that evening is one of much hugging and back slapping, and some tears. It is never mentioned, but we learn later that there was great relief that a long-standing record of no crew losses still stands.

The 'long-standing record' to which Ray refers was a 410 Squadron run of 50 missions without loss. While the Graves crew sorted out a way of returning to England, the rest of the 3rd Bomb Division accomplished their task. But what of poor *Mission Mistress*? Sitting forlornly on a recently-liberated French meadow, she now became an assignment for the 1st Strategic Air Depot (SAD), Flight Test Division at Honington, commanded by Capt Robert Hughes. Their rôle would be to bring her home after temporary repairs by a mobile repair unit. *Mission Mistress* would then be returned to full operational standards at Honington, where 1 SAD had the full range of necessary equipment. Bob Hughes, a combat-experienced pilot, decided to lead the team fetching *Mission Mistress*. Owing to the battlefield situation several days elapsed before a signal arrived saying that their charge should at least fly.

Scheduling his men into a Service Command C-47 which was routed to Normandy and British Strip Number Two, Bob Hughes took two flight crews, because they now had another B-17 to deal with as well. If they could achieve their aims with *Mission Mistress*, Bob would have the distinction of piloting home the first crash-landed bomber repaired on French soil.

Picking its way carefully around London, the C-47 crossed the Channel to make landfall near Cherbourg, where it dropped to low altitude and flew east for the fighter field. This was literally no more than a 'mowed strip in a nice long, green pasture'. Dropping off Bob and his flight crews, the busy transport quickly departed while they went to preflight *Mission Mistress* and her sister.

As Bob recalled: 'We found *Mission Mistress* had been ravished. Her side windows, sliding, bullet resistant and comforting, had been removed. Most likely they were resting on the windshield of some enterprising GI's Jeep. Pre-flight would not help this situation a bit. We knew that it would be a draughty flight back to Honington. We found good power on all engines and all flight controls functioned properly. Gas load was light, which would make for a short take-off roll. Colonel Fargo [the 8th AF Inspector General] and I decided to take *Mission Mistress* with all of her free air-conditioning. In late afternoon, after our other flight crew returned, we briefed for our return trip.

'Colonel Fargo and I boarded *Mission Mistress*. The navigator and engineer flew in the second aircraft because it was more complete and much less draughty. The pasture grass was tall, two to three feet, and made taxiing a bit tentative because you could not see holes or objects lying on the ground. I believe the worst objects we hit were cow paddies, mostly mature ones. We reached the take-off end of the flying strip and found we were pointed directly towards the enemy battle line. The decision was made then and there to make a short field take-off. We ran our engines

Almost home. Mission Mistress *under repair at 1 SAD, Honington, with Capt Gospodor (left) and Bob Hughes.* (Russell J. Zorn.)

up for mag. check. The mags checked OK, and we squared into take-off position. We brought our power up to "quiver" position, released the brakes and forged ahead, and at about 3,000 ft we lifted in the air as the lull of battle was shattered by two B-17s circling low over the beach head to pick up a heading for Cherbourg.

'At Cherbourg we made identification manoeuvres, picked up our heading for the south coast of England and passed over the largest collection of vessels of war that any of us had ever seen. To say the sight was awesome would be like polishing a diamond with chalk – would not scratch the surface. Conversation between pilots in *Mission Mistress* was impossible except by intercom. After several attempts to speak we resigned ourselves to intercom and proceeded to the English coast, where we picked up the flight corridor for safe passage west of London. My flight record indicates that it was a two-hour flight . . . *Mission Mistress* was speedily repaired and returned to combat, where it carried the ball many more times.'

'*Mission Mistress* did, indeed, 'carry the ball', but by November 1944 she was a weary old bomber that some were reluctant to fly. John MacMillian flew her several times and, after the mission of 30 November, his crew reported her as unstable and difficult to control when fully loaded. *Mission Mistress* disappeared to a repair depot for rectification of any ailments and, on return to Rougham, Lt Jack

Major John Rooney and enlisted new crew show their 'respect' for the symbol of a Nazi tyranny draped from the nose of a restored, combat-ready Mission Mistress. *(Russell J. Zorn.)*

Collins felt satisfied after taking her on a mission. MacMillian thought he was crazy, and felt that the airborne geriatric would kill someone. Nevertheless she was assigned to Collins, adding to her mission tally until 6 January 1945.

That morning armourers loaded six, 1,000 lb bombs intended for marshalling yards in what remained of Hitler's tottering Reich. At 8.15 a.m. Collins taxied *Mission Mistress* to the eastern end of Rougham's main runway. Once again she quivered with the power of her four Cyclones. Final checks complete and brakes released, *Mission Mistress* rolled, speed building up. With such a large load in her belly the B-17 needed every inch of runway, every ounce of power. Beyond the point of no return, during the take-off's most critical moments, her number four engine faltered. Unable to climb, she was doomed.

Accustomed to the airfield's morning activity, civilians living nearby went about their own daily chores. In *Mount Farm House* Mrs Hedi Lawson was preparing breakfast, and a succession of bombers kept the crockery rattling as they thundered overhead. Her house lay directly in line with the runway and barely a quarter-mile distant. Hedi heard the bomber in trouble. It was not climbing like the others, and its engines sounded sick.

A little way off, in the garden of the *Cottage*, Moreton Hall, Sally Booth was

Hedi Lawson and her daughters dived for cover into the Morrison shelter. (Mrs H. Lawson.)

about to get her bicycle from the garden shed. She saw the bomber approaching, rapidly losing what little height it had, and felt sure it would hit either Mount Farm or her own home. Perhaps Jack Collins realised this, for, when only 60 yards away, the bomber veered to port and tore into Home Covert. Flames immediately engulfed the wreck, and Sally heard men screaming for help, struggling to escape. Sally started climbing through the garden fence, but her father ran out and ordered her to get off to work. Ammunition was cooking-off, and bullets were sent zinging from the wreck as Joseph Booth ran to help the unfortunate airmen.

Heroically, others also raced to the scene. Philip Lawson had been working in the farmyard with Jim Newman, and both men did what they could. Philip helped one severely burnt flier carry a more badly burnt crew-mate to Mount Farm. Sadly, the man later died in hospital. Fearing for her three daughters, Hedi hurried them downstairs and shoved them into the Morrison shelter, a steel-framed table in the kitchen. Just as the last little head ducked under, a terrific explosion tore through the house. Ceilings collapsed and windows were blasted in. As she dived beneath the table, a dagger of glass pierced Hedi's left arm, and all four were left choking and coughing., covered in debris and dust, and badly shocked. Outside, Philip was unhurt, but a piece of shrapnel hit Jim Newman in the leg.

Four bombs had detonated six minutes after the crash, leaving a crater 30 ft across and 12 ft deep. Sally Booth had not gone far, and was terrified when debris rained around her. Scared also for her family, she hastened home. As she cycled up the drive she saw that the chimney and walls were intact, but there was a hole in the roof and all the doors and windows had been blown in. Her mother, Nellie, still in her nightie, was covered head-to-toe with soot blown from the fireplace. Tears streaked sooty lines down her face – tears for 'the mothers of the boys out there'. Still sobbing, Nellie fetched the teapot but, before they could take a sip, American airmen came and told them to evacuate because more bombs remained in the wreckage. Nellie Booth's response was that she would finish her tea and not leave until she was dressed decently.

The reaction by base personnel was swift. Richard M. Jones, an aircraft controller just coming off duty, leapt into the ambulance driven by medics Cpl James M. Smith and Pte Joe E. Thompson. They were tearing towards *Mission Mistress* when the bombs exploded. The ambulance screeched to a halt and the men dived for cover as bomb and aeroplane fragments clattered off the ambulance. Heavier chunks of wreckage, some on fire, thudded like meteorites into the ground nearby.

As they approached the wreck one survivor, Sgt Cecil H. Schermerhorn, staggered towards them and was given first aid by Joe Thompson. Trying to avoid stray bullets and see below the smoke, Jones and Smith crawled towards the flames, dragging a stretcher. Someone was heard pleading for medics, and they found the seriously wounded tail gunner, Sgt Nicholas A. Urda, and stretchered him to the ambulance. Finding no other survivors, they started for base hospital. En route they found Lt Robert J. Doran, the co-pilot, suffering from concussion and being cared for by a civilian. With Doran was his rescuer, ball-turret gunner Sgt Ony M. Carrico. Jack W. Collins, the pilot with faith in *Mission Mistress*, perished in her, along with four of his crew.

Fifty years later, Mount Farm has gone. New houses and a public house stand near the scene. When they visited the site in 1988 the authors found the overgrown crater blasted by *Mission Mistress*. Beneath the dead leaves were scraps of aluminium – tattered, insignificant remnants, yet also tokens of the courage of the many fliers which *Mission Mistress* brought home and a reminder of those she did not.

The end for Mission Mistress – *twisted fragments in a misty covert.* (Russell J. Zorn.)

21: Little Boy Blue

RELICS OF ANOTHER veteran Fortress still litter fields at Thurston, in rural west Suffolk. During 1986, East Anglian aviation archaeologists Jeff Carless and Clint Cansdale organised a dig for remains of *Little Boy Blue*, a B-17F-125-BO from the 388 Bombardment Group, following local reports of wreckage being pushed back into the crater. Enthusiasts clustered eagerly around the hired mechanical digger as it bit deeply into the recently-harvested field. Initial optimism faded when it became apparent that most of the bomber had been removed in 1944. A few lumps of torn aluminium, a section of tyre, pieces of the ball turret, Perspex, bomb fragments and a machine-gun emerged. The gun now resides in an American aviation museum. Sad reminders of the lives lost were the remains of an airman's flying goggles, a few scraps of an A2 leather jacket, and a boot. Those items contribute to the proud heritage of the Eighth Air Force. In England, they sit alongside artefacts from Roman, Saxon or Viking warriors, who also left their own legacies in Britain. However, items relating to the more recent American warrior can be tied to specific events and dates.

Wednesday, 19 July 1944. The early-morning skies over East Anglia are in tumult again as bombers form to attack an old adversary, the ball-bearing works at Schweinfurt. Waist gunner, S/Sgt Harold V. Hagerty tried to be as comfortable as possible sitting on an ammunition box in the open waist of a B-17. His squadron, the 560th,

Left: A relic is recovered from Little Boy Blue *in 1986. An earth-caked .5-calibre machine gun seen here with Jeff Carless and, nearest camera, Terry Spruce. (Ian McLachlan.) And right: An airman's boot lay buried amid pieces of his bomber. (Ian McLachlan.)*

388th BG ground personnel saw Little Boy Blue *proudly home from 66 missions until a turbo-supercharger failure led to disaster.*

had taken off from Knettishall between 5.10 a.m. and 5.27 a.m. to begin their laborious assembly procedure. The 388 BG launched 39 bombers, comprising both 'A' and 'B' Groups, to fly in the lead and low positions of the 45th 'A' Combat Wing. The formation slot assigned to Hal Hagerty's *Little Boy Blue* was number five position in the high squadron. While Hal shuffled uncomfortably on his box, the two pilots, Lt Walter H. Malaniak and Flt Off Aaron L. Brinkoeter, were fully occupied keeping formation. Malaniak, an experienced pilot with 360 hours and 19 missions to his credit, nursed the old bomber steadily higher and kept a good position in the group. Their troubles started as the formation neared 16,000 ft. *Little Boy Blue* had flown 66 missions, as the weathered and worn, olive-drab paintwork testified.

By now, 'F' model B-17s had all but vanished from front-line inventory. One troublesome feature of the variant was the need for frequent manipulation of the hydraulically-controlled, turbo-supercharger system. Height and temperature changes caused problems with oil viscosity, which unbalanced regulator settings. A supercharger malfunction caused power loss at high altitude, and Brinkoeter now faced problems in giving his pilot enough boost from their number three supercharger. Laden with fuel, ammunition and five 1,000 lb bombs, *Little Boy Blue* fell behind and below the 388 BG formation. Determined to regain their position, Malaniak boosted the remaining engines while his co-pilot tried to rectify the troublesome number three. As the aircraft dropped further behind, the two pilots discussed aborting the mission but decided on another, remedial effort.

Closing on the 388 BG from astern were the B-17s of the 96 BG, intending to start Wing assembly. In number four position of the low squadron, high group, was B-17G 43-37623, flown by Lt Ralph M. Colflesh and crew. Ralph saw the ailing *Little Boy Blue* lose position and drop below his own aircraft. Blending airspeeds, the two formations merged.

Below, the pilots of *Little Boy Blue* were still distracted by the malady afflicting number three supercharger. Just then, Brinkoeter reported that he had cleared the problem and power surged back. Malaniak said: 'OK – let's catch the group'. Intent on regaining his own formation Malaniak pulled up into Colflesh's B-17G. At 7.25 a.m. the two aircraft collided.

Hal Hagerty suddenly found himself without an aeroplane. (H. Hagerty.)

To Hal Hagerty's terrified astonishment, the floorboarding in front of him seemed to explode and a chunk of plywood hit him in the face. In a flash, Hal grabbed his parachute. The next instant there was complete silence. No engines. No tearing metal. No aeroplane! He was falling in a wide-open sky. Firmly gripping his parachute by its canvas handle, Hal calmly clipped it on the harness and pulled the rip-cord. The shock of it opening snapped off his boots and flying helmet, but he was otherwise unscathed.

Some 20 ft along the fuselage from Hal, S/Sgt James H. Bennett, the tail-gunner, was thrown on to his guns and winded by the impact. Turning to check what had happened, he discovered nothing but air where there should have been 60 ft of fuselage. Jim's escape hatch, below the starboard tailplane, was distorted and jammed, so, crawling around the tail wheel well, he came to the opening where the tail had been slashed away. As it fluttered earthwards the severed rear fuselage retained some crude aerodynamic qualities, enabling him to pause at the lip of the opening before slipping off as easily as sliding into a swimming pool. After falling a few feet he rolled over and, with some consternation, realised that the tail was still directly overhead and apparently pursuing him to earth. If he opened his parachute now it might allow the broken tail to catch him up, so he decided to out-fall it, and risk a delayed drop. As he hurtled down, outdistancing the unwelcome rear fuselage, a P-47 appeared and followed his descent. The Thunderbolt pilot must have grown increasingly alarmed as they rapidly approached the Suffolk countryside. Seeing that the B-17s tail no longer threatened him, Jim deployed his parachute.

With horror and fascination, eyewitnesses watched the last moments of *Little Boy Blue*. Jack Meyers, an engineer in the 388th formation, glimpsed a shadow from the corner of his eye. 'I whipped around and, for a millisecond, the two halves of the plane were suspended in front of me and then they fell from sight. Debris streamed out of the front end – papers, ammo belts, bags, oxygen bottles. I believe that the front section left a trail of debris for at least a mile.' After nosing up steeply and breaking in two, the tailless B-17 narrowly missed another Fortress before entering a flat spin. As it revolved with deceptive slowness, centrifugal reaction trapped all but one of those left on board. Seconds before impact, a third parachute was seen. Opening just above the wreck, it vanished in the explosion of five bombs.

Hal Hagerty and Jim Bennett both landed safely. Understandably shaken, Jim was found by a young woman and taken to her home. A few minutes later, after leaving his parachute as a welcome source of material for ladies underwear, Jim was driven to the crash site to help identify the bodies. This inconsideration only deepened his shock and, unable to stomach the ghastly scene, he was eventually taken to hospital.

Jim's distress can be readily comprehended. Six bodies should have been accounted for. A seventh, that of S/Sgt William W. Klemm Jr. was found near Shepherd's Grove. Klemm, the other waist gunner, had either died in the collision or been injured and unable to reach his parachute as the B-17 disintegrated. The bodies of three of the crew, Malaniak, Brinkoeter and radio operator Tech Sgt Ronald Grey, were never recovered. So violent was the explosion that nothing could be found of them. All three names are listed with 5,122 others on the Wall of the Missing at the Cambridge American Military Cemetery and Memorial. The grisly task of collecting human remains was conducted in and around a crater 15 ft deep and 25 ft in diameter, surrounded for several hundred yards with pieces of aircraft. Several properties had been damaged, including the Black Fox public house, which

Pictured in 1987, Hal Hagerty (left) and Jim Bennett reminisce about lost comrades and their own lucky escapes. (H. Hagerty.)

Three of the crew seen here were never found. Standing, L to R: Aaron Brinkoeter, Hal Hagerty, Jim Bennett, John McClusky, Leo Ramos and Walter Malaniak. Kneeling, L to R: William Klemm, Ronald Grey, Norris Thomas and Amos Force. (H. Hagerty.)

Disconsolate onlookers and service personnel ponder pieces of B-17 and lumps of soil discarded by blast. In the centre foreground, at the airman's feet, is a section of armour plating. A solitary engine lies in the middle distance. (Russell J. Zorn.)

was about 100 yards away. The pub and other dwellings suffered collapsed ceilings and broken windows, but there were no serious civilian casualties.

For that day at least, fortune smiled on the Colflesh crew. Immediately after the collision their pilot rang the bale-out alarm and three, the navigator, bombardier, and engineer, parachuted safely.

The remaining seven suffered a bumpy, frightening descent until Colflesh and his co-pilot, Elmer H. Wenzel, regained control and rescinded the bale-out order. *Little Boy Blue* had badly chewed the underside of their B-17, damaging the ball-turret; the flaps; the number one engine nacelle; the number two engine, propeller and supercharger; the number three supercharger, and numerous wing panels. The number two engine vibrated so badly that Colflesh feathered it, and Snetterton Heath control ordered that their bombs be dumped in the North Sea.

Rattling and shaking their way on three engines, they flew 40 miles seaward to avoid friendly shipping lanes and dumped the bombs. A safe landing at Snetterton was then accomplished. Ten days later, Colflesh and seven of the men who survived this incident perished on a mission to Leuna.

22: 'Do you Yanks always fly in this condition?'

GERALD HOLMES NEVER forgot the comment made by a British doctor on 27 July 1944. The former 34th Bombardment Group Liberator pilot recalls: 'We were bombing a German radar factory on the north-west edge of Brussels at 21,000 ft. The bomb run from IP to target was from north to south, and exceptionally long. Flak was light to moderate but very accurate. I noticed a four-gun battery

The crew of B-24 42-94930 with their regular aircraft and groundcrew. Rear, L to R: Henry Jensen, Charles Grzelak, Kivett Ivy, Dale Granger, Gerald Holmes, Hank Lambert and W. Berry. Front, L to R: Charles Smith (assistant crew chief), 'Shorty' (ground crew), Lee Weaver, Pete Gray (crew chief), Harry Petersen and Claude Gibbs. (G. Holmes.)

firing at my altitude, straight ahead, which seemed to halve the distance each time it fired. A few seconds before bomb release it hit us hard in the aft part of the fuselage. My rudder pedals went slack. We released on target and the group made a diving turn to the right.

'Without rudders I was unable to follow them, and continued straight ahead. We drew all of the flak after the group turned. After sorting out all of the yelling on the intercom, it was determined that Lee Weaver, left waist gunner, had been hit and was down. I sent Kivett Ivey, the flight engineer, aft to see about Weaver and to see if anything could be done to regain rudder control. He reported that Weaver had a hole through his leg about the size of a golf ball, a few inches above the knee. He put a tourniquet on him and injected a tube of morphine. This was rather ironic, because Weaver said that the only medal he ever wanted was a Purple Heart. "Just a scratch", he always said. He got it!

'In trying to steer the ship to England, with the engines, I noticed that there was no throttle control to number four and that it was trailing oil at a rapid rate. Also I had very limited elevator control due to binding. It was possible, however, to make a let-down to get the crew off oxygen. England was socked in and raining, so any instrument let-down and landing attempt was out of the question. The navigator and I decided that the only alternative was to jump, once we were certain that we were over land. The plan was to point the ship south and let it crash at sea. On signal, the aft crew punched Weaver through the camera hatch on a static line and followed him out. This upset the centre of gravity to such an extent that it was not possible to keep the nose up with limited elevator travel. Bad planning on my part.

'The ship went into a dive and gained airspeed rapidly. The forward crew jumped, and the navigator and I made a flying leap through the bomb bay, which had been left open since the bomb drop. There was a loud explosion immediately after clearing the aircraft. I thought that the ship had exploded because there were heavy gas fumes in the cabin.

'Because of the explosion, I delayed pulling the rip-cord until just before enter-

Looking like a beached whale, the inverted fuselage rests in a ditch near Hadlow. (Russell J. Zorn.)

ing the clouds, so that no falling part would hit my canopy. That was another stupid mistake, because the clouds were right on the ground. I think I hit the ground on the first swing. I broke an ankle and incurred internal injuries. The navigator hit a tree and broke his back. He and I were in the hospital for six weeks. The flight engineer had a scalp injury from hitting his head on a rock. In all, we were pretty lucky.

'I landed in a farmer's chicken yard behind his house. As I was frozen stiff, he sat me in front of a roaring fireplace and fed me a whole bottle of rum from a water glass. He got on the phone and had the local police round up my crew. By the time an ambulance picked me up I was as drunk as a skunk. A doctor at Tunbridge Wells hospital took a look at me and asked, "Do you Yanks always fly in this condition?" '

Happily, Gerald recovered from both the hangover and his injuries. For many years he fretted that his crashing Liberator 'might have killed someone', but research for this book confirmed that B-24H 42-94930 caused no injuries when it fell on the outskirts of Hadlow, in Kent.

23: Working together

BERLIN – THE CAPITAL of Germany and the hub of Hitler's Reich. For thousands of Allied airmen the unveiling at briefing of a long, red ribbon to 'Big B' produced fear; sometimes plated with humour, but fear nonetheless. The first series of American daylight raids were fiercely countered by fighters and flak, but diminishing interceptor strength reduced their ability to contest every assault. Flak, fliers knew, was always there.

On 6 August 1944 the Eighth Air Force demonstrated diversity and strength when over 1,000 bombers and 700 fighters raided airfields, oil installations and 'V' sites

Henry Jones brings B-17G 43-37528 back to Great Ashfield from an earlier Berlin mission with numbers one and three feathered. Don Noe's return on 6 August 1944 was more spectacular. (H. I. Jones.)

The officers of Don Noe's crew. L to R: William Feuerstein, Don Noe, Dan Milligan and Glenn Souik. Don is holding a pink elephant soft toy won at a carnival.

in Germany and the occupied countries. The second Russian 'shuttle' also saw an attack on aviation-industry targets at Gydnia in Poland, en route to the Soviet Union.

This massive fist of air-power comprised nearly 12,000 airmen, each wrestling with the anxiety felt when curtains parted to reveal routes and targets.

At Great Ashfield, 385th Bombardment Group aircrew winced when the objective of Mission 166 was revealed as an aero-engine plant in Marienfelde, Berlin. More than one hundred 385 BG airmen were missing in action from previous attacks, and this was the group's thirteenth visit. Later that morning the B-17s were growling higher through the undercast to form over radio beacon 'Buncher 12' near Bury St Edmunds. Homing on its transmissions, each bomber adhered to a predetermined rate and pattern of climb until it emerged from the murk. Flying his eleventh mission, Lt Don Noe was unperturbed to discover that the undercast was thicker than briefed – the met officer's predictions rarely proved accurate in such detail. He climbed another 2,000 ft, and his B-17 broke into brilliant sunshine over an angel-white carpet. A few minutes later Don's Fortress eased into number four position of the lead squadron. Looking both near and far, high and low, Don saw other B-17s sliding into their assigned slots; squadrons into groups, groups into wings. Powering towards Germany, the assault force climbed to 21,000 ft in three stages and then, after landfall, the B-17s completed a final altitude step to 25,000 ft, hoping that height might reduce the potency of anti-aircraft fire.

High over Germany, at precise points in the heavens, men had already died, but the emphemeral nature of air combat quickly cleansed the atmosphere. The aftermath of aerial battle lay in the countryside and cities below. Nearing Hamburg, aircrew saw the black blood of Hitler's Reich haemorrhaging skywards in the form of huge oil fires created by Second Air Division Liberators. Every gallon of gasoline consumed in the conflagration meant one less for enemy fighters and, today, the Mustangs escorting Don's formation were unchallenged. This factor, plus CAVU (Clear and Visibility Unlimited) conditions, presaged both accurate bombing and accurate flak.

Approaching Berlin, the 385th undertook a gentle 'S' pattern to avoid over-running the low group of the leading combat wing. With the distance safely adjusted, bomb doors whirred open. After synchronising airspeed and altitude, and fine-tuning the trim for optimum stability, Don relinquished control to his bombardier, Lt William J Feuerstein. During the next perilous two minutes Bill flew the Fortress from controls within his bombsight linked to the bomber's main systems. Their entire *raison d'être* was concentrated in these crucial seconds from Initial Point to release. Now, Bill's task was to fulfil the efforts of aircraft assemblers, munitions workers, seamen, planners, ground personnel and his fellow crew members. Their contribution and sacrifices would be rendered useless if Bill wasted the bombs. Studying the closing cross-hairs on his bombsight, Bill sought the accuracy demanded of him. Far below were people providing tracking and fire-control data to gunners – another team determined to expend its country's resources well; seeking the accuracy demanded of them.

Each side attained some of its aspirations. Bill's bombs were on target; so were the responding shells. Moments after releasing its bombs, Don Noe's B-17 was bracketed by flak. At least three rounds exploded in close proximity. As the stricken Fortress dived steeply from formation, another shell exploded near the nose. Shrapnel tore into the aircraft, savaging flesh and ripping through vital controls. Startled but unhurt, Don and his co-pilot, Flt Off Glenn G. Souik, strove to recover from the dive. The elevator and rudder response went slack immediately they were hit because control cables through the fuselage were severed. Pulling out and staying airborne demanded fine pilotage.

Waist gunner Bill Espolt, left, had an eye pierced by shell-splinters, while Jack Thomas, right, had the door blown off his ball turret and was also badly wounded. (D. Noe.)

Glen Souik (nearest camera) with George Runge, who was hit in the back by shell fragments. (D. Noe.)

Wind, shrieking through the shattered nose-Plexiglas, eerily orchestrated the drama as Don, contradicting instinct, applied enough power to encourage the B-17s inherent tendency to nose up. It worked. As the Fortress curved out of its dive the airspeed slackened towards a stall and Don reduced power, the nose dipped and the roller-coasting process began again. 'Horsing' the throttles and manipulation of what flight controls they had demanded co-ordination from both pilots. Having regained limited control, Don sought further assessment of injuries and damage. Part of the oxygen system had been shot out and George Runge, the radio-operator, quickly issued portable bottles until they descended to 13,000 ft. George had been hit in the back by shell fragments, but the wounds sustained by waist gunner Bill Espolt were grievous. One of Bill's eyes had been pierced by metal splinters, pulping the eyeball. Other vicious particles peppered his face, and blood oozed from his wounds.

When they were hit, Jack Thomas, the ball-turret gunner, had been tracking bomb-fall, so his turret was positioned with guns vertical and the turret entrance aligned inside the fuselage. The blast tore off the turret door and smashed the rotation mechanism. Had the door not been aligned, Jack would have been trapped, but George Runge found him dazed, half out of the turret and into the fuselage. One arm was badly injured and useless.

Bill Feuerstein went aft to help George give first-aid and report additional damage. Their Fortress was a wreck. There was no hope of splicing the shredded cables, the right waist-gun position was destroyed and Dan Milligan, their navigator, had lost maps vital for avoiding flak areas. In order to survive, the crew had to work together to sustain flight, avoid flak, tend the wounded and be ready to defend themselves. Each crewman's leather flying jacket bore a posed Betty Boop carica-ture adorned with few clothes but numerous good luck tokens. Now they needed their 'Lady Luck'. Don could only keep control by jockeying throttles backwards and forwards and carefully using aileron and power co-ordination for height and direction changes. Despite intense pain, Bill refused to be dropped over Germany in the hope of earlier medical aid. A brief discussion discounted Sweden as an option, and they voted for a run to friendly territory, perhaps even home. Limping alone from Germany, the B-17 was easy prey for prowling fighters and a low, steady target for flak, but 'Lady Luck' flew a charmed escort for nearly four wearying hours until they reached Great Ashfield.

The extent of the damage made landing impossible, and Don decided to parachute his crew over the airfield. Contacting the tower, Don approached at 8,000 ft while his crew rigged a static line for Bill Espolt, whose head was now swathed in bandages. Bill was pushed out, followed by Jack Thomas, also on the static line, and George Runge. Easing into a gentle circle, Don recrossed the base and four more parachutes appeared, leaving only the two pilots to fly the B-17 seawards and jump. Over the sea, two escorting P-47s would destroy the empty bomber. However, near the coast Don encountered increasing turbulence and Col Elliott Vandevanter ordered his pilots to bale out. Holding the B-17 steady while Glenn jumped, Don knew that his own departure would have to be speedy in case the bomber spun before he got out. Preparing himself, he released the yoke, slid from his seat, and leapt from the bomb bay. Moments later he was floating earthwards while the B-17, far from spinning, sailed serenely eastwards. Army Air Force B-17G 43-37528 seemed destined for a watery end, but the bomber confounded plans for its demise.

As he descended, Don found that the back-pack parachute was causing him to drift with his back to the direction of travel. Frequent glances over his shoulders revealed clumps of trees which he correctly calculated he would avoid. Next came a large meadow with only one, tall tree. Don hit it. Plummeting through a green cascade of leaves, snapping twigs and broken branches, he was knocked cold on hitting the ground. When he came round, the first thing he noticed was his continued grip on the parachute 'D' ring, then he saw a cluster of curious children and some adults wondering what to do. Next a jeep bounced into view, and two GIs checked him for serious injuries and then transported him to their base, a nearby bomb-dump. A tumbler full of 'Old Grandad' saw the exhausted aviator sound asleep in moments. His crew had landed without further mishap, and the wounded were quickly despatched to the 65th General Hospital. There the story may have ended, but for the strong homing instincts of Don's bomber.

Near the coast, the Thunderbolts lost their charge when it vanished into cloud and failed to emerge where predicted. Later that evening, teenager Cyril Brown was in the bedroom of his home at Thelnetham, not far from Great Ashfield, when he

Lady Luck *stay with me. Don Noe struggled to keep the Fortress airborne, hoping that the motif on his jacket would work its magic.* (D. Noe.)

Frog's Hall *was burnt to the ground, leaving only the chimney stack and remnants of a Flying Fortress.* (Russell J. Zorn.)

Visiting the site in 1988, Don Noe (kneeling) and Russell Pleasance of the 390th BG Memorial Air Museum pick pieces of Flying Fortress from recently-ploughed farmland. (B. Pleasance.)

heard an aircraft, low and coming closer. Then came 'a loud crashing noise' which sent Cyril dashing to his window to behold 25 tons of errant bomber crunching through tree tops towards his home. Yelling at his family to get out, Cyril leapt the stairway's length and fell near the front door. In the moments it took him to stand, the bomber's course was diverted by a solitary ash adjacent to his house and it smashed into a neighbouring cottage, *Frog's Hall,* about 20 yards away. As he ran to the crash site with his father, they both feared for the bomber crew and Mrs Rush, the widow living in *Frog's Hall* with two young evacuee girls. Fuel had already ignited the cottage as Cyril's father dashed inside, but luckily it was empty. Clambering into the bomber's broken fuselage, Cyril found that the only trace of its crew was a discarded flying helmet. The flames burnt both the B-17 and *Frog's Hall* to the ground, so Mrs Rush returned from chapel to find her home in a smouldering ruin, from which little was salvaged. Had the planned family tea taken place that Sunday, the outcome could have been tragic.

Like many others, Don went home, raised a family, and set the events of 6 August 1944 behind him as best he could. Bill Feuerstein never made it, and died two months later with another crew attacking Berlin. Forty years on, Don tried to trace survivors from his crew, but found out only that Bill Espolt died in 1977. Visiting the crash site in 1988, he searched a recently-ploughed field for evidence of that drama in his life, and recovered some spent cartridge casings, fragments of aluminium and Perspex, and some square steel plates from the flak-jackets worn by his crew. Mingled with the reminders of war were domestic artefacts from *Frog's Hall* — pottery shards; part of a door catch, and a piece of brass bedstead. Perhaps this record of the fate of Don's B-17 will prevent future archaeologists from being perplexed by this strange mixture.

24: For dear life

BY OPERATIONAL PREFERENCE, and to ease maintenance logistics, Eighth Air Force commanders decided in 1944 to standardise on the B-17. An initial phase entailed concentrating all their Liberators in the Second Air Division, which meant some 3rd Air Division groups relinquishing B-24s for B-17s. The conversion period provided a brief respite from combat, but arduous training was essential for a rapid return to operational status. In August, the 490 Bombardment Group at Eye bade farewell to the B-24 and began intensive training on their new Boeings. Sunday the 13th found a practice mission scheduled to continue the familiarization programme.

Lieutenant Andrew Korothy felt good that morning: 'It dawned sparkling clear – a great day for flying. A clear day over England was a rarity, and I looked forward to enjoying it'. Weather records show that by the time the B-17s left Eye there was five-tenths cloud, but with a gentle wind and good visibility. Weather is unlikely to have been a factor in the tragic events that followed.

Andrew's pilot, Capt Norman Cosby, had 1,467 flying hours, but only 20 were on B-17Gs. His Fortress, which would be leading the low group, climbed untroubled to the assembly point, Splasher 6. Peering from his position in the B-17's nose, Andrew maintained a cheerful disposition, helped by the facts that practice missions did not involve being shot at, and their bomb bay ordnance comprised only two 100lb M38A2 practice bombs. Sun, streaming through the Plexiglas nose, buoyed his happiness, and as he was not on a combat mission he allowed himself the comfort of leaving his parachute harness unbuckled. The canvas pack lay nearby, and fastening the straps in case of emergency was a simple task.

Reaching 8,000 ft at 8.40a.m., Capt Cosby eased into a gentle left turn and Andrew saw their right wingman, Lt Ketas, arrive below as was normal in the forming process. Over the intercom Andrew informed his pilot of the sighting and of the

Sunlight glistens on 490th BG Flying Fortresses. The group flew 40 Liberator missions, but changed to the B-17 in accordance with Eighth Air Force policy. (S. P. Evans.)

Teenager Greta Youngman was enjoying a Sunday lie-in when a ball of flames hurtled past her bedroom window. Then came a tremendous explosion. (Mrs G. Patrick.)

other bomber's position – it would be the first to ascend and form on them. Watching the B-17, Andrew felt some apprehension at the rate and manner of its approach, and notified Cosby that their wingman was: '. . . coming along very fast and coming up to our altitude extremely quickly'. Before Cosby could respond, the other B-17 struck them, shearing away their right wing at the inboard engine.

Andrew relates: 'We immediately nosed over and went into a spin in a clockwise direction. I forced myself to a standing position from my seat behind the bomb-sight and, bracing myself on the fuselage, tried to buckle my parachute harness in place. Try as I might, I was unable to buckle both legs. I saw the altimeter spinning wildly, so I concluded I had better get out. For several seconds I had a very strong urge to remain with the 'plane because of my great faith in our pilot. After all, he always did bring us down safely before. I located my chest pack, snapped it in place, and left the 'plane out of the emergency escape hatch. I just missed being struck by the crippled aircraft. With only one leg strap buckled I received a terrible jolt as the chute opened. I grabbed the parachute lines and held on for dear life.

'Floating down to the beautiful, lush English countryside, I watched as the wing-man's 'plane spun into the ground and burst into flames. Our 'plane soon followed, and I worried that I might drop into the flames. I followed several other parachutes to the ground and I knew immediately that we all did not survive.

'Local citizens helped me out of my parachute harness and took me to their home for tea. Some other crew members were also brought to the house, where we waited for the Air Force ambulance to transport us to a local field hospital, where we spent the night.'

One of the 'local citizens' was young John Meen, who was on his uncle's farm at Roydon Green when he heard 'a distinct bang' in the sky and, looking up, saw pieces of aircraft tumbling to earth. Several parachutes appeared and two airmen landed nearby, so John ran to help. John recalls one flier 'shaking like a leaf' from shock as he was helped out of his parachute harness, and John led him gently to the farmhouse for a strong cup of tea.

Other local inhabitants found themselves dramatically involved. At number 3 Factory Lane, Roydon, 15-year-old Greta Youngman was awake but enjoying a Sunday lie-in. Her father, Bertie, was needed for a special job at the nearby brush factory, and she heard him preparing to leave in the yard outside. Suddenly he yelled for his family to take cover, but Greta had no time to react before an enormous ball of flames hurtled past her bedroom window. Moments later the whole house shook as an explosion blew Bertie indoors and a still-smoking aero engine crunched down on the spot where he had been and bounded into the house behind him, smashing into the larder. Outside, another chunk of wreckage struck their home, collapsing a section of exterior wall. In less than 20 seconds the family's peaceful Sunday had become a day of terror. Picking himself up, Bertie urged his wife and three children from their home in case it caught fire. His son, Ivan, had a friend staying but, apart from fright, all emerged unscathed.

Next door, the Farrow family found that a bomb had smashed through the back door and landed in the kitchen. An ordnance report shows how lucky they were, because the spotting charge had been ripped off before it entered the house. Practice bombs carried an explosive 'spotting' charge to indicate the point of impact on bombing-range targets, the detonation of this indoors might have been lethal.

Outside Greta's bedroom window lies a jumble of twisted aluminium, part of the rear fuselage from John Ketas' B-17. (Russell J. Zorn.)

The burnt-out remains of Norman Cosby's B-17G, 43-38051, is examined by Lt John Aslip (left) and Lt Ed Hill, both Air Inspectors from 1 SAD Honington. Some parachutes descended into the flames. (Russell J. Zorn.)

As residents hastily vacated their homes they met with a terrible sight. Wreckage was scattered for hundreds of yards, but the bulk of Capt Cosby's B-17 lay blazing in an adjacent wheatfield. Emerging from her nearby home, 21-year-old Pauline Madgett was distraught to see airmen descend into the flames and vanish beneath parachutes settling like burning shrouds. Pauline had made friends with airmen from Eye, and feared for their safety.

The grim task of gathering the dead revealed that eleven young Americans perished on that sunny Sunday. Mrs Youngman contracted diabetes and died three years later, her grieving family convinced that the shock of the crash caused the onset of the disease. Andrew Korothy's account is confirmed by the *Report of Aircraft Accident* in the author's possession. However, official records do not relate how fortune favoured one young flier who left his harness undone and hung on 'for dear life'.

25: The lucky crew

THE IDEA OF a crash contributing to survival seems strange, but one former flier feels he lived because of the circumstances in which his bomber was lost.

On 11 September 1944 Lt Ferdinand Herres' crew hoped to complete their tour with the 100th BG on a mission to oil installations in Ruhland, Germany. Navigator Lt Alvin Ringhofer recorded their departure from Thorpe Abbots at 7.54 a.m. The miles droned steadily by until they neared Koblenz, when the number four engine of B-17 *Now an' Then* faltered. To make matters worse, the malfunctioning motor resisted all attempts to feather the propeller, and their aircraft was unable to maintain formation. The sky seemed large and lonely as they dropped back and Herres requested a course for home. Alvin then found that his gyro compass had failed, so Herres used the cockpit magnetic compass to steer for England.

Now An' Then *at Thorpe Abbots, with her Cyclone engines singing. On 11 September 1944 one of them went out of tune, creating a bad luck/good luck situation for the crew.* (A. Ringhofer.)

At 11.06 a.m. the bombs were jettisoned to maintain their airspeed of 125 m.p.h. without additional stress. If they went faster, the friction from their wind-milling propeller might overheat and ignite the number four engine. Gently shedding height, *Now an' Then* crossed the channel, reaching Dover at 1.02 p.m. Welcoming the white cliffs, Alvin gave his pilot a heading for base. A minute later their optimism slumped when the number four engine erupted in flames. A fierce cutting-torch of fire scorched greedily through the nacelle, and each passing second risked a violent explosion tearing away their starboard wing. The fire's intensity overwhelmed the engine's integral extinguisher system, giving Herres no choice but to issue the bale-out command.

Beached and burnt. The remains of Now An' Then *on the Isle of Sheppey sandflats.* (Russell J. Zorn.)

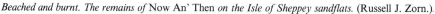

The lucky crew. Standing, L to R:: Duell Barnes, Alvin Ringhofer, Fred Herres, B. Conover and Robert Mulgrew. Kneeling, L to R:: Nester Nesser, James Morrow, Andrew Main and Wilbur Williams. (A. Ringhofer.)

As the emergency hatches tumbled away and bomb doors creaked open, Alvin noted time and altitude – 1.05 p.m., 16,000 ft. The cold blast of slipstream swirling through the B-17 emphasised the drama on board but did not disturb the crew's disciplined behaviour. Herres held the B-17 steady for his crew's departure, and Alvin followed the bombardier to the bomb bay. On the narrow catwalk, the dark surroundings contrasted sharply with the brilliance of light outside. It seemed as though the bomber was fixed and the landscape was sliding beneath. A final check on the security of parachute attachment, perhaps an inward prayer, and then the short, breathtaking step off the catwalk. As Alvin fell he hit his chest on a bomb door, and learnt later he had torn some muscles, but he descended near Manston aerodrome without further mishap.

Setting the auto pilot on a seawards heading, Herres also parachuted safely, and was delighted to learn that there were no serious injuries among his crew. *Now an' Then* crashed and burnt out on the shoreline at Harty Ferry on the Isle of Sheppey.

Had they continued, Herres' crew might have been numbered among the tragic losses the 100th suffered soon after their departure. Eleven Flying Fortresses were cut down during one of the Luftwaffe's now infrequent but highly effective concerted attacks. Engine failure had probably saved their lives. As Alvin recalled: 'Weren't we the lucky crew?'

26: Half 'n' Half

THE SKILL AND dedication of Eighth Air Force ground personnel and support services is beyond the scope of this book. However, their commitment, often when exposed to England's cold, arthritic environment, was an essential element in any mission. Aspiring to feats of great ingenuity, they frequently returned many seemingly-ruined bombers to combat. One such aircraft was a B-17G serial 42-97940, *Half 'n' Half.*

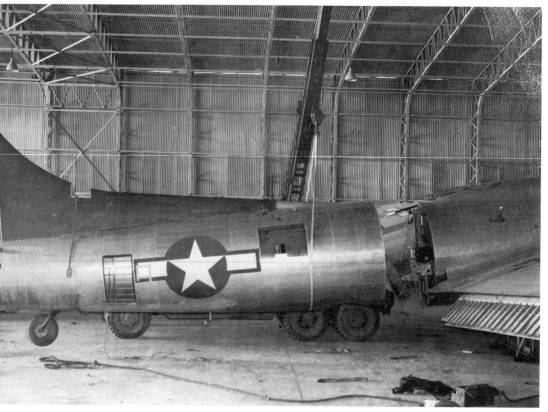

Eighth Air Force engineers blend two halves of a B-17 fuselage together. In this fashion they created the 385th BG's Half 'n' Half. *(Russell J. Zorn.)*

George Barnett with a British girlfriend in London. (G. Barnett.)

Confronted with two badly damaged airframes, maintenance personnel amalgamated the front of one with the rear of the other to produce one good Fortress. The battle-damaged 385 BG Fortress *Dozy Doats* contributed one half and, on return to Great Ashfield, the 'new' bomber was understandably renamed *Half 'n' Half* — also the name of a beer combination popular with the Americans.

On 13 September 1944 Tech Sgt George W. Barnett flew his first mission as replacement engineer for the crew of *Half 'n' Half*. The target was the Sindelfingen oil installation near Stuttgart, an objective notorious for its anti-aircraft defences. Shortly after bomb release, accurate anti-aircraft fire burst amid the 385 BG formation, and George recalls: 'We picked up a lot of flak that day and the left waist gunner was hit. It almost severed his right leg at the knee. I came out of the top turret but, by the time I got there, one of the other crew members had already given him morphine.'

Flak also struck the port wing and number two engine, but *Half 'n' Half* accomplished the mission and struggled back to England. Nearing the coast, they lost the number two engine completely and, even more alarming, a small fire started at the rear of their number two nacelle, possibly in the undercarriage compartment. George thought the turbo-supercharger had been hit, because the smoke filtering into the fuselage was white, not black – the sort of smoke associated with burning hydraulic fluid.

Despite the risk of rapidly spreading flames, the crew kept going because their badly wounded gunner, Joe Sturdivant, needed medical attention. While the flames were contained they had a chance of getting Joe safely home, but hopes vanished when a loud explosion shook the B-17 and thick black smoke poured from the port wing. The left main-wheel tyre had ignited and burst. *Half 'n' Half* had little time left.

Parachutes donned, the crew groped aft, carrying Joe between them. In the confusion they either failed to realise, or never knew, that a lanyard could have been hooked to Joe's parachute for opening by a static line. George remembers: 'We were a bunch of green kids, scared to death, with absolutely no training in first aid and damn little in emergency procedures. You have to take into account an

Half 'n' Half in half near Kentford, Suffolk. This time the battered bomber was beyond redemption. (Russell J. Zorn.)

The grave of Joe Sturdivant at Madingley – a life lost for want of a lanyard. (J. Ford.)

aircraft on fire at less than 1,000 ft and going down fast, a bunch of shook-up kids, and you have a recipe for disaster'. In pain and weak from loss of blood, Joe was pushed from the rear exit and, through all the years since, George has dwelt on what happened. All of the crew landed with no more than minor injuries except for Joe Sturdivant, whose body was found wearing an unused parachute.

Half 'n' Half came to grief near the Suffolk village of Kentford, and was wrecked beyond the best endeavours of even the most skilled repair service. Sergeant Joe P. Sturdivant rests with his comrades at Madingley; a life lost for want of a lanyard.

27: Death by misadventure

'IT'S SOMETHING YOU never really forget . . .' says Mrs Joyce Felton when recalling the events of 15 October 1944. A child at the time, Joyce Smith lived with her family at Woodhall Farm on the outskirts of Sudbury, in Suffolk. That morning, the early hours presaged a clear, autumnal Sunday, but not a day of peace. As the Smith family slumbered, 39 Flying Fortresses of the 486 BG were preparing to attack the marshalling yards in Cologne.

Woodhall Farm was about half a mile south-west from the main runway of Station 174, but Joyce's father, Major Smith, was accustomed to the bombers and slept soundly as the first five Fortresses, straining off runway 250, climbed almost directly overhead. The sixth, piloted by Lt Clarence B. Herrmann and crew, turned into what little support a 5 m.p.h. wind offered and paused, waiting for the green. Racked behind Herrmann were 14 250 lb bombs and four Type M17 incendiary clusters – each containing 110 individual M50 incendiary bombs – an additional 2,000 lb overall.

Not a cloud shielded the stars, and night visibility was 3,000 yards with a hint

A Fortress of the 486th BG over Cologne on 15 October 1944. Far below the clouds, smoke-pots can be seen obscuring the city. (S/Sgt Peter 'Rupy' Ruplenas.)

of ground mist, but conditions were fine for a semi-instrument take-off. Herrmann appreciated the clarity because he had accrued only 49 night-flying hours in the last six months – about 17 per cent of his total experience on B-17s. After nudging the big silver bomber on the runway, Herrmann and his co-pilot, Lt Robert N. Etter, set brakes, checked trim-tabs, and exercised turbos and propellers. With the engines pounding on 1,500 r.p.m., the turbo controls were manipulated through several settings, checked, and cleared. Propeller pitch ranges were run from low to high r.p.m. and back, and the instruments indicated that all was well. A final, visual check of the four cowlings, a go-ahead from the tower, and Herrmann's aircraft, fuselage code H8-N, started rolling towards a niche in American and English history.

Mechanics, armourers and other ground staff, their tasks complete, watched the group taking off. Master Sergeant Joe M. Bruce, an 834 squadron line chief, had seen H8-N shuffle from hardstand 14 because, although the B-17 belonged to the 835 squadron, its hardstand encroached into his squadron's area. Joe now saw the Fortress rolling and heard engine power building towards the climax necessary to achieve take-off. An experienced mechanic, he was attuned to healthy aero engines and, amidst the regular drumming of other radials, the discordant rhythm of a sick Cyclone drew his attention. The surging number four engine of H8-N had faltered. Joe's alarm eased with the sound of restoring power, but the relief proved fleeting as the engine spluttered again. Beyond the point of no return, Herrmann's B-17 was clearly struggling for airspeed. Surging again, the wavering engine offered hope, then withdrew it in a vacillating stammer of failing energy.

Visibly, three of H8-N's turbos emitted a strong, consistent glow, but number four exhaust emitted no flame. To Joe, a dark slot devoid of power pinpointed the problem but he, like the others, stood helplessly unable to provide a remedy. He knew that an imperfect fuel mixture could dampen flame emissions and still provide sufficient power, but felt that this was not the case for H8-N. Others, in the tower, anxiously observed the B-17's plight as it lifted unsteadily, striving for altitude. If power was lost when burdened by bombs, fuel, ammunition and nine airmen, there was no hope of a normal climb-out. Watching its wing-lights, eyewitnesses saw the starboard wing dip and H8-N canted right, losing what precious height it had. Executing a slow, flat turn, the B-17 slid into the dark landscape southwest of the airfield. There was a flash of flame, then an explosion boomed across the countryside and a strong, steady glow illuminated the distant darkness.

Major Smith was thrown into startled wakefulness when a tremendous crash jolted Woodhall Farm house. Momentarily he felt that the entire building was collapsing. His wife lay in bed screaming, and his two terrified daughters ran into the room. Gathering his senses, Major realised that his son, Raymond, had not appeared, and one glance on the landing told him the boy was trapped upstairs, with the loft and upper house burning furiously. Helping his wife, his daughters and their grandmother negotiate the rubble-strewn stairway, Major took them into the front garden before dashing back to fetch his son. The last flight of stairs to Ray's room was blocked, and his bedroom was already on fire. Shielding himself from the heat as best he could, Major called to his son, and to his relief the boy answered, saying he was all right. Frantically throwing aside the debris, Major created enough room for Ray to escape, and the lad emerged with a badly burnt face and hands but at least able to walk.

Outside, it looked like a grotesque bonfire, with their home the unfortunate centrepiece. The roof had been ripped away, and flames from burning rafters reflected in pieces of shiny aluminium littering the garden. Two twisted propellers lying near the house confirmed what had happened. A neighbour, Tom Byford, found his own

The B-17 tore the roof off Woodhall Farm house, setting the upper storey ablaze. (S/Sgt Peter 'Rupy' Ruplenas.)

garden soaked with blazing fuel and hurriedly helped his family escape before rushing to aid the Smith family. They had taken shelter in their barn – someone had slipped a coat over Ray's shoulders, and the youngster was bravely saying he felt all right despite grievous burns. Then, seeing clearly the state of his hands and feeling the pain, he started screaming: 'Look at my hands, look at my hands!' Trying to console Ray and his family, Tom suggested they go to his less-damaged home until the ambulance arrived. After walking only a few paces Ray asked Tom to pick him up, and slumped into Tom's arms while the boy's father frantically ran from person to person trying to find transport – no ambulance had arrived. First on the scene was an American jeep, into which Ray was gently placed and driven to Sudbury hospital. Joyce clearly remembers how Ray's pyjamas had been burnt off, exposing flesh that was blistering and peeling in strips from his back, hands and face. Her brother seemed too shocked to cry, but their mother sobbed as the jeep sped away.

Dawn's strengthening light revealed a scene of utter devastation on Woodhall Farm. After striking the house, H8-N had scorched a burnt smear across an adjacent, winter-tilled field. Little could be identified of aircraft or crew, and only Clarence Herrmann had survived, if survived is the right terminology for horrific burns and brain damage. His injuries ruled out any hope of a normal future, and 32 years elapsed before events that morning took their final victim from a veteran's home in New Bedford, Massachusetts.

Ray reached hospital in terrible pain but fully conscious. While his wounds were being tenderly dressed, the youngster suffered three attacks of respiratory failure. Doctor R.W. Rix pulled him through these, and through a fourth occurrence half an hour later. Ray recovered from these, but the following morning a fifth attack killed him. Two weeks later Mr Alan Phillips, the Sudbury Borough Coroner, heard

Scorching a burnt smear across an adjacent field, the crashing Fortress left a trail of debris. (S/Sgt Peter 'Rupy' Ruplenas.)

USAAF personnel remove a hideously burnt corpse from the wreckage. (Russell J. Zorn.)

that death was due to 'acute odema of the lungs and shock following extensive burns'. He returned a verdict of death by misadventure.

Joyce Felton feels no bitterness when she remembers her brother, because she realises that nine young Americans, not very much older than Ray, were also victims of the same sad, misadventure. Clarence B. Herrmann died in 1976. That year,

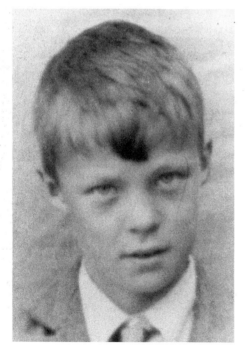

Young Ray Smith suffered serious burns and shock.
(Mrs J. Felton.)

A propeller found in the moat of Woodhall Farm now serves as a fitting reminder of courage and tragedy.
(R. H. Nolan.)

England was enjoying the peace for which he had given so much. Suffolk sweltered in record-setting temperatures, and the old moat surrounding Woodhall Farm evaporated into a cracked, crazily-paved pathway providing an interesting new walk for local people. Then, among the guilt of untidiness and a few redundant rowing boats, a large metal cylinder was revealed. Was it a bomb?

Consternation spread amongst those aware of the farm's history, and the police were called. Word of the discovery travelled swiftly, soon reaching two aviation enthusiasts, Chris Richards and Bill Hurley. Following closely behind the local constabulary, they helped identify the mysterious cylinder – it was the hub of a partially-buried Hamilton-Standard propeller. Digging revealed that two blades were still attached, and the decision was taken to retrieve it for museum display. The following week a small team, encouraged by an abundance of local children, winched the propeller out of its resting place and on to the moat-bank. From its sojourn in the moat, this relic of a wartime tragedy began a journey which ultimately took it back to America. Its first destination was Duxford, where it was cleaned, varnished and displayed in one of the amateur collections co-existing on the Imperial War Museum site.

The following year, Chris Richards decided to clean some of the parts gathered by children, who had been diverted to this duty to enable recovery of the propeller to proceed unhindered. An assortment of aircraft-type debris had been separated from household rubbish, and Chris began cleaning an hexagonal object about 12 in long. Removing most of the mud, he felt convinced it came from the B-17 but could not identify it. As he was at Duxford, he wandered across to *Sally-B,* the only airworthy B-17 in England. The obliging crew, equally puzzled, let Chris search for a fitting or part comparable with his hexagon, but he was unable to make a match and returned to his workshop. A thin film of mud remained on the base and, as he scraped it away, Chris identified his trophy by the letter and number code revealed: 'M50' – it was an incendiary bomb! Hastily immersing it in a tub of water, Chris called the police and bomb disposal personnel. A remote dispersal bay was chosen, and a small charge of plastic explosive destroyed the unwelcome souvenir.

In 1985 the 486th Bomb Group Association asked Stan and David Brett of the Rebel Air Museum if the propeller could be donated to become the focal point of a proposed 486th BG memorial at Barksdale Air Force Base, Louisiana. The brothers agreed, and passed it to US Strategic Air Command for transportation to the USA. Today, the twisted relic stands proudly on a plinth raised in tribute by 486th BG veterans to their fallen comrades who 'grew not old'. Raymond Major Smith grew no older than fifteen, so the propeller also forms a memorial to a young boy who died before he was old enough to go to war.

28: It helps when you pray

IN NOVEMBER 1944 the 100th BG were training to use Micro-H, a new beam-radar bombing system linked with H2X. On the 7th, poor continental weather prevented operations, but the opportunity was taken for over 500 bombers to practise attacking tactical targets. The advancing armies frequently needed air support, but bombing close to Allied lines demanded great accuracy and, where necessary, skilled use of the more sophisticated radar systems becoming available.

As an eighteen-year-old tail gunner, Sgt Cornelius 'Joe' Romano was unconcerned about details of the new apparatus. To Joe they were just 'trying out new secret equipment'. Their bomber was an elderly ship named *Batchelor's Heaven,* but it was distinguished by the type-suffix B-17GSH, the 'SH' denoting a PFF 'Mickey' ship. In this rôle *Batchelor's Heaven* would lead the low group, and other B-17s would form on them. Joe gained the awesome impression that the whole Eighth Air Force would be following them in serried ranks of B-17s and B-24s: an airborne army at the peak of its power. Their key task meant that a Command Pilot, Capt Stanley A. Clark, was on board. He was due to be promoted to Major on December 1, and had considerable PFF mission experience. Alongside him in the cockpit was Lt John T. Dyatt, while some of Joe's other regular crew took their usual slots, just as on a normal mission. 'Gus' Gustavson was the engineer, and one of his jobs would be to fire flares indicating their position as lead ship. In the nose were navigator Ralph Bohlsson and bombardier Preston Wallace, while Nelson McClain was radio operator and August Kienitz took charge of both waist guns – few crews carried two waist gunners at this stage of the war. Harry Tennebaum had been borrowed from another crew as 'Mickey' operator.

Joe's diary takes up the story: 'Nov. 7, 1944. Today WE HAD IT!! Took off about 11.00 a.m. – it was a practice mission. Flew in an early model B-17 number 42-97561, call letter "W" . . . Gus shot off a flare to indicate we were the lead ship and to form up on our 'plane, but as far as I know the gun went off on the flight deck. There was a hell of a jolt, the 'plane went into a dive – I landed behind the ammunition boxes. At first I thought it was prop wash. I started to plug my intercom cord back in and looked out of my window when there was another jolt, and I saw that we were pulling out of formation and diving down. After a third jolt I started to look for my 'chute – it was way back by the tailwheel. I made one dive for the 'chute and crawled back to my oxygen line, took some deep breaths of oxygen, and tried to hook up my 'chute to the harness. My mask was in the way so I ripped off mask and helmet and hooked up. Then I kneeled by the tail door (it helps when you pray) and looked towards the waist section. I saw Mac kick the waist door off, so I did the same to the tail door. Then, for the first time, I saw flames shooting out of the radio room and 'Mickey' [Harry Tennebaum] crawling out. I kept hearing little explosions, and was waiting for the ship to blow up. Looking out of the tail door, I saw pieces of the 'plane going by – I motioned to Mac, 'Mickey' and Augie [Kienitz] to jump – they did from the waist and I left from the tail. The last I saw of our ship was when the tail passed me. I then decided to pull the rip-cord, and there was a terrific jolt and I twisted around in the air but was as happy as hell to see the 'chute had worked.

'I heard someone shout, "Hello there," and before I could answer 'Mickey' had collided with me in mid-air. Knowing that, if our 'chutes were to tangle, they would collapse and both of us fall to the ground a lot faster than we should, I began to push and curse him. Next thing I knew we were separated – I said all the prayers I could remember as loud as I could but still heard 'Mickey' yell to me how he left his Parker 51 pen in the 'plane. Strange what goes through your mind at such times.

'I saw Mac and Augie K in the air and felt good. Someone landed near a little stream – it must have been Wallace. Looking down, I figured I was about 200 ft from the ground and I started to whistle *I Walk Alone* — don't ask me why. Guess I wanted to be cool and I was happy to be that close to mother earth. I landed hard and hurt my knee and back, and the wind was knocked out of me, so I just let the 'chute drag me for a while until I caught my breath. Finally, I dug my heels

Smoke shrouds the devastated Coast Guard cottages at Felixstowe where three airmen of the RAF Regiment perished. (S. P. Evans.)

RAF airmen clear the debris of their billet. Leaning against the left chimney can be seen the B-17's tailplane, with some of the fuselage spilling towards the camera. A propeller blade protrudes from rubble on the right. (Russell J. Zorn.)

and elbows into the ground and slipped off my harness. A P-47 and a P-51 buzzed
our position. I saw Augie K about 100 yards away and we both ran and limped
towards one another, hugged and kissed. Three girls came by to see if they could
help, then 'Mickey' came by in a small truck with an Englishman driver and Mac
came by in a larger truck. We all went to a P-51 base control tower, and there
we learned that Dyatt had landed in a nearby wood without 'chute or harness.

'In trying to figure out what had happened, Mac said he felt a jolt and saw
'Mickey' trying his best to get down from the ceiling. Mac then opened the bomb-
bay door and saw fire – tried to use the extinguisher but to no avail. Then 'Mickey'
tried, but no success – they both went to the waist, near the door, not knowing
whether to stay with the 'plane or bail out. Augie K said he, too, knew there was
trouble when he felt a hard jolt, he hit the ceiling and next noticed Mac and 'Mickey'
fighting the fire in the bomb bay. Mac's 'chute didn't open properly, and he had
to peel it out of the pack with his hands. He landed safely, but Augie K hit his
head and hurt his side on landing. 'Mickey' said he thought the flares blew up and
started the fire. He landed safely. Wallace said that the flames gushed down into
the nose and burned his face. He tried to crawl to the flightdeck to fight the fire
and met Dyatt on the catwalk, but doesn't know why Dyatt was there. Wallace
continued to the flightdeck, received more burns and his clothing caught fire, but
he beat the flames out with his hands as best he could. He saw Gus having a hell
of a time with the fire – called to him but got no response. He and Bohlsson then
bailed out through the nose hatch.'

Joe's diary continues later: 'Saw Wallace in the hospital. His face burnt bad and
swollen to three times normal size – second and third degree burns. Wallace has
a lot of courage and guts to go through all that, and yet tries to laugh when you

*The nose section detached and fell separately. Note the oxygen bottles in the foreground and the pilot's
control column in the cockpit.* (S. P. Evans.)

kid around with him. Wallace was at the 65th General Hospital – Bohlssen is in an English hospital attached to the navy – severe burns about the face and hands. Both Wallace and Bohlssen bailed out before the boys in the waist – guess they knew how bad the ship was. Dyatt, I think, bailed out first, I am not sure. Gus and Capt Clark were found in the ship. The 'plane, we are told, landed on a row of buildings, killing three more people.'

Batchelor's Heaven broke up in mid-air, and the wingless fuselage plummeted on to some former coastguard cottages being used by the RAF Regiment in Felixstowe. Three British airmen perished: Cpl D. Postlethwaite with LACs L.P. Orrom and A.C. Coward. Flight Lieutenant Duckworth King, second-in-command of Number 3 Anti-Aircraft Practice Camp, was seriously burnt and taken to hospital. It is possible that Capt Clark was trying to take the burning B-17 nearer the coast before he parachuted. An East Suffolk Police Report describes a glow being seen in the aircraft when it was over Ipswich and, at about 2.45 p.m., an airman was seen falling from the distressed aircraft. The body of John T. Dyatt was found in a field near Holbrook Road, Wherstead village, a few miles from Felixstowe. As Joe recorded, he was not wearing a parachute – perhaps flames destroyed it, but only God knows the unfortunate man's anguish. A Felixstowe schoolboy, John Watling, saw the B-17 break up and two bodies fall out. The courageous Capt Clark, one of the group's finest pilots, perished in Langer Road, Felixstowe. The broken and burnt body of Gus Gustavson was found nearby.

Fifty years on, the coastal cottages destroyed by *Batchelor's Heaven* have been repaired. Residents still find the odd bullet or aluminium fragment, and Felixstowe's Flying Fortress is now as much part of the Suffolk seaport's history as Landguard Fort, attacked by the Dutch in 1665.

29: Boyd's Boids

ON 21 NOVEMBER 1944 the Eighth Air Force continued pummelling Germany's petroleum industry when over 1,100 bombers thrust eastwards from England.

For the crew of a 96th BG B-17, *Boyd's Boids,* the day did not go well. Over Germany the pilots, Lts John K. Boyd and Robert H. Ashley, faced a malfunctioning propeller governor on their number one engine. They throttled back on number one and partially feathered the propeller to maintain some contribution. With compensating power applied to their good engines, they held formation and continued towards their objective, a synthetic-oil production plant near Merseburg. After some time the additional stress caused mounting oil pressure on number three engine. When oil began spurting from the breather, Boyd had no alternative but to feather a second engine and abort the mission.

The engineer, Tech Sgt Ernest T. 'Mo' Moriarty recalls that they were unable to maintain airspeed or altitude, and rapidly had to select a target of opportunity. The bombs were dropped on a railroad. This lightened *Boyd's Boids,* but the problems intensified a few moments later when the number two engine failed, leaving only a partially effective number one and lots of prayers to keep number four going. Rate-of-descent calculations indicated that they would run out of air before reaching England. 'We looked around to see what else could be jettisoned,' Mo recalls. 'The armour plate, ammunition, guns went first. I held the ammunition and

Technical Sergeant Ernest 'Mo' Moriarty, flight engineer and top turret gunner. (E. T. Moriarty.)

guns for the top turret in case we had fighters attack us. Everything else was ripped out or torn up and thrown out the windows.' Fortunately they were not intercepted; nor did they experience any flak, but, on reaching the Zuider Zee, they had only 1,000 ft left.

Resolving to reach England, they flew on as mile on slow mile slid by over a sea of foreboding. Soon, they were so low that swelling waves threatened to snatch them into the water's icy clutches. At times, the two propellers still turning blew bursts of sea-spray from wave-tops only inches below. John Boyd asked Mo if they should ditch while some form of controlled impact remained possible. To Mo a sea-landing, controlled or not, offered only two chances – a swift or a slow death. Repeated 'Mayday' transmissions by Tech Sgt Nick Corleto might have got through, but the chances of being found before freezing to death were slim.

They elected to press on, drawing some encouragement from the occasional, slight lift prompted by exterior air currents and skilled flying. At such a low speed their journey seemed interminable, but the sea-grey horizon eventually broke to reveal land and the jubilant aircrew felt like ship-wrecked mariners crawling ashore.

Soon an airfield appeared, but, with spirits boosted, they opted for Snetterton Heath and Nick contacted base control. After explaining their condition Boyd was granted immediate clearance for a straight-in approach. Positioning himself between the pilots, Mo called off airspeed as they edged towards Snetterton's south-north runway. Undercarriage down and locked: height so preciously fought for and conserved was now eased away on a long, gradual approach.

Moments before touchdown another B-17, firing red flares to show that it had wounded on board, cut in front of *Boyd's Boids*. The two pilots strove desperately

Some of Boyd's Boids. L to R: William Carey, Dale Parcher, Robert Ashley, John Boyd and Nicholas Corleto. (E. T. Moriarty.)

to pull up and go round again, but it was too late. Mo felt the B-17 sliding sideways, right wing down. A crash was inevitable. Jumping into the flightdeck tunnel, he yelled forwards to navigator William J. Carey and togglier Louis T. Wallace, warning them to take up crash stations in the radio room. Carey made it, but Wallace had no time and, in the last instant before impact, he jumped for cover behind Ashley's armoured seat. Mo sought a similar slot behind Boyd as both pilots still fought to lift the right wing. With a tremendous crash, they smashed on to the main

A bustle of activity surrounds the wreckage of Boyd's Boids *as 96th BG personnel strive to clear the blocked LNER railway line.* (G. Ward.)

Wreckage was hurriedly hauled aside, enabling a railway gang to repair the line. Self-sealing fuel tanks from the bomber's wing lie in the left foreground, and others are visible where the aluminium skin has been torn open. (Russell J. Zorn.)

London and North Eastern Railway line, close to Bryant's Bridge and mere yards from the runway. Mo felt the left wing jar into the railway embankment and, in the ensuing cacophony and chaos of a disaster's microseconds, the fuselage tore apart spilling bodies into the railway cutting. The centre section then crunched heavily on to the broken rear fuselage, crushing the radio compartment.

In the sudden silence that followed, Mo was amazed to be not only alive but almost unscathed. Others were less fortunate, and his first action on extracting himself was to haul a badly-injured Nick Corleto to safety on top of the cutting. Ignoring the reek of aviation gasoline and the settling tinkle from hot engines, Mo clambered to the flightdeck again and found Boyd just regaining consciousness. As he helped his pilot clear Mo was relieved when assistance from the base arrived and took over the rescue operation.

Incredibly, there were no fatalities among *Boyd's Boids,* but the crew never flew together again. Some were too injured, others healed on different timescales and recovered to join new crews. They all survived the war.

★ Releasing the bombs with the formation leader meant that highly trained bombardiers could be replaced by toggliers on many aircraft. The togglier watched the leader and operated a toggle switch for simultaneous release.

30: Grateful to the Almighty

NO LANDING IS complete until engines are shut down and the crew safely disembarked. Those final moments of flight, gently settling to the ground, were comforting, with the promise of rest and relief after an exhausting, nerve-wracking mission. At the last moment things could go wrong, however, and the loss of Lt Owen W. Winter and crew of the 94th BG illustrates a haunting misfortune.

Following most mishaps a War Department, Army Air Force Form 14 *Report of Aircraft Accident* would be filed. The report on the loss of the Winter crew, dated

Lieutenant Norman Hochberg knew the impact was serious. (N. Hochberg.)

on 7 December 1944, reads as follows: 'On 30th November, at approximately 1645 hours, a 38-aircraft formation returned to base from an operational mission over Germany. Landing by peeling off from sections proceeded according to Standard Operating Procedure. At 1651 hours two B-17Gs were about two miles away from the field on final approach for landing on runway 275. Due to a restricted visibility of approximately 3,900 yards, it was impossible to ascertain the exact closeness of the aircraft from the control tower or from the caravan at the landing end of the runway. A "broadcast" was made to the aircraft on station frequency, "Darky" frequency and Channel "A" for the two aircraft on final approach to use caution and observe other aircraft on approach. As they approached the field, it was possible to tell that one aircraft was directly over the other by a vertical spread of approximately 100 ft. At this time, the higher aircraft was at an altitude of about 300 ft. Red flares were fired from the caravan and tower and a "broadcast" for both aircraft to go round was made. The lower aircraft pulled up rather violently, gaining sufficient altitude to collide with the airplane above, was broken into two sections by the propellers of the upper aircraft and immediately crashed and burned. All members of the crew were fatally injured. The second aircraft maintained sufficient power to execute a crash-landing immediately north of the main field without further damage to the aircraft and without injury to any crew member.'

Lieutenant Norman Hochberg, who was on board the second bomber, recalls what happened: 'Our crew was a Lead Crew, and on November 30, 1944, our 14th mission was to Lutzkendorf, Germany, which was an 8½-hour flight. I was Co-Pilot of the aircraft and Neil Pratt was the Crew Commander.

'That day, an officer from Headquarters was assigned to our 'plane as Command Pilot, and he flew in my co-pilot position. I was assigned as Flight Controller for our echelon. I do not recall the weather or other details of the mission, as nothing stands out in mind as being especially eventful until we returned to our field at Bury St. Edmunds.

'As I was not acting as co-pilot and my duties for the mission had been completed, I went into the nose of the 'plane. I had placed my chest parachute and harness in my flight bag and then sat in the bombardier's seat in the Plexiglas nose of the 'plane immediately over the twin .50-calibre machine guns.

'The normal procedure used upon returning to the airport was to join the traffic pattern, and follow the 'plane in front at a reasonably safe distance. When the 'plane rolled on to the final approach leg, the right wing was dropping and the 'plane began levelling. I looked out to the right side of the 'plane, and I was staring into the eyes of the pilot of a 'plane to our right. That 'plane was slightly below ours and slightly ahead of us. As the right wing levelled, the propellers of number three and four engines struck the other 'plane's fuselage immediately behind the trailing edge of the left wing, and our 'plane seemed to nose up and stutter. I knew the impact was serious, and I felt that our 'plane was about to lose airspeed and stall; and I was waiting for the resulting drop to the ground. However, the 'plane retained sufficient airspeed to maintain flight.

'On take-off for the mission that morning, a fuse blew out so that the landing gear failed to electrically retract. The wheels had to be cranked up on leaving the field, and they were cranked down in preparation for the landing; and it is to this fuse problem that I attribute the saving of the lives of my crew and myself. After the impact of the two 'planes and our retention of enough speed to be airborne, our 'plane veered off of the final approach but continued outside of the perimeter of the airport, parallel with the runway on which it was intended that we land. The wheels being down rather than retracted, as would be normal, caused the 'plane to hit the ground in a brussel sprout patch, then bounce into the air and fly over two stone walls lining a dirt road between the two brussel sprout fields. The 'plane then rolled to a stop, and all of us scrambled from it in case a fire or explosion ensued.

'When no fire or explosion occurred we returned to our 'plane and made a cursory inspection of the damage and I saw that the Plexiglas on which I was sitting, as well as the Plexiglas which was in the nose of the 'plane, was gone. The twin .50 calibre machine guns in the nose were gone, the bombsight position was ripped out. The third and fourth engine propeller tips were torn off and the blades, immediately inward of the tips, were bent; the trailing edge of the 'plane's right wing and

Stranded in a sprout field, the B-17 has had its chin turret torn off and damage to the wing trailing edge is evident. (Russell J. Zorn.)

Owen Winter's B-17 plunged into this meadow at Battlies Corner near Rougham, killing all nine crew. (Russell J. Zorn.)

right wing flaps between the third and fourth engines were chewed up and ripped apart where the propellers of the other 'plane came into contact with our 'plane. Needless to say, we were all shaken by the incident and grateful to the Almighty that we were spared from physical harm.

'I do not remember when we learned of the enormous tragedy which befell the Winter's crew in the other 'plane. I don't recall whether the information was related to us while we were in the farm field or at the debriefing; but I was dumbstruck by the tragic and untimely death of nine good, innocent people whose lives came to an abrupt end at their home base and not in pursuit of action against our enemy.'

31: No more Christmases

LOSSES TAKING OFF; losses landing; combat casualties and the constant struggle against the European climate. A human drama – young men facing adversity to overcome evil. It is no wonder that the essence of such events remains vivid to veterans and permanently etched into the history of many British communities.

The Suffolk hamlet of Parham was projected into the newspapers on 27 December 1944, when a crashing B-17 destroyed the village chapel. Hidden from the tiny rural community by sloping farmland, the 390th BG airbase had become operational in August 1943. In those grim days of war and rationing, friendships quickly formed between 'limey' and 'yank' so, by Christmas 1944, the airfield hosted a party for over 270 local children. Summarising the successful occasion, 390 BG records posed a poignant question prominent in the minds of Parham's provisional American population – 'Next Christmas – where?'

During December fog, snow and ice kept bombers grounded, but any opportunities to fly were seized and the 27th saw plans to pulverise German marshalling yards

Flight Officer James McGuire and crew perished when this Fortress crashed in Parham village. Serial 42-107010 was a B-17G-35-DL built by Douglas. (S.P. Evans.)

A scene of destruction at Parham – 500 lb bombs, bits of Boeing, and debris from the village chapel. (Russell J. Zorn.)

yet again. Hitler's last thrust west, the 'Battle of the Bulge,' was being strenuously resisted, and smashing the transportation system throttled the opposition's supply resources. While guns thundered around Bastogne, Parham awoke to rime ice creating Christmas-card pastoral scenes. The ice-covered B-17s also looked picturesque, but behind the beauty lay the potential of frozen controls, engine failure, and unpredictable aerodynamics owing to ice accretion. As Flt Off James E. McGuire's crew taxied out, fog obscured the tower and radio contact seemed more detached than ever as the controller's ethereal voice came from beyond the grey mists surrounding the cockpit. Only the nearest of the 34 taxiing bombers could be seen from the control tower in visibility cut to 200 yards. McGuire's Fortress 'sounded all right' as it stereoed from right to left on the take-off. A few seconds later came the horrific noise of a crash and the thunderous blast of bombs.

Within moments the crash trucks roared into action and went racing into the mist as a further blast boomed over frozen farmland from the direction of Parham. Some records mention failure of a port engine; it was also felt that a frozen pitot tube caused an erroneous indication of airspeed. Instead of climbing, McGuire's B-17 sagged into the declining contours towards Parham and hit a tree. The left wing and elevator sheared off, and the bomber smashed into a railway embankment on the village outskirts. Continuing on a swift and ghastly trail of disintegration, the bomber hit a roadside and exploded. To Mr H.W. Richardson, the village storekeeper, 'It seemed like an earthquake' as doors blew in, ceilings fell, glass shattered and tiles hurtled skywards. The chapel vanished in a roar and blast of bombs which spewed bits of building and bomber for hundreds of yards.

Mrs Snowling, the railway station gatekeeper, was blown from her kitchen into an adjoining room, but bravely kept her wits and telephoned an alarm to stop trains approaching the scene of the disaster. A local reporter said: 'The village resembled a battlefield,' but there were no serious injuries among the population. It was grimly evident, however, that the bomber's crew had perished. For nine sons there would be no more Christmases: James E. McGuire, pilot; Hamilton H. Swasey, co-pilot; Albert V. Banning, navigator; John F. Crahan, togglier; and the gunners: Pleasant D. Ralston Jr; Dominick Licata; Devore Murdock, Francis R. Tornabene; and James L. Trotter.

32: Happy New Year?

FOUR DAYS AFTER McGuire's fatal crash, the 390th BG suffered another casualty at the opposite end of a mission, when a new B-17 crashed on landing. Not only had the aircraft logged few flying hours, but the crew were on their first mission. Ben Holman, the engineer and top-turret gunner, recalls events leading up to 31 December 1944:

'We were assembled at Drew Field, Florida, in August of 1944, took our overseas training, then went by train to Savannah, Georgia, to pick up a new 'plane. We flew up the east coast to Bangor, Maine, in the last week of October 1944, and then to Gander, Newfoundland, on 31 October 1944.'

Following a now well-established route, Ben and his fellow crew members, commanded by Lt Robert Penovich, waited for clear weather and departed Gander for Prestwick, Scotland, at the end of November. On arrival the new bomber disap-

Would 1945 be a Happy New Year for Bob Penovich's crew? Standing, L to R: Lloyd Chapman, Smith (assigned after injury to Gleason), Richard Myers and Wilson. Kneeling, L to R: Ben Holman, Bob Penovich, Robert Taggart and Maurice Stanton. (B. Holman.)

peared to a modification centre while Bob and his men entrained for the Replacement and Control Depot at Stone in Staffordshire. After they had paused a few days to await a combat unit assignment, their next rail journey took them to Framlingham, Suffolk, an historic town which had given its name to the airfield at Parham for the duration.

Ben continues: 'I think we got there about 3 December 1944. This was buzz-bomb alley, and many nights the doodlebugs could be seen heading for London with fire shooting out of the engine. They would be a couple or so hundred feet up. We had a month of training at the base, which was AAF Station 153, 570 Squadron, 390 Group.

'On the evening of 30 December 1944 our name was up on the board to fly the next day. I was so excited that I did not sleep all night. Breakfast was at 0300 hours, briefing at 0400 hours, and take off at 0600 hours. It was still dark, but the weather was clear with unlimited visibility. We were very pleased to be assigned to such a 'plane as B-17G 44-8273 for our first mission. It was practically a new 'plane that had been given to one of the older crews. It was clean, engines were A1, everything functioned perfectly, all ammunition boxes were full and everything as it should be. We were carrying ten 500 lb general-purpose bombs and were heading for Hamburg, Germany where we were to bomb the Rhenania Oil Refinery. We circled for two hours and got into formation at 25,000 ft. The weather was clear, and at 0800 hours we headed north-east along the Dutch and German coasts. At 1115 hours we got to the estuary of the Elbe river. Off to the left I could see the Island of Heligoland, of which I had read much in relation to World War One. We headed east-south-east along the Elbe river and at 1145 hours were at the IP.'

The records of 390 BG add to Ben's account: 'The route out was flown south of course, taking the division line over the Frisian Islands. However, the column corrected course and crossed the enemy coast at the briefed point. The Initial Point was made good and the run was started by squadrons . . . Intense flak about two minutes before bombs away spread the formation and caused a poor pattern.'

Ben says: 'I had heard all about flak and the death and damage it could deal to any airplane and crew. The weather was clear, the sky was bright blue, and the sun brightly shining. We started on the bomb run straight and even. German flak blasted us right and left. Hundreds and thousands of black puffs appeared, each the size of a fifty-gallon oil drum. As far ahead as we could see these puffs made a black cloud through which we flew, and at times was so thick that it obscured the forward vision. High-speed steel slivers from the exploding flak penetrated the 'planes from nose to tail.

'Enemy fighters were in the area, but did not attack, and one fighter could be seen going down at a distance. The 95th Group was ahead of us and the 100th Group behind us. They took an awful beating from the intense flak and each Group had several of their 'planes blown up and fall to the ground in so many flaming pieces. Just before bombs away at 1200 hours the 'plane to our left took a direct hit and was set on fire. It turned down at a steep angle with the flames engulfing the tanks on its right wing. Trailing flames and smoke, it was soon out of sight. Another 'plane also went down due to the heavy flak.'

The official account supports Ben's recollections. Two 390 BG ships succumbed to flak. Aircraft number '247, Lt W.J. Monit and crew, was hit by flak over the target at 11.54 a.m., just after releasing its bombs. From 25,800 ft the B-17, its port wing ablaze, peeled out of formation to the left and then exploded. No parachutes were seen as flaming debris cascaded earthwards. Lieutenant R.J. Nash's aeroplane, number '632, was also hit, and slid out of formation followed by a loyal wing-man for a short distance. Unable to help his leader, the wingman resumed his position and Nash's straggling bomber was pounced on by a Messerschmitt Me 262. Ben's observation that the 100th 'took an awful beating' was an understatement. Twelve of their B-17s were hacked from the heavens by fighters and flak.

His account continues: 'After bombs away we made a left turn to the rally point and headed south-west for home. The pilot, Bob Penovich, called for a check on the crew and battle damage. Everyone seemed to be alive and talking, so I thought it a little strange. However, I soon changed my mind when I looked out my turret to the right and in the wing was a large hole, the size of a wash tub, with a big piece of jagged aluminium attached to the edge of the hole and flapping in the slip-stream. The 'plane had dozens of fist-size holes, but fate deemed that none of the crew were struck.

'We headed back along the Frisian Islands, on which were many of the heavy 88 flak guns. They fired at us, but we were out of range. We were able to relax a little, and at 1500 hours or a little later were back at the base. The weather was clear with a solid cloud cover up to 10,000 ft or so.

'We landed in the usual manner with about a mile of runway ahead of us. We coasted toward the end of the runway, but as we approached the end I was cons-cious of the fact that we were still travelling at a high rate of speed. The brakes had failed! We shot off the end of the runway. In a flash we were across the dirt and Penovich called: "Brace yourselves". Instantly I put one hand against the rear of the pilot's seat and the other around one of the uprights to the turret, with my left foot against the catwalk to the nose. There was a pond of water with thick ice 300 or so feet off the end of the runway. We hit the ice with a terrific crash

A splendid view of Bob Penovich's bent bomber. The hole cut by Ben Holman can be seen in the nose. (Russell J. Zorn.)

that sounded like a hundred garbage cans hitting the pavement at once. This was followed by a second and harder collision that almost broke my grip as we ended up against the bank on the far side of the pond.

'Machine guns broke loose from their mounts, ammunition belts went flying through the air, the nose of the 'plane folded up against the cockpit. A flying ammunition can ripped the armpit out of my flying jacket. The landing gear was wiped out, and number three engine was pulled under the wing, where it sizzled in the water, which was covered with big chunks of ice. Bob Penovich and W.M. Hayes, co-pilot, unstrapped themselves from their seats and started through the two small sliding windows on either side of the cockpit. They were both big men and I thought they would never make it out. Hayes got out first on the co-pilot's side, and I dove through the window behind him. It was a long way to the ground and I hit hard, but no injuries. Bob Penovich had cut the main switch as we went off the end of the runway, but we still had a thousand gallons of gas left in the tanks and I was afraid it was going to go up in a big explosion. However, after a minute or so, it appeared as though there would be no blow-up.'

Bob Penovich provides the pilot's point of view: 'The intense flak about two minutes before bombs away caused damage to other sections and parts of the 'plane. These included the hydraulic brake system. In preparation for landing, the hydraulic accumulator was started and pressure built up normally for flaps and other landing procedures. After landing and applying the brakes near the end of the runway, they did not respond. In addition, the co-pilot's efforts to disengage the tailwheel lock failed, and our attempt to turn off the runway by powering number one merely resulted in increasing our speed straight off the end of the runway and into the pond.' W.M. Hayes had replaced their regular co-pilot, Bob Taggart, because it was standard practice to assign a combat experienced co-pilot to new crews on their first mission.

Ben remembers: 'In the nose section, Roy Golder, navigator, and Jim Gleason, armorer-togglier, had been rendered unconscious by the terrific crash but had come to and were talking, although they could not move as they were held down buried under hundreds of pounds of chin turret, ammunition, machine guns, navigational and bombing equipment. The smaller of the station fire trucks (the large one was busy at another crash) followed us off the end of the runway. A large group of onlookers soon assembled, and after a few minutes I set to freeing the two men in the nose. I begged a long pry bar, and sledge hammer and an axe from the ambulance crew. I got down in the deep mud on the lower half, right side of the nose section just ahead of the windshield. In about fifteen minutes I had cut a hole about three feet by three feet. The Medics were able to crawl in, free the trapped men, slide them out.

'Roy Golder was OK after three weeks, and was able to resume flying with the crew. Jim Gleason was so badly injured that his flying days were over. He was sent back to the States. Maurice Stanton, ball-gunner, and Lloyd Chapman, tail-gunner, were shaken up and bruised but were none the worse for the experience.

'We went for debriefing and interrogation and then supper. I walked back to the hut past the coal yard, wondering about my chances for 34 more missions and if I would ever see my parents, sister, girlfriend or home town again.'

Happily, Ben survived his missions and returned to his family physically unscathed but, with the advent of each of the many subsequent New Years, he has recalled the dramatic events and uncertainties which faced him on New Year's Eve 1944.

33: Over-excited

ANOTHER INCIDENT ON Sunday 31 December 1944 saw a B-17 with a full bomb load crash close to houses in the village of Little Cornard, near Sudbury.

Thirty-eight aircrews from the 486th BG were also briefed to hit oil-industry targets in Hamburg. Commanding one of them was 2nd Lt Virgil G.F. Raddatz, a

B-17G 3R-C 43-37910 (nearest camera) forms up for a mission. (R. Andrews.)

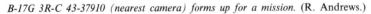

The Raddatz crew, 832 squadron, 486th BG. Standing, L to R: Frederick Koehn, Harold Paetz, Russell Humphries, Captain Simpson and Virgil Raddatz. Kneeling, L to R: Harry Tekler, Aloysius Ontko, Robert Corman, Robert Holan, unknown. (R. Andrews.)

skilled pilot with 694 flying hours. He and his co-pilot, 2nd Lt Kenneth C. Hart, completed their take-off checks and noted nothing unusual. All four engines were run up several times – propeller-pitch checks and turbo settings showed no symptoms of the trouble ahead. Confidently, Raddatz started to take-off run and the B-17 became airborne as normal. Then, when the bomber was only 20-30 ft up, Hart was startled by stabs of crimson flame spurting from their number three engine. The fire was small, but the intensity was magnified by surrounding darkness and, before he could react, the engine revolutions surged out of control and a massive oil loss made feathering impossible. Understandably, Hart was frightened and quickly became 'over-excited', repeatedly yelling that they had a fire. His agitated state did not help his pilot.

Climbing unsteadily, Raddatz kept control and immediately tried alerting the airfield on his command radio but, owing to pre-mission activity, he was unable to get through. Switching to VHF, he tried again, banking the B-17 into a return pattern. Contact with control was finally established on channel 'A', and all take offs ceased to enable the emergency on aircraft 910-C to be dealt with.

Seeing the landing lights of the distressed bomber on approach, control realised that Raddatz was too high, and ordered him to break off and go round again. The unfortunate pilot's predicament now seriously worsened as he attempted to climb away – the main gear refused to retract. Ordering it to be hand-cranked, Raddatz now juggled with an engine fire, a wind milling propeller and the additional drag of exposed main wheels. Fortunately the blaze burnt itself out, but Raddatz dared not risk restarting the engine, even though he desperately needed more power to compensate for the drag from his undercarriage.

From the tower his Fortress was seen to lose altitude while making a slow, left turn beyond the west end of the runway. As the bomber sank from view in the darkness, radio contact ceased and observers feared a repeat of Herrmann's crash

Guarded by the local constabulary, 3R-C rests at Little Cornard. (Russell J. Zorn.)

in October. As they were unaware of the crash location, little could be done until word arrived, and mission 123 resumed. At 7.30 a.m. the telephone rang. Instead of a call reporting the blazing destruction of their missing B-17, Raddatz was on the line, asking to be collected.

Flying Fortress number 43-37910, now lay on a meadow in the village of Little Cornard, about four miles south of Station 174, guarded by the local 'Bobby'. None of the crew was injured, nor were there any civilian casualties, although the B-17G was a write-off. Responding to Raddatz's call, Capt Rumisck, the Flying Control Officer, sent a crash truck and personnel carrier. The station Bomb Reconnaissance Officer also set off to check the ordnance and assess the risks to civilian property. He found that Raddatz had achieved an amazing crash-landing in almost total darkness. The B-17 had chewed into some treetops before slithering to earth and ripping away its starboard wing. Its chin and ball turrets were smashed as it swept through a hedge and barbed-wire fence and slewed violently to face the way it had come. As the aircraft slid backwards the number two propeller was torn off, and the wreck finally stopped only feet from the nearest dwelling. Despite such rough treatment, not one of the 20 300 lb M31 bombs exploded, and all were defused by 6216 RAF Bomb Disposal Squadron and returned to the 486th BG.

Mistakes had been made and a young officer became 'over-excited' – very human in such circumstances. Senior 486th BG officers attributed most of the blame to material failure and, happily, the Raddatz crew went on to complete the remainder of their tour.

34: Flaring personalities

HARMONY AMONGST AN aircrew was essential, given the reliance they had to place on each other, but sometimes operational stresses could fracture relationships under pressure. This happened to the crew of a 388th BG B-17, *Mary's Sister*, on 5 January 1945.

Captain John B. Brinegar, who was Lead Pilot for the mission to Hanau marshalling yards, recalls that the 388th flew as the second of three groups in the 45th Combat Wing. 'Take off was made before daylight in heavy snow using a 4,000 ft runway because of a strong north wind 90° from the main 6,000 ft runway,' he relates. 'Although the briefed assembly altitude was 17,000 ft, cloud and contrails prevent assembling the group until 25,000 was reached. We departed on course a little late because of the difficulties in assembling, with the 96th BG leading, followed by the 388th BG and 452nd BG. Large cloud formations reaching our altitude caused some deviations from the prescribed route to avoid them. The ground was obscured by cloud as we entered Germany and navigation was by radar.'

Confusion regarding target identification resulted in the 388th and 452nd separating from the 96th. Led by Capt Tom Dennis as Command Pilot, the 388th spotted their objective through a break in the undercast and bombed visually. Flak over Hanau was described as 'moderate accurate tracking', and a cluster of bursts caught *Mary's Sister* on the bombing run. On board as radio operator was Tech Sgt Ray Ward. That morning, when talking to crew chief George Pilgrim before take-of, he asked what had happened to the original *Mary*. The jaundiced response was that she had gone down a long time ago, and George followed this with an expressed desire for someone to belly her sister so he would have a newer, less troublesome ship to maintain. Now, bouncing in the flak-punched sky over Hanau, with two engines out and the bomb doors jammed open after release, Ray felt that the disgruntled crew-chief would get his wish.

Mary's Sister dropped from formation and her pilot, Lt James F. Reuther, asked Ray to radio the nearest continental airstrip. Anticipating this request, Ray had already established contact, but an argument now developed between Reuther and the navigator, Lt H.W. Swanson, who for some reason insisted that they try for England. Swanson eventually got his way – with disastrous consequences. Flying a course for the emergency airfield at RAF Manston, they steadily lost height as they approached England. Ball-turret gunner S/Sgt Marlin H. Smith felt very uncomfortable as the bomber edged nearer the sea.

When the English coastline became distinguishable it became evident they were slightly adrift from their intended course, and this provoked another row between Reuther and Swanson. Matters were decided by *Mary's Sister* when another engine

The cockpit roof ripped away. Still strapped to their seats, both pilots were thrown 50 ft from the wreck. Snow has decorated the debris. The cockpit roof with the top turret aperture can be seen lower right. (Russell J. Zorn.)

started spluttering. The nearest airfield was RAF Hawkinge, and the ailing B-17 sagged wearily in to land as her crew took up their crash stations. Swanson did not leave the navigator's position. Hawkinge was an RAF fighter field unsuitable for heavy bombers, but *Mary's Sister* left no choice and Reuther settled close to the threshold, giving himself the maximum of space available. Cutting throttles, he applied braking pressure and discovered that the brakes had been shot out. There was no response.

As they sped across the turf, an effort to gun the two remaining engines and go around again only veered the B-17 to port. Seconds later, *Mary's Sister* slammed into an air raid shelter and tore open. Swanson died instantly. The cockpit roof ripped away and Reuther, still strapped to his seat, was thrown nearly 50 ft from the wreck. His co-pilot, Lt Raymond Helminiak, followed a similar trajectory, but both survived. Less fortunate were Tech Sgts J. Haskett, togglier, and F.P. Thielsks, the top-turret gunner. Staff Sergeant Virgil Koon, the tail gunner, also perished. Just before impact Marlin Smith braced himself, hands behind his neck, against a bulkhead. In the tumbling jumble, noise and chaos of the crash one of the waist guns tore loose, hurtled forward, and hit Marlin violently in the back, dislocating both shoulder blades and ripping his shoulder muscles from the bone. As the cacophony ceased, those who could do so clambered from the shambles of *Mary's Sister* in case it exploded. Fortunately, the wreck did not ignite, and rescue services worked during the darkening afternoon to extricate both living and dead aircrew. Swanson's adamant stance on returning to England had cost him his life.

With hindsight, Ray Ward felt they had been a highly competent crew but that there were '. . . too many flaring personalities'.

35: Incident over Bury

THE EYE-BASED 490th BG were not operating on 5 January 1945, but a training accident that afternoon exacted a toll heavier than on many missions.

Newly arrived aircrew needed additional training before being allowed on operations. Assembly skills, formation flying, navigation and simulated bomb runs were the order that Friday, a beautiful day of sharp winter-blue skies flecked with few clouds and crystal clarity. Yesterday's snow iced a landscape patterned with dark woodlands and the stark, individual outlines of villages and towns presented precise targets for practice bombing runs.

However, one flier was too scared to enjoy the scenery. Roger Coryell, an experienced radio operator on Roy White's crew, felt that his initial reluctance about flying with neophyte birdmen was proving well founded. His rôle was to check out a recently-assigned radio operator in customs and procedures used over England. With over 30 missions to his credit, Roger wanted no more flying than was necessary to complete his tour. Hoped-for snow failed to arrive to scrub the mission, and soon his B-17 was undulating upwards on winter-thin air. Concentrating on instructing, Roger introduced his fledgling to Eighth Air Force techniques and British terminology. At one point they tuned in to transmissions to bombers in combat over Europe before returning to their base frequency. Such preoccupation prevented him from seeing how their assembly was proceeding and, when a cry of alarm cut across the intercom, he was startled to see the great silver belly of a B-17 poised

Ernest Langholz had his fingers 'rather neatly amputated'. (E. Langholz.)

only 15ft overhead. As they manoeuvred away, Roger peered out and: 'Instead of each ship gradually working his way into the formation and then closing in tighter, slowly, all the ships were jerkily diving into and out of their right places. Planes were sliding back and forth, from side to side and up and down. In the short space of thirty seconds I must have seen four near collisions.' In time, the ragged assembly settled into an order of sorts, and three mock bombing runs were flown, along with some navigational instruction.

At 2.30 p.m. the formation flew at 12,000 ft towards the distinctive features of Bury St. Edmunds. On board B-17G 43-38050, near Roger's ship, was Lt Ernest F. Langholz, an Instructor-Navigator who recalls: 'Aircraft 43-38050 carried four instructors along with the newly-arrived crew. Major Ed Blum was 849 Squadron Operations Officer, and was Instructor Pilot in our aircraft. We flew in the lower left position of the formation so that Blum, riding in the co-pilot seat, could observe the formation. [Lieutenant Harold Adelman was the pilot.] During the course of the mission, on several occasions, 43-38111, which was above and to the right of us, failed to hold position. I noticed this, as did Blum, who talked to 43-38111 about tightening up.

We were flying along smoothly when suddenly there was a bump and a "bucking" of the aircraft. I somehow sensed it was time to get out, and tried to get to the forward escape hatch; however, before I could make it, a ball of flame came out of the bomb bay area. The next thing I was aware of was falling through the air with pieces of wreckage going by me. Fortunately, I had obtained a back-pack type parachute which came through the wreck intact. But when I put my right hand up to get the rip cord handle on the left shoulder, all I had was a thumb. Four fingers had been rather neatly amputated, probably by a prop or heavy piece of metal. I got the 'chute open with my left hand and floated down into the middle of a beet field, where two elderly men working there came up to me and escorted me out to the road. Some people at the base near Bury St. Edmunds had seen the accident and had a jeep on the road waiting to take me to the base clinic. From there it was the 65th General Hospital near Diss for skin graft, etc, and then to

B-17G 43-38050 burns furiously in a field on Hall Farm. (Russell J. Zorn.)

The photographer photographed. Russell Zorn stands centre left, beyond the tailplane of 43-38050. Symbolically torn, the fuselage star-and-bar is crumpled in the foreground. (N. Offord.)

the Walter Reed Hospital in Washington.'

Of ten men on board, only Langholz, Blum and Lt Harold K. Hatrell survived, the latter spilling from the broken fuselage as the B-17 exploded. Both he and Blum suffered only minor injuries.

Aircraft 43-38111 was flown by Lt Donald L. Wood under the instruction of Lt Paul E. McGee, and the left wing of their aircraft struck 43-38050 in the waist. For a few moments the B-17s fused together, then Adelman's ship broke apart near the radio operator's position. The forward section fell and then blew up as the carcass of Wood's bomber turned on its back and spun towards Bury St. Edmunds. The airmen inside were pinned in an aluminium coffin which plummeted into the beet sugar factory sewerage purification pool on Hollow Road. Adelman's exploding bomber scattered wreckage for four miles between Bury St. Edmunds and Fornham St. Martin. The bulk fell blazing onto farmland at Hall Farm, where it was photographed by Russ Zorn, who was returning from another assignment. The ominous pall of smoke told its own, sad story, and Russ reached the crash before the crash trucks but could only watch helplessly as flames incinerated bodies not thrown clear. One corpse crashed through a glass roof in the sugar beet factory, another thudded on to a frozen tennis court as lighter debris fluttered down like metal snowflakes and settled in fields and gardens on the outskirts of Bury.

A roll-call revealed 16 fatalities, with several bodies unaccounted for, presumably trapped in the submerged hulk of 43-38111. That evening schoolboys, with the usual callousness of their species, began gathering and exchanging souvenirs. A more grisly task facing a detachment from the American 453rd Sub Depot was the recovery of bodies from the sewage purification pool. When Russ visited the scene to take official photographs, an oil and gasoline covered lake was being dragged without success. An airman sitting astride the inverted fuselage yelled at Russ not to smoke because of high-octane fumes hanging in the atmosphere. Even though the sluice valve was opened to reduce the water level, a layer of sludge still handicapped the

The inverted hulk of B-17G 43-38111 in the purification pool on Hollow Road, Bury St. Edmunds. (Russell J. Zorn.)

search. For several days the sombre task continued in freezing temperatures and
snow squalls. Eight days after the crash, two bodies floated to the surface and were
found near the shoreline. On 13 January, in intense cold, the pool was again unsuc-
cessfully dragged for the last victim. The following day a thaw set in and receding
snow revealed his corpse, not in the purification pool, but laying in a snow drift
near the factory gates.

Several days passed, then the *Bury Free Press* published 'an appeal for the
assistance of the public' from the Chief Constable of West Suffolk, who was anxious to recover 'all outstanding parts' from the crashed bombers. A reminder was
issued, stating that it was '. . . an offence under the Defence Regulations to retain
any part of a crashed aircraft.' A few junior culprits were caught out, but without
doubt, some souvenirs still exist in the town, and pieces of Ernest Langholz's B-17
are extant on Hall Farm. Today, a licence under the Protection of Military Remains
Act 1986 is necessary before any parts can be recovered, but an ageing airman,
Ernest F. Langholz, hopes that someone may hand on a small token from the incident over Bury.

36: Scared all the way

THE LAST EIGHTH Air Force bomber group to become operational was the
493rd, from Debach, on 6 June 1944. Eventually they faced their hundredth mission, to the Hohenzollern railway bridge near Cologne, in bitter winter conditions.
The Flying Control log commented: 'It is sincerely hoped that no future mission
will be as difficult to get airborne as was the Group's one hundredth mission on
10 January 1945. To say that trouble was around that day would certainly be a
case of gross understatement. It had snowed immediately before take-off, making

The last Eighth Air Force bomber group to become operational – a formation of 493rd BG Fortresses.

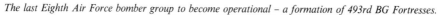

Bill Stepp was terrified at the prospect of flying with a different crew. He nearly climbed Jacob's Ladder that day. (W. Stepp.)

taxiing in the darkness even more tricky than usual, with the result that several aircraft got stuck off hardstands. After the first few planes were airborne, Lieutenant Butler's plane crashed and exploded two miles north of the field.'

'Crashed and exploded' – those three words cover the tragic departure of souls and, occasionally, cases of miraculous survival. Sergeant William H. Stepp recalls his career, and how he avoided climbing Jacob's Ladder that bleak, winter Wednesday: 'I entered the service in July 1943, trained in the States as a radio operator and gunner, assigned to a flight crew piloted by Lt Adalai S. Munday from Peoria, Illinois, and co-piloted by Jack Martin from Missouri. We arrived in England after training completion in Walla Walla, Washington. We had trained in B-24s, and felt sure we were slated for the South Pacific, but we found ourselves headed for England in November 1944, by boat landing in Glasgow, Scotland, on Thanksgiving Day. We went by train to Ipswich, England, and then motored to Debach air base, located just a few miles outside Ipswich. We knew we would be flying B-17 Flying Fortresses, because B-24s were mostly used for combat in the South Pacific. My pilot had had no training on B-17s, but the co-pilot had. The pilot flew one mission with the squadron commander and then we were assigned a ship of our own that we christened *Peoria Belle* after the pilot's home town and the ground chief's girl friend, Belle. The crew liked the B-17 because we believed it was a safer ship. Take-off and landing speeds were less than the B-24, it was not as big, and it would glide better in case of an emergency.

'We had finished six combat missions into Germany, hitting airfields in Cologne and Coblenz, and oil targets in Hanover and Merseburg. We had force-landed twice in France, and had our share of flak holes during these six missions. Any member of a combat crew knows the feeling of teamwork and the confidence each member places in the other. You eat, sleep, work, play, and fly together. You become so close that nothing else, it seems, really matters now except the safety and well-being of each other. You become almost inseparable.

'You are alerted the night before a combat mission. The name of the pilot is posted on the squadron bulletin board if his crew is scheduled to fly the next day. The crews were usually posted by 10.00 or 12.00 at the latest. There was always activity around the bulletin board every night until you found out whether or not your crew was scheduled to fly the next day's mission. If you were posted, the next thing was to try and get some sleep. If you were posted I can assure you no one got too much sleep. There would be chatter, and I know a lot of silent prayers were said. Just about anything you wanted to know about someone would be revealed. You could ask a question any hour of the night and get an answer from a buddy that wasn't sleeping well either. The nights that you weren't posted to fly were nights of relief and relaxation, because at least you would have another day.

'January 10 1945 was to be another day for me of relief and relaxation because the night before our crew was not posted to fly. We sat around the barracks, talked, planned, played cards, checkers, etc. I suppose I hit the sack about 12.30 for a good night's rest. It was between 3.00 a.m. to 3.30 a.m. that I was awakened sharply and told to report to breakfast and then to briefing on the double. I told the corporal whose job it was to awaken the crews that were flying, and who had just about shaken me out of my bunk, that he must be off his rocker. I said my crew certainly had not been posted, and that he should check his roster before waking people who were entitled to sleep once in a while. He then told me that another pilot had three men off sick and that I, the navigator, and the bombardier of our crew was assigned to fill in for this pilot on this mission.

'I was terrified – the tension, apprehension, or whatever comes over you; the thought of being taken away from the crew that you had trained so well with, that you knew everything about and depended on and they on you, to fly with a stranger that you didn't even know; an airplane that you weren't familiar with, the little things or malfunctions that you know about and learn to correct on your own 'plane. It was like being in a strange far-off place where nobody cares. Of course they care, but, nevertheless, this is the feeling you get when separated from your own crew, the guys that you depend on are suddenly not with you this trip.

'I got dressed and headed for the mess hall for breakfast, which always consisted of eggs (fresh) sunnyside up or any way you wanted them, hot biscuits, the whole works. Nothing was too good for you because you were probably headed for a rough day and one of which no one could know the outcome until late in the evening, when those that made it would return. At the least it was your day for the breakfast you wanted so much because, if you weren't scheduled to fly, you were served powdered eggs from the can, warmed. I have been in the mess hall when they would be serving the sunnyside-ups and the mission was scrubbed, the sunnysides cancelled and back to the powdered.

'After the breakfast I hurried to briefing, took a seat, listened to the briefing officer explain that the target was . . . and then I must have drawn a blank, all I could think about was: "I'm not flying with my original crew". I left the briefing room not knowing how long or where the target would be. I went outside to board the truck that was always waiting to take you to the 'planes. The navigator and bombardier were already in the truck, and they told me who we were flying with and that the target was a bridge just inside the German lines. I could sense their feelings, and knew that they felt as tensed as I because they both remarked that they wished they were flying with "Ole Dad" this morning – that's what we called our own pilot. We were driven to where the 'plane was parked, met and introduced ourselves to the pilot and his crew, and then climbed aboard to our stations. Their stations were up front, and my radio room was in the waist of the 'plane.

'It was a terrible day. It had been snowing for several days, there was at least six inches of snow on the ground, and it was still snowing. The ground crew were busy servicing the 'plane and two men were on the wings trying to scrape the snow and ice off. This is a must if the 'plane is expected to get off the ground.

'The feeling of fear and uneasiness was still with me, and it got worse, especially when the engines began to start up. I was praying they would scrub this mission and we could get back with our own crew. I really felt that the ground crew hadn't had enough time properly to clear the wings of the heavy snow and ice. The tower ordered us to line up for take off. I was still praying for a scrubbed mission. Our crew had been ready several times, even at the head of the runway ready to go, when the control tower would inform us to taxi back to the hard-stand, mission scrubbed. I knew by experience this could happen, but evidently not this morning. The pilot was taxiing towards the runway and I kept waiting for him to stop and check out the engines, release the brakes and then you're on your way. This is what our pilot did and when he started down the runway nothing short of engine failure could keep him from getting the 'plane in the air. Again the expected didn't happen. The 'plane moved slowly towards the runway and never stopped. I knew that this would be another experience for me, as evidently this pilot was used to gaining the needed power on the engines as he started down the runway to get the 'plane airborne. Maybe this is done and done to perfection, but it wasn't this particular morning.

'We had a gas load of 2,700 gal, we had four 1,000 lb bombs, and several hundred pounds of what we called chaff, which was like Christmas tree icicles, that we used to throw out over the target and before we reached the target area, to mess up the German radar. These icicles would show up on their radar screen, and they would be shooting at these strips until they got our range. Lots of times we could see the ack-ack flak exploding behind us, as these metal strips were being shoved out of a chute in the rear and sides of our 'planes.

'As we were going down the runway I was sitting in my radio room. The windows were all covered with frost or snow and I couldn't see out. It seemed as though we would never leave the runway, and I knew that we had to be past the point of no return, the point that all pilots fear. If something goes wrong you have almost run out of runway and are too fast to stop, so you must get airborne. I must have been pretty close to being in shock from fright, because the 'plane began to vibrate something awful. It sounded as though someone was outside shovelling gravel and throwing it on the 'plane. The next thing I remember was a flash of light that came through the radio room, and then the room was full of a tremedous amount of sparks and smoke. I found myself lying across the radio room on the opposite side from where I was sitting during take-off. Finally I was able to get up, and knew I had to get out. With my hands over my face I made it to the waist of the plane and found the ball-turret gunner and waist-gunner trying to kick the side door open. It was jammed. We did not know if we were on the ground or in the air, all we knew was that we had better get out of there, and in a hurry.

'I couldn't find the tail gunner. I even looked for him in the tail of the 'plane, and no tail gunner in his right mind ever gets in the tail position until after take-off. We decided that he must have stayed up front during the take-off, because he was nowhere in the back stations. We finally managed to kick the door open, and then we could see that we were on the ground and on fire.

'We started running as fast as we could. I lost one of my boots, fell several times, but got up and kept on running. I yelled to the top of my voice: "Get away from those bombs".

'I ran through bushes, jumped over ditches, I couldn't seem to get far enough away to suit myself, especially with the heavy weight of the flying suit and heavy snow to run through. I finally stopped and said a brief prayer, thanking God I got out safely. Then the bombs went off! I hit the ground and kept watching for anything that might hit me. I saw flames over 200 ft high during the explosion. I then got up and yelled: "Art, hey, Art" – that was the name of the waist gunner. He and the ball-turret gunner were in another field, and answered my call.

'We then got together and started towards a farmhouse about half a mile away. We met about six farmers and a couple of kids coming towards us. For a minute we all had thoughts that we might be in enemy territory, being dazed and not knowing for sure what had really happened. When they spoke we realised they were English. One of them took us to his house, gave us tea and brandy, and made us comfortable by the fire. The ball gunner and I bathed Art's head; he had a small cut that didn't amount to much but was bleeding a lot. I tried on four or five shoes, trying to find one to cover my left foot, which felt like it was about to come off.

'The farmer took us back to the 'plane, and it seemed like it took hours to get there. When we arrived, ambulances and a lot of military personnel were there, looking over the wreckage. About half of the 'plane was left. I was busy looking for the bombardier and navigator when a captain told me the navigator was taken to the hospital, badly burned. He told me the control tower watched us stall out at about 300ft and come down, hitting some trees. Part of the right wing had fallen off before we hit the ground. He said that we were about three-and-a-half miles from the base. I found the bombardier in an ambulance. I offered him a smoke and tried to comfort him; he kept saying: "I can't hear you, open the door and come on in, my head hurts". I put my jacket under his head and stayed with him.

'We were brought back to the base hospital and treated. The navigator and bombardier were given treatment at the base and then sent to the 65th General Hospital and sometime later discharged. I was kept at the base hospital for several days, along with the other two gunners. The tail gunner died on the way to hospital, the pilot, co-pilot and engineer were dead instantly on crashing. The five of us that survived and those that didn't get a scratch will always wonder how we did it. Maybe, as some feel, it just wasn't our time. After a few days in a rest home I was back with the old crew to fly 19 more missions, scared all the way but able to perform my duties and wishing all the time that this thing had never happened.'

The bombardier and regular crew-mate who Bill Stepp comforted in the ambulance was 2nd Lt Carlyle E. Bradbury, who suffered major injuries and amnesia following the crash. Recuperating in America before returning to civilian life, Brad lost touch with his crew for over 40 years. In 1988 a letter from an old comrade, navigator Robert E. Gaustad, revealed both of their stories. 'I have thought of you many times over these bunches of years,' Gaustad wrote. 'It's good to hear that you have been enjoying a normal life – marriage, complete with kids and grandkids. It's also a miracle that all this has come to pass. Maybe your kids and grandkids would be interested in knowing just how close they came to not being born.

'You have told me that the amnesia has stayed with you regarding the day of 10 January 1945; that you have no memory of getting out of bed, going to the briefing room or the take-off, or any other events of that day, until you woke up in hospital . . . The way things were, whenever a scheduled crew was short one or more people, somebody in headquarters would spin a wheel of fortune and come up with necessary replacements to fill the shortages. Thus, you and Bill Stepp and I drew the lucky numbers, since the fates arranged for this crew to be in need of a bombardier, navigator and radio operator . . . Well, we took off – you and I were in the nose, right back from the Plexiglas nose cone. While assembling we all had responsibilities to watch out for other aircraft so as to avoid mid-air collisions. God knows how many crews were lost in this manner. Visibility was terrible, and the sky full of airplanes circling around like a flock of geese over a feeding area . . .

'After take off we didn't get very far. We were airborne for only two or three minutes when I felt a giant vibration, then I could see nothing but flames. Next thing I knew I was out in the snow, standing up watching this airplane burning like I was watching a movie. Obviously I was in shock, because it took some moments or minutes, I really don't know how long, for me to realise that I was a part of that scene, that the 'plane had bombs which had not yet exploded (at least I didn't think so), and that I was about to be blasted into eternity. Right close by was a big ditch, later explained as an anti-invasion trench, which I stumbled into. Then the bombs did go off. My senses were so numbed that it sounded like nothing more than a Fourth of July firecracker.

'While I was in my trance, before the bombs went off, I had a clear image of you sprawled out in the snow like you were taking a coffee break. And, to tell the truth, I have always felt guilty about not helping you or at least not trying to. Probably I couldn't have, what with a couple of useless hands, but it has bothered me for years. After the bomb blast I didn't just think you were history, I KNEW IT! You couldn't have been more than 30 or 40 feet from the point of explosion, and if ever there was a survival miracle, you are it. I thought I was the only survivor . . . my hands were badly burned and face not quite so badly.'

Following hospitalization and treatment for burns, Bob Gaustad resumed flying until VE Day. What caused the crash of B-17G 44-8304 remains uncertain, but Bob believed that an abrupt and massive mechanical failure had occurred. Other records pinpoint ice on the wings as the case but, whatever the case, it took the life of Lt William H. Butler and three of his crew. From Debach, the Fortress was seen to make a gradual left turn at low altitude and fall into the ground about two miles north of the airfield. It tore down a large tree on Rookery Farm, Monewden, caught fire, and slithered across snow-clad farmland, coming to rest in a ploughed field. Between three and five minutes later two of the four 1,000 lb bombs exploded. Their

The fuselage of 44-8304 'E' has vanished, leaving only the shredded tail unit on Rookery Farm, Monewden, Suffolk. (Russell J. Zorn.)

two companions were each blown more than 30ft from the wreck. One was found in a highly dangerous condition, with the arming screw sheared off and the striker forced to within a fraction of detonation. The second unexploded bomb had the nose arming vane broken, but its safety discs were held in place by the cap. Had the full load detonated, the casualty list might well have been longer and 493rd BG veterans reunions several members fewer.

37: Ice

ICING CLAIMED THE lives of more airmen on 28 January 1945, when the 94th BG left Rougham to raid railyards at Hohenbudberg, Germany.

Engine start was before dawn, and myriad snowflakes flurried through the brilliance of B-17 landing lights as they inched warily round the perimeter track. Falling snow blotted out guiding lights on the taxi way, causing disorientation even before take-off. Mercifully the snow abated as dawn greyed reluctantly, revealing 32 bombers on a giant white table beneath a dismal cloudscape. Nearly 300 men prayed for mission cancellation, but the urgency of hitting Hohenbudberg prevailed,

Icing proved the downfall of the Weiss crew. Standing, L to R: Wilmar Weiss, Charles Weber, David Smith and Leon Rondeau. Kneeling, L to R: Edward Kelly, Paul Pidgeon, Wayne Ward, Ralph Peeples and Henry Ollerdessen. Weiss, Rondeau and Peeples perished in the crash. (C. Weber.)

The process of dismantling 44-8600 is under way. Note the reversed 'S' stencilled on the bomber's fin.
(Russell J. Zorn.)

and ground staff busied themselves see-sawing ropes across the outer-wing panels to remove snow. The mission was on.

To make matters worse, the wind direction meant that one of the short runways was being used – if they could find it. To delineate where it lay, a jeep was driven the full length, providing some perspective for the first B-17 flown by Lt Frank Halm. With the Halm crew was Lt-Col Bertram Witham Jr, as Command Pilot. Slush slowed acceleration essential for take off. Using every foot available, their B-17 just made it, but not without the landing gear swiping a fence nearly 200 yards off the end of the runway. A second Fortress followed Frank's tracks. Then came the turn of Lt Wilmar G. Weiss and crew.

Fresh snow was falling on the wings of B-17G 44-8600 as it began rolling. Co-pilot Lt Charles V. Weber followed through with his pilot's throttle advance, ready to take over while Weiss concentrated on achieving lift-off. Alarmingly, Weber realised that the B-17 was lagging, and tension accumulated as four engines screamed to overcome an impending disaster. As the bomber shuddered skywards its four whirling propellers clutched like cliff-hanging fingers, sliding remorselessly into an abyss. In those final, desperate seconds Charles Weber felt convinced that they lost power. Moments after taking off, the big bomber stalled before sprawling into a field adjoining the runway. Charles has no memory of hitting the ground because he was catapulted through the cabin roof and landed several hundred feet away as the B-17 burst into flames. Moments later an ugly, black smoke-pall brewed into the snow clouds. Another B-17 scraped overhead before a change of runways avoided further casualties.

Charles Weber spent twenty-two months in hospital and on light duty assignments before being discharged. Wilmar Weiss and three others died in combat – not because of fighters or flak, but owing to the presence of frozen water on an already laden bomber.

38: Into parish history

ONE LEGACY LEFT by the Eighth Air Force is a sense of pride by association in numerous British parishes. Many villages found that neighbouring airfields dwarfed them for the duration and then vanished, to become enormous, ghostly edifices, fast fading into the soil from whence they came. The villages often claimed history and traditions stretching into a past incomprehensible to the brash young boys from a much newer nation. Sometimes these foreign youths made their own tragic contribution to the continuing history of ancient hamlets. So it was for the two Norfolk communities of North and South Lopham on 29 January 1945.

That day, 17-year-old Tom Emms was working on Hall Farm, South Lopham, where his father was foreman. As he was an ardent aircraft enthusiast and Air Training Corps cadet with 1070 (Diss) Squadron, Tom's attention was often distracted from farm duties to watch bombers heaving majestically heavenwards from nearby Snetterton Heath. By 9.05 a.m. his father was at least getting value for money, because the climbing Fortresses were now lost from view, assembling above clouds. Farmwork continued against the familiar background rumble of aero engines, and Tom and his father were just crossing the road from the farm to their cottage when they heard a higher-noted 'vroom' overhead. As they looked skywards there was a big flash through the clouds, and then a loud bang echoed earthwards. Tom knew what had happened, and the grim evidence emerged from cloud moments later. A section of Flying Fortress wing, the engines still churning, tumbled to earth on fire. Man and boy stood mesmerised, frightened but fascinated. Streaking down, some ammunitions boxes clattered as they bounced on the hard, frosty ground. Lighter pieces floated, drifting like leaves. The main section of burning bomber impacted and spat exploding ammunition viciously across open countryside. Debris of all shapes and sizes showered over the Lophams. Later, Tom found a Christmas card inside a piece of fuselage. It read: 'To Roy, with love, from all at "Tibbetts" '.

Working at Fersfield, Leslie J. Burrows saw the collision through a break in the clouds. One aircraft hit the other at right angles, breaking it to pieces. Among the falling debris he discerned bodies, but no parachutes appeared. The second bomber fell almost lazily in a flat spin, but no one escaped as far as Leslie could tell.

On leave from the RAF, Eric Meeks was enjoying breakfast at Meadowhurst Farm when he heard a 'terrific bang in the sky'. Rushing outside, he saw half a B-17 tipping over and over as it fell. His mother-in-law was gathering eggs when she and the chickens were startled by the blast. Retreating from the hen-house, she heard a thump on the roof and, once outside, found the cause. A blood-stained parachute, still bundled, had fallen on top of the shed. Nearby she saw a pair of brown boots; in the adjacent field lay their owner's broken body.

From Gables Farm Vic Gilbert saw: 'a big black fireball' coming down. 'The

Vic Gilbert found the crushed corpse of Sgt William Brauner inside the severed tail of 43-38746, BX-G. (Russell J. Zorn.)

sky seemed full of small black pieces getting bigger as they fell,' he recalled. 'I noticed the tail section looking as if it were going down over East Harling – all the time the black pieces were coming closer, sounding like pieces of galvanised metal as they hit the frosty ground. Meanwhile, the tail section seemed to have changed direction. It finally dropped into a ditch opposite the farmhouse, 100 yards from where we had been having breakfast. I ran over and the rear gunner was still inside. The body seemed just pulp to me.'

Cleaning down the cowshed of Grange Farm, Eric Reeder was startled when a loud explosion boomed through the village. Twelve 500 lb bombs from one aircraft landed in North Lopham, but only one detonated, about 200ft behind *The Limes,* doing superficial damage to the house, the stables nearby, and two greenhouses. Three unexploded bombs buried themselves in gardens behind the Methodist Chapel, and three more landed in a meadow on Grange Farm itself. The others, also unexploded, fell in open countryside. From the second B-17 another dozen bombs landed west of North Lopham. Five exploded, but did little more than leave 15ft-deep craters across the countryside. Seven vanished, leaving hard-to-find points of penetration only 18in across.

'It only seemed a short while before the whole area was alive with USA jeeps and ambulances, says Vic Gilbert. 'Because of the hard frost and a few inches of snow, the vehicles could run about over the fields anywhere looking for airmen. Later in the day I found another airman lying flat on his back – he had made an impression in the ground of some eight inches. His boots and socks were missing, and his face also was squashed out, poor devil. I saw two more bodies, and another which had hit an electricity cable as it came down. It was several days before they found the last of the crew – he was in a bit of wreckage in another field some 500 yards from the tail-piece.'

Eighteen unexploded bombs lay in and around North Lopham, and the emergency evacuation of some 15 families occurred. Traffic was diverted while lost UXB's were located and dealt with over several days by 6219 Bomb Disposal Flight from RAF Feltwell, acting on 'A' class priority orders.

Eighteen bodies also lay amid the bombs and debris strewn over a wide area. The precise cause remains unknown, for there were no survivors from either crew. The 96th BG had been forming for yet another assault on the transportation system within Hitler's deflating Third Reich. This time it was the marshalling yards at Bielefeld. At 11,000ft B-17G 43-38746, flown by Lt Alex Philipovitch, crashed into 44-6137, carrying Lt George J. Peretti and crew. The latter had been flying straight and level when Philipovitch flew across his path. The port wing of '746 struck '137 amidships, and then Philipovitch's aircraft exploded. Peretti's aeroplane broke in half, and the forward section fell spinning and on fire into the history of the Lophams.

39: Tragedy came to Prickwillow

'TRAGEDY CAME TO Prickwillow . . .' – so opened a brief contemporary newspaper account describing events in the fenland village on 6 February 1945.

The day started normally for Mrs Gladys Howe in *Lilecote Cottage*. Trying not to waken the children, or her mother asleep downstairs, she tip-toed to the lavatory before scurrying back to snatch a few more precious cosy moments in bed. Hardly had she snuggled back when the door opened and her daughter, Janet, then aged seven, crept in beside her.

Outside, her brother-in-law, farmworker Reg Howe, was approaching the cottage to collect his milk, which was delivered there for him. Another early riser was Sid Leonard, who sat in the lorry-yard warming his hands on an early morning 'cuppa'. As he sipped the hot tea his attention was drawn to an aeroplane circling the village. It was low, and making a 'funny sound'. Then, materialising from the mist, he saw a big four-engined bomber diving at a shallow angle – straight for the village.

Unseen and unheard by Gladys until it was too late, the giant machine swept down on her home. Some 55,000 lb of death and destruction tore the gentle domesticity to pieces in an enormous crash. Suddenly the ceiling collapsed, burying both mother and daughter in rubble. Flames engulfed the house as bricks and bits of bomber whirled into a terrifying, devastating maelstrom. One engine tore in through the bedroom and out again, landing in the garden. A machine-gun sliced the lavatory pan in two. Screaming, Janet tried to hide as the wardrobe toppled towards her. A mother's protective instinct is powerful and, desperate to save her child, Gladys struggled free from the rubble covering the bed. Alongside, Janet had disappeared beneath plaster, dust and the crazily-tilted wardrobe. Choking on inhaled smoke and dust, Gladys clawed at the rubble, pulling her child free. Flames seared her left arm as she fought to escape, shielding Janet.

Reg saw the B-17 hit the Legge family bungalow and flip over the high drainage bank, to crash violently on to *Lilecote Cottage* on to the opposite side. Both dwell-

The scene at Prickwillow on 7 February 1945. Only one exterior wall of the Legge family bungalow still stands, centre-left. The tail of B-17G 43-37894, 'R', can be seen in the garden. (Russell J. Zorn.)

lings vanished in a raging fireball as Reg ran to help. Dashing to the cottage, he saw Gladys emerge on the verandah, still protecting Janet from the flames. She had clambered through the hole created by the bomber's engine. There was only one way that Reg could reach them and it meant walking through a pool of blazing gasoline. Without hesitation, Reg strode bravely towards Gladys. As she handed her terrified daughter across the rubble Gladys saw that Reg's trousers were alight, flames flaring upwards from his ankles. Courageously he helped them escape, suffering terrible burns himself. Nearby, Gladys' mother emerged unscathed despite an already infirm leg. Searching frantically, Gladys realised that her 16-year-old daughter Doreen was still inside. Luckily, Doreen's room was away from the brunt of the impact, but her bedroom door had jammed. Tugging hard, she managed to free

Edith Legge, her husband, and 18-month-old Josephine. The chubby, cheerful toddler died and her mother suffered permanent injuries when the fully-laden bomber destroyed their home. (Mrs G. Howe.)

it, and fled with flames surging behind her and bullets exploding in all directions.

Outside, villagers were rallying to help where they could. Two distinct explosions occurred after the crash itself, and intense heat made rescue attempts very hazardous, quite apart from the risk of stray bullets. Mr Legge's bungalow was blazing furiously. Sid Leonard knew that Mr Legge was away on war-work, but his wife, Edith, their baby daughter, Josephine, and a ten-year-old evacuee girl from London, Pamela Turner, were inside. Warding off the heat as best they could, Sid, William Bennett and Ralph Rice fought their way into the shattered bungalow. The prone figure of Edith Legge lay in her burning and rubble-stewn bedroom. Heroically, the men rescued the grievously injured woman, but nothing could be done for 18-month-old Josephine. A wall had collapsed on her cot, killing the child. Retrieving the tiny body, they searched for Pamela until driven back by flames. The dead girl's body was recovered from the smouldering ruins some hours later. As they withdrew, Sid heard someone swear and then shout: 'Get moving – she's loaded!' A bomb had been seen in the wreckage.

A doctor attended Edith in a neighbouring home and, although she lived, the poor woman never fully recovered. Seriously brain-damaged, crippled, and always suffering the loss of her daughter, Edith passed away in December 1989.

As Gladys and her children were helped from the scene, Janet crying for her lost golliwog, the National Fire Service arrived from Ely, but little was salvaged from *Lilecote Cottage*. About two hours after the crash a USAAF car arrived with some members of the bomber's crew. Surveying the burnt dwellings, the downcast young fliers knew they had had no alternative but to bale out, but this did not help their remorse.

The Flying Fortress, number 43-37894, came from the 490th BG. Manned by Lt John W. Hedgcock and crew, it had taken off from Eye at 5.45 a.m., intending to attack the Bohlen-Rotha Synthetic oil plant, vital to German war economy. Climbing over their Buncher in haze and partial darkness, the crew were alarmed as they thumped propwash from other, unseen bombers climbing nearby. The collision, when it came, was mild compared with some. The two bombers locked their port wings, almost gently, but seriously enough to set in train a sequence of events leading to disaster.

The bombardier on Hedgcock's crew was Lt Al Elias, who recalled: 'For the first time (I usually had a crew member do it) I personally went into the bomb bay to remove the arming pins from the bombs when we reached 4,000 ft. The fog was very thick, but I asked our navigator, John Roschen, to keep his eye on the nose as well as the sides for – whatever. I removed pins from ten bombs when there was a loud noise. I could see that number one engine was stopped and the cowling over it was loose. At approximately six o'clock the pilot sounded the emergency (bale-out) alarm, then followed up with an intercom message to stand by. At that time I started to get the pins back into the bombs, and when I had finished with number eight the alarm went off again.'

Hurrying to the waist, Al joined the gunners parachuting clear. 'I landed in a farm field next to a creek. Art Fleischer [radio operator] was several hundred yards behind me, and when I ran back to him I noticed he had a compound fracture of the leg – a fragment of bone was protruding. Pete Nicoliasen landed in one of the two trees in the area and had a broken hip. Help came for both – Pete had to be lowered by pulley. All in the area were taken to a hospital in Cambridge, where we linked up except for Ed Tijan [tail gunner], who was first out of the 'plane. We later learned he was dead, and speculated that he either hit the tail assembly on the way out or waited too long to open the 'chute.'

New homes now occupy the site. Gladys Howe, left, with her daughters Doreen and Janet, still lives in the village and can never forget the events of 1945. Janet, right, always flinches at the sound of low-flying aircraft. (Ian McLachlan.)

Sid Leonard's home is on the crash site, and reminders of the drama still surface in his garden. (Ian McLachlan.)

The more seriously injured crewmen were evacuated to America, while the rest re-formed a new crew with their replacements and flew until the war ended.

The other Fortress, a 388th BG machine aptly named *Miss Fortune,* lost a section of wing and crashed on Bracks Farm, Soham, where all ten 500 lb bombs exploded, leaving a huge crater 40ft deep and 75ft across. Luckily, the only damage to buildings were broken windows in the grammar school and some nearby houses. All of the crew baled out, but another parachute problem cost the life of co-pilot Lt Wettersten.

At Prickwillow and other nearby villages a relief fund was set up, and raised the then worthy sum of over £427.00 for victims of the tragedy. Official compensation provided new homes where the destroyed dwellings once stood, but nothing could console Edith Legge for the loss of her daughter, her impaired faculties, and her callipered legs. Gladys Howe was in hospital for seven weeks. Shrapnel was removed from her right thigh and treatment was given for her severely burned arm. Happily, she made a full recovery, as did Reg Howe. Today, Janet flinches whenever an aircraft screeches low overhead, reminding her of a traumatic childhood experience.

More tangible evidence still appears in local gardens. Sid Leonard now lives almost on the site, and in 1989 his wife was planting a rose bush when her trowel struck something solid. Clearing the soil, she discovered a fuel filler cap from the lost bomber. A more frightening find was made when tractor driver, Sam Leggett, ploughed up one of the 20 200 lb fragmentation bombs. A report dated 7 February 1944 noted that ten bombs were unaccounted for, and one hopes that the spectre of that incident will not visit further drama on peaceful Prickwillow.

40: The loss of Lil Edie

TROUBLES COME IN groups or, on 6 February 1945, for a Group – the 490th. Even as the wreck at Prickwillow burned, another of their Fortresses fell in East Suffolk. The authorities in that region have demonstrated a sense of history by preserving police reports on aircraft crashes. That dated 7 February 1945 and submitted to Superintendent Hopes by Police Constable 127, William D. Martin, is a splendid example, giving great detail.

'I beg to report that at 8.10 a.m. on Tuesday 6 February 1945, an American Fortress bomber, number D 33805, piloted by Second Lieutenant Lawrence M. Flannelly, 851 Bomber Squadron, APO 559, home station Eye, crashed in two fields about 300 yards north of the LNER Station, Darsham. The aircraft was completely wrecked and parts burnt out. Wreckage was strewn over two fields, one field being within the boundary of the parish of Darsham and the other within the boundary of the parish of Yoxford.

The crew of nine men baled out and landed safely. One man was slightly injured. Two men landed in Yoxford, and it is believed five landed in Darsham. It is not known where the other members of the crew landed.

The aircraft was laden with fragmentation bombs and was going out on a mission. Evidently trouble developed whilst the aircraft was in flight. It circled Yoxford and watchers on the ground saw that one of its engines was on fire. As it

Wreckage of B-17G 43-38054 strewn across a field near the LNER line at Darsham, Suffolk. A freight train chugs slowly up the track. (Russell J. Zorn.)

came round a second time fire appeared to have spread to the cockpit. The sound of machine guns was heard from the aircraft, and shortly afterwards its bomb load was released. Two bombs fell in the Egg Depot Yard, Darsham, about 150 yards north-east of the LNER Station, Darsham. Two sows were killed, also three fowls, and about two or three fowls injured. Fowl houses and pig pens and a pigeon loft were damaged, and an orchard of young fruit trees was badly damaged. This property is owned by Frederick George Hammond, Egg Depot, Darsham, manager. One of the bombs in its descent struck an oak tree and smashed it off about twelve feet from the ground. The tree was about twelve to fifteen inches in diameter at the point where it was smashed off. This bomb appeared to have exploded either when it hit the tree or immediately afterwards, there was no crater, only the top earth being disturbed. Windows and skylights were smashed in the Egg Depot mill house and a brick wall split. This property is owned by Sir Guy Hambling, Bart, Rookery Park, Yoxford. Damage to the Eileen Cafe nearby was reported, windows being broken and cafe shifted on its foundations. It is owned by Mr A.E. Kirridge, Station Garage, Darsham.

Eighteen more bombs fell at Oven House Corner, Yoxford Road, just within the boundary of the parish of Darsham; map reference M857870. About 150 yards south west of the LNER Arch, two of the bombs fell in the roadway and did slight damage to the road surface, which was quickly repaired. The remaining sixteen fell in two fields. Two cottages at this point, owned by Mr J.E. Thurtell, Yoxford, were damaged; a large number of tiles were displaced and broken, windows smashed and brickwork punctured by flying fragments. Household furniture owned by Mr Ransby, in one of the cottages was damaged. His wife is living c/o Mrs Self, Westleton. Household furniture owned by Mr W. Ringwood, the other occupant of the cottages, was also damaged.

Ringwood is a builder and has a small yard close to the cottages. Small buildings in this yard were damaged by fragments and his pony was hit in the offside rear leg, fracturing the bone about six inches above the fetlock. It was destroyed by shooting by the USA Military Police. A gent's pedal cycle was damaged beyond repair by bomb fragments. It is the property of a lad named Poulson of Middleton, employed by Ringwood, Yoxford. A roadman, Mr Leverett, of Yoxford, had a narrow escape at this point, he dropped flat on the road near these cottages as the bombs exploded.

The aircraft crashed just as a fast train to Ipswich was travelling along the LNER about 150 yards away.

It was ascertained that the number of bombs of this type carried is twenty.

The largest crater is ten foot in diameter and three foot deep. The others seven foot in diameter and two foot deep.

A pair of flying boots and oxygen mask were found at Grove Park, Yoxford.

PC Allum of Westleton and PC Leeks of Southwold were present at the scene of the crash. Mr A.G. Starling, head warden for Yoxford, and ARWs [Air Raid Wardens] Godward and Andrews, Yoxford, and SC W.G. Holmes were also present. Useful assistance was rendered by Mr A.G. Starling and SC W.G. Holmes.'

Understandably, PC Martin did not know what caused the crash, but two crew accounts explain what happened. Firstly, that of Sgt George W. Irwin: 'It was to be our second mission, scheduled to hit Berlin. Our B-17, *Lil Edie,* was hit on our first mission, and a new upper turret was installed, along with other repairs which I cannot recall. Our first mission was to a place called Hohenbudburg on January 28 1945. Our navigator, Scott Grandy, was hit in the hip by a piece of flak and was hospitalised. He was not with us on February 6. He was replaced by Herman Pinkleman. I was the waist gunner at that time, Leon Hatch was the ball gunner, Jim Underwood the tail gunner; Joe Huttlin the nose gunner (and "togglier" – we did not have a bombardier after mission number one); Cliff Gross the flight engineer and upper turret gunner; Jim Gardner, the radio operator, Larry Flannelly the pilot, Walt Cansdale the co-pilot, and Herman Pinkleman was the navigator.

'After the routine pre-flighting of the 'plane, we took off and began to climb

Pictured while training on the B-24, Lawrence Flannelly and crew pose for a photograph typical of those sent home before a crew departed overseas. Standing, L to R: George Irwin, Joe Huttlin, Clifford Gross, Jim Underwood, Leon Hatch and Jim Gardner. Kneeling, L to R: Scott Grandy, Lawrence Flannelly, Walter Cansdale, unknown (did not stay with the crew). (G. Irwin.)

to altitude for rendezvous with the rest of the squadron, heading for the North Sea coast. At about 11,000 ft we went on oxygen, and that is when the 'plane shuddered and went into a steep dive. I could see sparks and flames rushing past the waist window. I tried to get the pilot or someone up front to find out what was wrong on the intercom, and so did Jim Gardner, but we couldn't raise anyone. A little while before this Leon had gone back to the tail to check on Jim Underwood, because he hadn't responded on the intercom about going on oxygen. Apparently his microphone jack was not working properly. Leon was just coming back from the tail when I yelled: 'Let's get out of here!' He had to fight his way back to the ball turret for his 'chute, since we were pinned to the wall by the 'plane's attitude. I crawled (and clawed) my way to the waist door, pulled the hinge release pins, kicked out the door, lost my grip, and was thrown back against the opposite wall again. I finally made it back to the door again, looked back, and saw Jim Gardner coming from the radio room, his oxygen hose stretched to the limit. Leon had his chute on. I baled out and lost little time pulling the ripcord. I was spinning head over heels and, just as my pilot 'chute pulled out the main 'chute, I was in a horizontal position looking up. What a beautiful sight to see that 'chute open. I got quite a jolt when it popped open, and both my flight boots jerked off, leaving me with just my electric heated shoes on my feet.

'Shortly after I jumped, the 'plane went into a steep spiral, and it passed right below me. I could see into the cockpit, and it looked like it was melting. Guns were "cooking" off, sending bullets and tracers out, and flares were blowing up – a pretty scary moment. It looked like I was over the water, but I was drifting back towards land.

'I watched the 'plane go all the way down in that spiralling attitude. At about 700 or 1,000 ft the bombs fell out and blew up part of a road and some fields. About the same time I saw another 'chute come out. That was Jim Underwood. I had seen others before, but couldn't tell how many. Things were happening too fast, and I was having problems trying to stop my 'chute from swinging and turning. I kept hitting propwash from the 'plane as it spiralled down, and couldn't sit in the harness . . . just hung by my crotch. Every time I dropped into the rough propwash I really took a good shaking. I was really weak. No way could I sit in the harness. I saw the 'plane, fire streaking out behind it, make about a half spiral after Jim got out. Then it splattered across the English countryside like someone had thrown a bucket of burning oil across it. At 8.00 a.m. (about the time this happened) it was still pretty dark, and that flaming wreck really lit up the area.

'There was a train coming down some railroad tracks, and I thought the plane would hit it, but it didn't. To me (I was still pretty high yet) it seemed to just miss it. I could see a 'chute that looked like it was going to hit the train, too. It turned out to be Leon. He missed it, though. Leon and Jim Gardner left the 'plane after I did, but were down before me. They must have delayed opening their 'chutes longer than I.

'Suddenly I noticed the ground coming up pretty fast, and I wasn't going to land right. I tried to straighten out by twisting the shroud lines, my legs flailed out, and I hit the ground with quite a smack. I twisted my knees, but other than that and a sore groin, I wasn't hurt. I came down in a wheatfield, where a small group of people gathered. They told me I was near the village of Leiston, Suffolk. I remember kissing the good old earth and saying: "Thank you, God". Another thing I remember while coming down – I kept calling for "Mom" and praying for all the guys to get out.

'I got up and realised I still had a ripcord 'D' ring in my hand. My oxygen mask was still on, with part of the hose still on it, and I noticed my gloves (three pairs) were shredded to the fingers, and the knees of my flight suit were also shredded to the skin. I must have really worked hard to get out of the 'plane. I asked someone for a cigarette (which I'd just sworn off of the day before), took a puff, and threw it away. English cigarettes aren't any good.

'I saw a "meatwagon" coming down a nearby road, gathered up my 'chute and started running toward it. Someone in another field shouted to me. It was Cliff. He had come down right near me. We made it to the truck and saw they had picked up Leon and Jim Underwood.

'We were taken to a nearby fighter base. I don't remember which one, except it was a USA base. We gathered in the CO's office, except for Jim Underwood, who was taken to the hospital. We made quick work of a bottle of spirits the CO offered and had some coffee. I was shaking so bad, as were the others, that I had some trouble holding the coffee cup. We were then taken back to our own base for debriefing. We were later told that a faulty upper turret base, where the oxygen and hydraulic oil entered the turret, allowed the oxygen and hydraulic oil to combine when the valves were turned on. That's all it takes for a big bang!

'Jim Underwood apparently was knocked out when his 'chute opened. He must have hit the ground like a rag doll. He had his face smashed in. We figured he must have hit his head with his knee when he landed. Later we learned he had crushed three vertebrae in his back, too. When I first saw him he didn't have a mark on his face, but at the hospital the left side of his face was so swollen so that there was only a slit where his eye was. The doctors said the inside of his face was smashed. Cheek, jaw and sinus bones looked like a hamburger. They worked on him, saved his sight, and rebuilt his facial bone structure. They did a terrific job on him. They found the back problem a day or so later, and he was put in a full body cast. I think he said the doctors decided to let the vertebrae fuse into solid bone. We would go to see him every chance we got, and aside from a sinus drainage problem that made his nose drip, and the body cast, he looked good as before and as humorously crazy as ever. He was later sent back to the USA. That guy has a lot of guts.

'The remaining eight of us were issued special orders to go to London for an interview with Lt Col Ben Lyon. We each told him our individual story. From that interview we were able to make the BBC broadcast to the USA on a programme called *London Calling North America* – Morning Special. My mother and father were notified of the forthcoming broadcast, and my mother was able to hear it at Holland High School, which had a short-wave receiver. The Superintendent of Schools, Mr B.J. Bishop, had the broadcast piped through the high school intercom, and I became somewhat of a celebrity for a while. I was graduated from Holland High School in 1943.

'Our crew returned to combat duty February 20 1945, picking up "pool" gunners to replace Jim Underwood. We flew 28 more missions after February 6 1945, and were made members of the International Caterpillar Club, receiving a small gold caterpillar pin with red ruby eyes.'

Also proud of his Caterpillar Club badge, Leon Hatch remembers striving to escape. 'We usually went oxygen at about 12,000 to 15,000 ft, and had already checked with each other to see if everyone was on oxygen and safe. I had not gotten into my ball turret, and that probably was the difference between living and dying. This gun turret was electrically powered, and since an electrical short circuit ignited the oxygen and hydraulic systems, the chances are this turret would have been inoperable and there would have been no way to get back into the 'plane. The next time we checked by intercom to see if everyone was OK, the tail gunner [Underwood] failed to answer. I was called to check on Underwood – the reason for his not answering was that he was sick and throwing up. Just as I got alongside the tailwheel well it seemed like all hell broke loose. I could see a mass of flames coming from the front portion of the bomber. It seemed there was an electrical short circuit at the base of the upper turret which ignited the hydraulic and oxygen systems, so it was a burst or explosion right behind the cockpit. This burst of flames caught the collar of the co-pilot on fire, and in his haste to get out of the seat, he pulled back on the controls and the 'plane went almost straight up then fell off into a spiral. While this was going on up front, I was virtually glued to the wall [fuselage], and could move only by "snaking" myself along on my belly and pulling on the ribs of the 'plane. As me and the waist gunner neared each other, he shouted to me: "Let's get the Hell out of here" – words which have rung through my mind seems like thousands of times. By this time the fire was coming all the way back through the bomb bay, where we were loaded with fragmentation bombs, and into the radio operator's room. It looked like the metal and fuselage was burning. I know the emergency flares were firing off or burning, and some of our machine gun bullets. It now looked like an arsenal being set afire – an array of colours and sounds.

'I made a habit of *always* keeping my chest pack 'chute between the ball turret and fuselage, but it seemed like an eternity before I could get to it. I still had problems because I had trouble fastening it to my harness. So much time had elapsed that I wondered if we were near the ground and the inevitable crash, or if the bombs would explode, making dust of everything. Still having a problem getting my 'chute hooked, I thought: "Time is short, and if I can get one side hooked, I'll bale out with only one side hooked". I finally got one side hooked and got in position to get at the escape hatch. The way the 'plane was spiralling down I could see out, and decided to try the other hook to my harness. This time I had no trouble. After that, all I had to do was get up to the hatch. Suction did the rest. I did sort of roll out so I would be a proper position when my 'chute opened.

'When I left the 'plane I was very much relieved, but not for long. The 'plane was going down at a 45° angle. After my 'chute popped it looked as if the B-17 was heading straight towards me with its propellers running wild. Once again I was spared as it went under me, but close enough that my 'chute momentarily collapsed as it passed through the 'plane's stripstream. I don't know how high I was when I baled out, but would guess about 3,000 ft. I landed on the edge of a small field with my 'chute partially caught in some tree limbs. A farmer and his wife were the first to reach me. Throughout the whole ordeal I never felt exhausted at all, until I had landed and tried to get to my feet. I honestly did not have the energy to get up . . .

'Looking back on those times, it seems to me that there was a lot of responsibility placed on some young lives. I was the oldest person in the crew at 21 years of age, yet I don't regret *one* day I served, because I believe it taught me to appreciate our country, the good things God has given us, and especially the young fellows I served with.'

Misfortune continued to dog the 490th BG throughout that mission, when two more of the group's B-17s collided in cloud over the continent. Four aircraft were destroyed, but not one was lost to direct enemy action.

41: Sack Happy

THE WAR'S END lay only weeks ahead, but the relentless grind of missions continued unabated. For 24 February 1945 a familiar adversary was chosen – the Bremen-Deschimag U-Boat yard, a tough target needing heavy ordnance.

This point was not lost on Lt Maurice F. Radtke of the 563rd Squadron, 388th BG, as he pre-flighted his battle-scarred B-17 *Sack Happy*. It would be his crew's fourteenth mission, and her seventy-first. Numerous flak patches over the aeroplane's skin were evidence of earlier trials from which she had always emerged tattered but triumphant. The loading list today was the heaviest Maurice had ever carried – seven 1,000 lb bombs for maximum effect against the U-Boat yard, now thought to be producing the latest 'Schnorkel' boats, capable of re-invigorating German submarine warfare.

Conscious of their burden, Maurice and his co-pilot, Lt Warren R. Headrick, ran carefully down their checklists. As the first engine turned and caught, a burst of exhaust smoke hovered momentarily and then whipped back as the number one propeller shuddered life into the dormant airframe. Soon, all four Cyclones pounded a familiar rhythm for taxiing. Numbers two and three engines idled around 500 r.p.m., while power applied to one or four helped swing the heavy bomber during turns. Nudging at walking pace from her hardstand, *Sack Happy* eased carefully into the line of Fortresses, an aluminium ribbon leading to take-off. Knettishall was vibrant, alive – fulfilling its purpose. Visibility was good, a mere 7 m.p.h. breeze

The 14th mission for Maurice Radtke and crew was the 71st – and last – for their B-17G Sack Happy. Standing, L to R: Louis Steele, Norman Snyder, Carl King, Irwin Nelson, George Rose and Billy Hardgrave. Kneeling, L to R: Warren Headrick, Maurice Radtke and William Meade. (C. King.)

Nose art of the veteran Sack Happy. *The broken Plexiglas nose permitted the crew's fast exit.* (Russell J. Zorn.)

offered no take-off problems, and the cloud ceiling was unlimited; two-tenths at 20,000 ft. However, nearly 800 hours of flying experience had taught Maurice always to expect the unexpected.

Sack Happy sat waiting for her take-off slot. Then the tower flashed a green and the elderly B-17 began what proved to be her final flight. Trembling with increased horsepower, the airspeed indicator moved purposefully round its dial. In the Pilot Training Manual it said glibly: 'When you have attained 110-115 m.p.h., moderate back-pressure on the control column will enable the aircraft to fly itself off the ground'. The guy who wrote that did not have 7,000 lb of bombs in his belly and nine men on a 71-mission ship. Maurice needed more miles per hour, and the straining Cyclones sought to deliver. Daylight had barely appeared beneath her tyres when the reduction gears on number three engine sheared, causing it to run wild. Maurice knew he was too far and too fast to abort the take-off. If he did, nothing would stop *Sack Happy* plunging into trees beyond the runway and exploding – *finis* nine men. He also knew that a B-17 could take off on three engines under 'normal circumstances'. Seven abnormalities sat in his bomb bay, but he had no choice.

Warren had already cut number three throttle and punched the feathering button, but the nature of the failure nullified his actions. The propeller would not feather. Thinking at lighting speed, Maurice elected to go, urging *Sack Happy* from the runway. As she wallowed airborne, the trees lay straight ahead.

In his radio room, Tech Sgt Lou Steele experienced 'stark terror'. Through his earphones, he heard the tower yelling with futility: "KEEP YOUR NOSE UP, KEEP YOUR NOSE UP!" They did. Just. There was barely enough lift and failing momentum to carry them above black branches beckoning like a demon's crooked fingers. There was no more. *Sack Happy* sank wearily into whatever fate lay in store.

Maurice's thoughts were to settle the 'plane as though making a normal landing. He was too busy to experience fear, but a swift, silent prayer put matters in the hands of the Almighty. As the B-17 settled he thought: 'It's all Yours'.

Their main gear was still down, and both pilots frantically chopped switches in

Souvenir flak patches can be seen dotted over the sadly-smashed Sack Happy. *Her flying days are over.* (Russell. J. Zorn.)

the seconds when *Sack Happy* dipped beyond the trees. Hitting a hummock with her wheels, she bounced over a small stream and swept between two telegraph poles, one of which demolished a section of starboard wing. The next obstacle was a grove of trees to port. These chopped away their port outer wing, which dropped into a pond. Still with residual speed, the B-17 then rattled her helpless crewmen over a ploughed field. As they shook and shuddered, Maurice saw a fine English mansion house nearby, and was grateful they had missed it. Abruptly, the left gear collapsed, skidding *Sack Happy* into her final repose, when a tree arrested progress with a sharp jolt. The smoking bomber lay about 2,000 yards off runway 27 and, although their ground travel had been only some 200 yards, they were the longest yards in the lives of nine airmen, whose common aim was now to get out – FAST.

Hot engines, fuel leaking from holed tanks, and 7,000 lb of bombs put in a cocktail-shaker spurred them on. The Plexiglas nose had burst, creating a convenient escape route, and nine fliers fled with wings on their heels. Diving into the first suitable ditch, hearts pounding, they waited. Nothing happened. *Sack Happy* sat ruefully mocking them, her flying days done. An ambulance arrived and took the crew to the infirmary, where, Lou Steele recalls: 'The 100 per cent proof medication was welcome, despite the early hour'.

The entire crew escaped. Next day they had another B-17, and flew the remainder of their 35 missions without serious mishap.

42: Nightmares

IT WAS OVER. Fireworks, celebrations, tears of joy – and some of sorrow for loved ones lost. The war in Europe ended on VE Day, 8 May 1945, when Germany unconditionally surrendered. Thoughts of home, half-stifled in preceding weeks, now flowed with relief into the hearts of Eighth Air Force combat fliers.

Lieutenant Wade D. Pratt had only seven missions left to complete his tour with the already legendary 100th BG. When they arrived on January 22, he and his crew found themselves in the ring delivering the final blows against an evil regime. But, reeling on the ropes, it still hit back. Wade had already bellied one B-17 into a Belgian field, and since his arrival the group had lost 14 bombers. Horrific images of friends flaming earthwards haunted Wade in recurring nightmares. Now, with the war over, he wrote to his parents: 'No need for worrying any more at all'. In a subsequent letter he told them: 'It's pretty nice to lay in bed in the morning – no dreading a hand on your shoulder at 4.30 in the morning; or 1.30 in the morning. "Breakfast at 2.00, briefing at 2.30, Lt Pratt." Get out of bed with the "shakes" (nervousness and butterflies in the belly), and keep shaking till the curtain is pulled at briefing. When you *know* where you're going, how many ack-ack guns and fighters expected – even on the toughest – the fear goes. It's not being fired at that bothers you: it's the worry – it's knowing you have 34 more to go then 33, 32, 31 and so on. Thinking, "By God, we'll never do 30 more like that. Wonder if we'll last 5 more!" Then, after 20 or 22: "Maybe we'll make it. Lady Luck, stay with us just a few more". Sweat out that gas, wondering if you have enough to make it across the channel. It's damn cold in that water, a guy lives less than a minute down there. You look at the co-pilot, he checks the gas and shrugs. Cut the power setting a little lower and start across. If there's an overcast when you get there and you have to use instruments to let down, you won't make it. Call the formation leader and ask to go straight on in. Finally, you sight the field and turn on the approach. Wow, what a relief. The flak is nothing, it's propwash, weather and gas that you really sweat; every mission.'

Lady Luck proved flirtatious. Although the guns were silent in Europe, there was a need for Occupying Forces, and the chilling, political temperature with the Soviets required a state of readiness by Western forces. Rumours also circulated in Thorpe Abbots about redeployment to Japan, still a fanatically defiant foe. So

Faces from a fading photograph – Wade Pratt's crew. Standing, L to R: William Lucas, Hansel Adkins, Ernest Damato, Robert Guidi and Anthony Szott. Kneeling, L to R: Wade Pratt, John Crotty, William Woodruff and Harold Rintoul. (G.M. Pratt.)

the need for training continued and, once the mass hangover had cleared, May 11 saw Wade taking his regular crew on a practice mission in their ship *Girdle Girty*. In addition, to keep his instrument hours and rating, Wade was scheduled for a night flight in a shiny new pathfinder B-17, 44-8790, 'V-Victor'. This would not involve keeping his entire crew awake, and only four went with him – Hal Rintoul, his co-pilot; Jim Brand, navigator; Tony Szott, engineer; and Bob Guidi, a gunner who went along for the ride. Ernest Damato, his radio-man, intended going, but changed places with a replacement, Vince Ferranco, who wanted the hours to make up his flight pay.

Eight Fortresses flew from Thorpe Abbotts at about 8.30 p.m., with Wade at the controls of the unfamiliar, 'Rubber-Victor'. All 418 Squadron aircraft were call-signed 'Rubber', followed by the individual letter. Half-an-hour later, weather conditions worsened and, anticipating a further decline, Maj Robert Stivers, the Air Executive, cancelled the training exercise and ordered recall signals to be sent. Visibility was about one mile but reducing rapidly as one of England's familiar fogs shrouded the countryside. One by one, all the aircraft, except V-Victor, responded and headed home. For 15 minutes the tower at Station 139 sought V-Victor without reply. Exasperated and anxious, the Flying Control Officer finally instructed the High Frequency Direction Finding station to seek their stray and send a 'Return to Base' command in code. Pulsing invisibly through the fog, the insistent transmissions vanished, unacknowledged, into the ether – 10.40 p.m., 10.41, '43; '46; '48; '50; '53; '57 and '59. No reply. Then, suddenly, at 11.06, Ferranco answered. He confirmed receipt of the recall signal – V-Victor was returning to base. Six minutes later the tower radioed landing instructions in clear voice transmissions, and these were acknowledged in similar vein for the first time since take-off.

Fog, swirling eerily around the tower, induced a sense of isolation but, down there, such emotions were synthetic. Up in V-Victor it was real, they were on their own. At 11.35 p.m. the B-17 was heard overhead but, peering into the gloom, Wade saw nothing of the runway lights nor the flares arcing skywards from the tower and runway control van. Their situation now caused increasing concern, and the tower told Wade to try an instrument landing on Runway 10, using his SCS51 localiser. This was an early, electronic-beam landing aid which worked on a signal aligned with the runway so that the pilot could follow the beam down both audibly and on a visual instrument presentation. A few minutes later Wade advised control that his SCS51 unit was unserviceable. So much for the brand new bomber! Putting their stray into an overhead holding pattern, the tower ordered generators to be started so that the base's powerful sodium lights could be switched on. Another option under consideration was to divert to Bury St. Edmunds, and contact was made to determine weather conditions further inland. Such was the concern by now that the 418th Squadron Flight Commander had been called. He told Wade to fly out to Splasher 6 at Scole and steer 90°, which should bring them in on Runway 10.

On board V-Victor the tension was evident as Wade eased lower, his mind absorbing vital information from his blind-flying instruments. His world had no other reference apart from the disembodied voice from control. Tony Szott stood between Wade and Hal Rintoul, his rôle being to monitor instruments and call off airspeed. Like a fog-bound ship approaching harbour on a rocky coast, V-Victor flew on to its destiny. Jim Brand sat in the Plexiglas nose, eyes strained for the runway lights or any sign of danger, but the fog was impenetrable. As they groped towards the earth Bob Guidi stared anxiously from the waist while Vince Ferranco kept at his radio. Wade began a normal, 160 m.p.h. descent from pattern – as 'normal' as being blind allowed. The main gear was down and locked, pilots and engines poised for a power-on climb-out if they saw any obstruction. A few minutes ago Wade had taken an altimeter setting from the tower. This vital instrument was still reading 450 ft when they hit a tree and tore off an aileron about six miles west of the runway. The altimeter was faulty. They must have been flying at nearly fifty feet for ages without knowing it.

When they struck the tree there was an alarming thump and the nose pitched forwards. Instantly, Wade tried pulling up, but the damaged wing failed to respond. Speeding at over 100 m.p.h. and beyond Wade's control, the B-17 smacked on to a wheatfield and raced across the rough terrain, shaking engines and propellers violenty from their mountings. Bounced off his feet in the waist, Bob clearly heard the buckling and drumming of the bomber's skin as it contorted to destruction. Yelling 'Mayday' repeatedly into his microphone, Wade fought hopelessly with the control wheel as V-Victor careered crazily onwards. Nothing he did could prevent what happened. V-Victor struck a ditch on the Diss-Shelfanger road and cartwheeled upside down. The mayhem of their bomber's last moments tore away the nose-section, throwing Jim Brand on to the road. The rear fuselage whipped, snapping off at the radio room. The cockpit and wings went nose down, through the vertical, and crashed inverted across the opposite ditch, blocking the road.

A climax of silence followed as V-Victor's skywards-pointing mainwheels slowly ceased spinning. Hal Rintoul had been thrown from the cockpit and lay stunned and bleeding, a shoulder and ankle broken but still alive. Vince Ferranco had also been tossed clear, but was sprawled unconscious, blood oozing from cuts and a wound caused by a piece of radio equipment which had embedded itself in his abdomen. Tony Szott could move, and clambered from the cockpit with serious leg and head lacerations. Additional movement aft came from Bob Guidi, seemingly the least injured, who struggled free with a dislocated knee. Trying to ignore the pain,

Hanging upside down and saturated in gasoline, the terrified pilot was trapped in the wreckage. (Russell J. Zorn.)

Bob Guidi clambered from the wrecked rear fuselage to search for his crew. (Russell J. Zorn.)

Bob stood up. The overwhelming silence was uncanny. Moving forwards, he found Jim Brand prostrate in the road. The navigator did not look badly hurt, but a severe blow to the skull had killed him outright.

Next, Bob helped Hal away from the wreck and began searching for the others. Szott and Ferranco lay in the ditch, which was now filling with gasoline draining from the hulk. Ferranco was unconscious. Szott had crawled from the bomber, fallen into the ditch, and was now too weak to pull himself out. Bob hauled both men clear and then heard Wade calling for help. The pilot had regained his senses hanging upside down by his seat harness, bleeding and saturated with gasoline. Reaching across, Bob snapped the harness release but, instead of falling free, Wade discovered his legs were trapped at the knees. From deep inside he felt fear rising. He knew the risk of fire – he knew that the crash had given him no time to turn off the switches. One spark and he would torch into flames. His nightmare seemed to be coming true. Only a month earlier Wade had witnessed the horror of crewmen cremated when a B-24 crashed at Thorpe Abbotts. The sight of a dying man, his face and arms burnt away, now arose grotesquely, taunting him. Wade's mind agonizingly immolated his body as he struggled against panic.

Bob was trying to help his friend when he heard a vehicle approaching. Nothing could get by because the B-17's carcass blocked the road. A jeep crawled from the fog and two soldiers got unsteadily out, both drunk but aghast at the spectacle. As they began inspecting the wreck Bob saw the glow of cigars, and yelled angrily to get them extinguished.

In a desperate attempt to reduce the risk of fire, Bob and the soldiers tried to block broken fuel lines with earth and sticks. Increasingly frightened, Wade made frantic efforts to free himself. How many minutes of horror had elapsed was unclear to Bob, but next on the scene was a police car, alerted by electricity and telephone lines torn down in the crash. Now the police tried freeing Wade, but without success. Unhappy with their progress, Bob grabbed an axe, chopping fiercely at the wreckage. Tormented and struggling like an ensnared creature, Wade was screaming with pain and terror when the base crash truck and doctor arrived. As the medic advanced with morphine, Wade's panic heightened. Yelling at the doctor, he threatened to shoot him if he came any nearer. Moreover, he ordered Guidi to do likewise if the doctor tried to sedate his pilot. A pair of Colt .45 automatics made the doctor mindful of his own health, and he wisely retreated. A few minutes later an English heavy-wreckage team arrived, and finally freed Wade about 45 minutes after the crash. Ambulances conveyed survivors to the 96th General Hospital.

The pilot's face was badly cut and he had concussion from the seat being thrown forward, smashing him into the instrument panel. His legs were lacerated but, physically, he was otherwise unharmed. Emotionally, the trauma returned in nightmares long after his wounds healed.

In a letter written on 13 May, Wade told his parents: 'Lady Luck done left me', but went on to allay their concerns by saying he was recovering and 'doing fine'. Jim Brand, joining a long, long roll call, was interred at Cambridge American Military Cemetery and Memorial, where he rests today with 3,810 of his comrades. Eventually Wade D. Pratt's nightmares faded. He died of cancer in 1966. Lady Luck abandoned Hal Rintoul in the early 1960s, when his light aeroplane crashed. Contact was lost with Vincent Ferranco, but, as these words are written, Tony Szott and the brave Bob Guidi can proudly recall their service with the 'Bloody Hundredth'.

43: Homeward bound

FOLLOWING THE WAR'S end, there began a massive movement of Eighth Air Force aircraft and personnel to America. Starting towards the end of May, more than 2,000 aircraft and upwards of 41,500 men left Britain, bound for home. Most flew from their bases to stage through RAF Valley in Anglesey, North Wales. At Polebrook, the group historian wrote: 'The beginning of the end of the 351st Bombardment Group is commemorated in a letter, Headquarters, European Theatre of Operations, dated 13 May 1945, subject: "Movement Orders, Shipment 10034". That letter, wherever it is, should be appropriately framed and incorporated in a shrine for war-weary veterans. It was the letter we had been sweating out for two long years – it meant that we were going home.

'Our first detachment of 'planes on what the Army coded "Home Run" movement took off on 26 May – ten B-17s each carrying a crew of ten and ten passengers. During the next two weeks the operations office was a mad-house, orders for the movement of more airplanes were given and then rescinded, and duty operations officers spent most of their time talking on four telephones at once. At last, by means of one of the those everyday miracles with which the Army continually brings accomplishment out of chaos like a rabbit out of a hat, the rest of our airplanes got off the ground on 9 June – 65 'planes each carrying a crew of ten and ten passengers, under the supervision of our Commanding Officer, Col M.I. Carter. This brought the total group personnel transported by air to 1,500 men.

'The first base on the Home Run trip was Valley Air Field in Wales. One of our 'planes didn't even get to first base.'

The hapless aircraft which failed to reach Valley was a B-17G, 44-6005, flown by Capt Joseph C. Robinson. It took off on the morning of 8 June with 20 happy, homeward-bound people on board. Dense cloud over Wales handicapped navigation, and the Flying Fortress got totally lost. Residents in the Welsh town of Barmouth heard the bomber circling in cloud, probably at the time Robinson was calling Valley for a 'QDM'. This involved a fix being taken on the aeroplane's transmissions, then a magnetic course to steer in degrees would be given to enable the aircraft to reach the airfield. Valley provided a course, but then a basic and tragic error appears to have occurred. The B-17 headed away from Barmouth on a reciprocal heading – flying the wrong way.

That afternoon Ifor Higgon was working in his garage at Arthog, alongside the A493 road to Dollgellau, when he heard a multi-engined aircraft approaching from Cardigan Bay. The cloud base was below 400ft, and Ifor grew concerned because he knew that the land rose steeply behind his garage to a plateau of rough pasture about 500ft high. Climbing beyond this were the crags of Craig Cwm-Llwdd and the Cader Idris, peaking at some 2,000ft. Listening, Ifor felt alarmed – the big aeroplane sounded too low, but there was nothing he could do as it passed, unseen, over his garage. A few moments later the terrible sound of a crash resonated from the hills and seconds after that Ifor heard 'a pronounced thud'; presumably the fuel tanks exploding.

Reaching the isolated site, rescuers found no survivors. Some of the 20 bodies, charred beyond recognition, were spread over a quarter of a mile on the burnt mountainside. When Ifor visited the scene his impression was: '. . . that the pilot may have caught a glimpse of what lay ahead and, in the last few moments, had banked steeply to the left, but it was too late'. Instead of welcoming home husbands, sons

Homeward bound . . . 20 tragic telegrams resulted from the impact on Craig Cwm-Llwdd, Wales. (Russell J. Zorn.)

Symbols of courage. Wings and a Distinguished Flying Cross lay hidden on a Welsh mountainside for nearly 40 years. (R. Handforth.)

and fathers, 20 families now received grim telegrams: 'The Secretary of War desires me to express his deep regret . . .'

Over 30 years after the tragedy, a new theory regarding the loss of 44-6005 was advanced by members of the Eighth Air Force Research Group (Wales). Roy Handforth, their chairman, had served in the RAF and worked on the R/T direction finding (RTDF) unit at Valley. In Roy's opinion the B-17 *had* flown a reciprocal heading to the course provided, but it might not have been entirely because of a terrible mistake made by the crew or the RTDF operator. When the RTDF operator used a special sensor switch to distinguish true from reciprocal, the signal strength was possibly influenced by high levels of iron ore in the mountains, and the voice transmission may have been misinterpreted, resulting in a bearing being given which took the aeroplane to disaster. Another theory was that magnetism affected the bomber's compass. To add to Roy's RAF experience, the research group visited the site several times, and were astonished to find their metal detectors registering constantly as they climbed Craig Cwm-Llwdd. This supported suspicions that external magnetism influenced the bomber's compass, perhaps causing the disaster. Following the group's exploits, a local newspaper put the suggestion to the University College of Wales Geology Department, which felt it was 'an interesting theory'. One geologist said he had observed compass deflection by rocks in the region and felt the idea had some merit, but another was more doubtful.

While the cause was mysterious, there was no doubting the depth of sadness research group members felt when they discovered relics from the lost bomber scattered across the bleak terrain. A propeller blade, an oil cooler, oxygen bottles and ammunition were retrieved from a shallow soil. Emphasizing the personal tragedy were a graduation ring, a set of captain's insignia, two officers' cap badges and, perhaps the most poignant find, a Distinguished Flying Cross with a set of airman's silver wings fused to it by intense heat. The DFC, recognition by the nation of an individual's courage, had apparently been placed in the owner's breast pocket; something to show his grandchildren.

The manifest for the aircraft lists three holders of the DFC: Capt Joseph A. Glover Jr, Lt Howard R. Hibbard, and Tech Sgt Paul Lucyk. When compiling information for this book, Russ Zorn discovered that the manifest had several errors in the crew and passenger list. At least three fliers named were alive, well, and had attended 351st BG reunions. Contact with the 351st BG British historians Ken Harbour and Peter Harris confirmed that three casualties were not on the manifest. Frustrated by the confusion, Russ finally wrote to his Congressman, Bill Paxon, who gained a response from the Department of the Army, listing only 12 names. Just who was homeward bound on that fateful flight is now difficult to establish, but the list given in the appendix is thought to be complete and accurate.

44: Scrap album

RUSS ZORN'S COLLECTION of crashed bomber pictures numbers in the region of 3,000, and this chapter presents a few more, with brief, accompanying accounts.

On 15 February 1944, Lt Emmett O. Watson and crew of the 445th BG were flying their B-24 *Kelly* on a no-ball mission. Over the target a flak-burst destroyed their left rudder and blew tail-gunner Sid Moore several feet back into the fuselage, fortunately without injury. The only wound was to bombardier, Lt Perry A. Freda,

B-24 42-7559 Kelly *at Manston after flak mutilated the left rudder. When told they had only one rudder, co-pilot Otis Rhoney kept crew morale high by retorting that they only needed one. (Russell J. Zorn.)*

Alexander's Ragtime Band *played her last gig at Mendlesham.* (J. Hood.)

who collected a piece of flak in the left foot.

Seeing the straggler, three Fw 190s swept in like wolves for the kill. Luckily, escorting P-47s saw their plight and rescued the Liberator, protecting it from further attack as skilled pilotage got it to RAF Manston for an emergency landing. Without flaps or brakes, the touchdown was fast and the left tyre blew, sending *Kelly* speeding uncontrollably towards airfield buildings. Fortunately the bomber's speed slackened before it reached any obstacles, and *Kelly's* 14th mission ended when she nudged, nose-on, into a wooden hut. A small fire started in the number two nacelle, but was quickly doused as her thankful crew scurried clear.

Firemen could do little for *Alexander's Ragtime Band* when the 385th BG B-17 bellied in at Mendlesham on 1 May 1944. The aircraft was hit by flak over Ostende, and Lt Russell A. Novotny lost his number four engine. Unable to feather the prop or extinguish a slight fire, Novotny tried for home, but gave his crew the option of baling out. Eight airmen parachuted near Lens, leaving Novotny and his co-pilot Lt Fred M. Hageter, to risk the Channel crossing. As they neared Great

Reduced to scrap, Alexander's Ragtime Band *exits stage right on cletracks.* (Russell J. Zorn.)

Bitten by a Vampire – Lt Ziegler's Liberator sans *tail at Lavenham.* (Russell J. Zorn.)

The lady that did the damage – B-24H 42-52745 The Virgin Vampire. *Blooded on seven missions, she was now credited with one B-24 confirmed destroyed.* (Russell J. Zorn.)

The end of a tail. A crane clears the rear fuselage of Lt Ziegler's 41-29482. The square 'P' is the 487th BG identification letter, the 'D' being the bomber's individual code. (Russell J. Zorn.)

Nose-turret gunner Joe Lisowski shot down one of their attackers. Note the thick bullet-proof glass screen in his turret and the slab of armour plating beneath the cockpit window. (Russell J. Zorn.)

Ashfield the fire's intensity strengthened, and the two pilots crash-landed on the then non-operational base at Mendlesham. Hastily vacating their B-17, the pilots watched as a crash tender raced up to foam the flames, but the equipment failed to work and *Alexander's Ragtime Band* burnt out where it lay.

On 30 May a Lavenham Liberator, the *Virgin Vampire,* flown by Lt Bernard J. Majerus, had been hit by flak and was coming in with number four feathered and a smoking number three threatening to ignite. Following 30 seconds behind Lt Arlon F. Ziegler, Majerus touched down and discovered that his brakes were out. Seeing the *Virgin Vampire* bearing down on Ziegler's B-24, the 487th BG Flying Control Officer warned Ziegler to pull off the runway, but it was too late. With an horrendous crunch the *Virgin Vampire* bit into her sister, tearing off the other aircraft's tail. Fortunately, Ziegler's gunners were standing forward of the ball turret, although S/Sgt Stanley M. Goldstein suffered a broken leg when the floor folded up on his foot. Staff Sergeant James D. Bond was also injured, but both crews realised that the mishap could have been much worse.

Flying an invasion-support mission on 22 June, Lt Guy M. Gipson's B-24 *Off Limits,* was hit by flak defending the target at Tournay Sur-Brie. Gipson shut down his number one engine, and *Off Limits* still reached the target and bombed with the 34th BG formation. Suddenly, two Fw 190s pounced in a classic out-of-the-sun attack which put paid to their number two engine. Sitting in his nose turret, Sgt Joe Lisowski caught one enemy fighter, which disintegrated in a long burst from his twin machine guns. This was possibly one of the five lost that day by Jagdgeschwader 26. Thunderbolts chased away the other Fw 190, but Gipson's crew faced serious problems. With both port engines feathered, the B-24 slewed across the sky in danger of spinning. Fuel was vanishing at an alarming rate because of higher power settings for their good engines and possibly also due to leaks from damaged tanks. Staff Sergeant Don Mann juggled with fuel transfer taps to use what they

Off Limits on the shingle of Denge Beach near Dungeness. Local schoolboys used her machine guns for their own crack at the Hun. (Russell J. Zorn.)

could and help stabilise the stricken bomber.

Lieutenant Alvin D. Lichtenstein, the bombardier, recounts: 'We were between 7,000 and 8,000ft when we hit the English coast south of London. We started looking for an airfield, losing altitude all the time. It seemed just seconds until the altimeter was reading 3,500ft, and we still hadn't found a place to land – then the numbers three and four engines spluttered and went out. Our gas was gone. The pilot gave the order to take ditching stations. He told me later he planned at first to ditch on the water, but shipping was too heavy so he picked out a spot on the beach. With all power gone, we were dropping 1,200ft per minute.

'We came in over the beach at about 400ft and discovered power lines above the spot picked out for landing. Without engines the 'plane couldn't be pulled up, so the pilot banked over and headed for a gravel stretch near the beach. I heard the nose gunner say: 'Uh oh, here it comes,' and the next few seconds were just a jumble of awful sensations. The jolt was terrific, and there was a peculiar dusty, salty smell and I was in the air, hurtling through the waist. I landed hung up on the sharp point of a strut from the belly turret which had snapped loose. The point had pierced my heated suit and 'chute harness, but hadn't scratched me. The waist was half-filled up with gravel. A .50 calibre from the ball turret which we hadn't thrown overboard had been catapulted up between the waist windows, pointed towards the tail. The inside of the 'plane looked like a 1,000 lb shell had exploded in the centre of it, and yet nine of us were able to pick ourselves up and scramble out.'

The unconscious top-turret gunner, S/Sgt William P. Stevens, was carried clear and given first aid by Alvin Lichtenstein, who continues: 'When we were all out, the pilot pointed to a levee or dyke of some sort that jutted about ten feet above the ground – "I didn't think we were going to get over that," he said . . . Another guy who deserves a lot of credit is the engineer. He had been busy strapping the pilot into his seat and, after everyone else had taken ditching stations, he went back into the bomb bay and closed the fuel cocks, getting back to his station just a second or two before the crash. That took guts. If the ship had crashed while he had been in the bomb bay, he wouldn't have had much chance. By his action he prevented possible explosion and fire.'

By a strange coincidence, Guy Gipson's brother saw the crash-landing. He was an infantryman on guard duty only 50 yards away. Another witness was 14-year-old Cyril Adams, and the wreck of *Off Limits* gave him and one of his chums a chance for their own crack at the enemy. Sneaking to the site on Denge Beach, near Dungeness, after dark, and while nearby AA defences drowned the noise, they fired one of the aeroplane's machine guns at a V1. Perhaps it is just as well they missed!

During July 1944 the Eighth continued supporting the invasion, and the 17th saw 100 BG aircrews briefed for a bridge at Auxerre. Lieutenant Joseph Trapnell's B-17 never got there, as his navigator, Lt Harold L. Heyneman, relates.

'We were in formation and doing OK when our number one engine started throwing oil and giving us a bad time. Finally, the damn thing ran away and we couldn't feather the prop, so it froze up. We left the formation and started for the channel to jettison our bombs. We dropped them and started back. During this time the ship vibrated so much that the nose shook like it was going to fall off at any minute. When we left the formation we were at 15,000ft, but now we were down to 6,000 and still losing altitude.'

Technical Sergeant Murray W. Holditch went through the aircraft releasing all the escape hatches. Ball turret gunner S/Sgt William A. Geigle remembers being

Clare Harnden expected an unwelcome dip in the North Sea, but landed in a tree near Kelsale, Suffolk. (C. Harnden.)

told to take a life preserver because they were running for the coast with their number one engine now well ablaze. It became a race to reach land before the burning wing exploded, but a dense undercast hid everything below. Heyneman takes up the story: 'I kept getting fixes on the GEE box which, by the way, was the first time we had had one, and found we were still over water. The fire was getting worse and parts were falling off the plane so Trap, in a very cool voice, said: "Men, I guess this is it". It got my last fix, and it showed us about one half mile off the coast – we waited for about a minute and Trap called; "JUMP everyone".'

GEE was originally introduced as a blind-bombing system, but jamming eventually restricted its performance. However, as a navigational aid it provided valuable support, and a skilled operator could swiftly interpret the signals on his CRT as co-ordinates, fixing his position within half a mile. The extra minute they allowed before baling out was just to be sure.

100th BG Fortress 42-102977 belonged to the 349th BS and was coded XR-L. The engines lay several hundred yards from the tail section, shown here in a beet field at Friston, Suffolk. (Russell J. Zorn.)

Tread marks on the turf show how Koreky's P51 hit a 385th BG Fortress, 42-107226, tearing off the tail unit. The burning fighter is in the background. (Russell J. Zorn.)

Tail-gunner S/Sgt Clare R. Harnden was surprised and greatly relieved to float from clouds and land in a tree alongside the A12 road at Kelsale in Suffolk. None of the crew was seriously injured, and an ambulance soon rounded them up. Their empty B-17 hit a tree in the grounds of Friston Hall, narrowly missed the hall itself, tore down some electricity cables and then scattered itself across a beet field. Clare Harnden was at least able to retrieve his torch and jacket from the broken tail section.

Normally, Russ Zorn travelled to crash sites, but sometimes they came to him.

A fiercely blazing fighter forms a young pilot's funeral pyre. Rescuers tried to reach him by placing a ladder against the fuselage, but were driven back by the intense heat. (Russell J. Zorn.)

One local account described the B-24 '. . . landing so gently that it came to rest barely damaged with its nose against the side of the house'. Russell Zorn's camera captures a different version of events at Holt. (Russell J. Zorn.)

Fireball *may have been slower getting her gear down than the nose-art and name imply. (S.P. Evans.)*

His rôle did not normally include photographing fighter incidents, but, on 30 July 1944, a crash occurred at Honington, only yards from his photo lab. The 1st Strategic Air Depot shared Honington with the 364th Fighter Group, who had just converted from twin-engined Lockheed P-38 Lightnings to the P-51 Mustang. Lieutenant James R.Koreky wanted to demonstrate his new fighter to his brother, who was visiting from the infantry. All pilots had been warned that engine torque was stronger on the P-51, but Koreky lost control on take-off. When the Mustang veered left, instead of cutting power he boosted into a take-off attempt and careered out of control into the tail of a 385th BG Fortress under repair. Two enlisted men working in the bomber, Pte Joseph F. Shafrath and Sgt William R. Sellers, were injured when the fighter severed the B-17's tail section before coming to rest engulfed in flames. The heat was too intense for rescuers to reach the hapless Koreky, and he burned to death in his cockpit.

As mentioned elsewhere, Third Air Division B-24 groups re-equipped with B-17s, and the last 34th BG Liberator operation was to Kiel on 24 August 1944. One Liberator was lost to flak over the target and another limped to Sweden, but the final casualty descended dramatically into the north-Norfolk village of Holt. Flown by 4 Squadron commanding officer Maj Joseph O. Garrett, aircraft 44-40443 suffered flak damage to its number one engine. Leaking gasoline, the B-24 headed home, but while it was still over the North Sea, the engineer reported that only three minutes' fuel remained. Knowing the B-24's notorious ditching reputation, the crew opted to bale out, and nine parachutes drifted seaward. As he left his seat Garrett got snagged on a piece of flightdeck equipment, and the B-24 keeled over into a spin before he escaped. Clambering back into his seat, the pilot regained control and decided to risk continuing until the fuel ran out. The minutes passed without a splutter from any of the Twin Wasps. Constantly tensed for a hasty exit, Garrett got to England, and then abandoned his machine, this time without any hitch. He was the only survivor.

Crossing over Salthouse, the B-24 nosed down at a shallow angle and crashed on the outskirts of Holt. Sliding across a field, it clipped a piggery before smashing into Pereers Farm house in Cley Road, knocking the building off its foundations. Happily, the occupant, Mrs Edwards, was visiting her sister, so there were no casualties. The house was destroyed.

Saturday 9 September 1944 saw 28 95th BG Fortresses depart Horham for targets in Germany. However, one Lt Billie Layl's *Fireball,* was soon back. High over the North Sea their number four engine failed and was feathered, forcing a return to base with five 1,000 bombs still on board. Billie Layl recalls the engine loss being handled in '. . . a routine manner (which was really no problem) – never any thought of having to bale out'.

Descending from 16,000 ft over Horham, *Fireball* emerged from cloud at 1,500 ft with the airfield in view. Abbreviating the landing pattern, Layl turned on to final approach. According to the Report of Aircraft Accident, 'Lowering of landing gear and flaps was delayed until well on the final approach'. Noting the absence of main gear, the control caravan at the downwind end of the runway anxiously flashed red to the approaching aircraft. Extending the gear took about 20 seconds and, just before flare-out, S/Sgt Benjamin F. Powell Jr, the engineer, reported that the tailwheel was not fully down and locked. Power was added to go round again, and Layl called for gear up. Unfortunately this did not happen, and the act of increasing power caused the B-17 to drift from runway alignment without giving enough to increase their altitude and climb away. With gear down, flaps up, and fast 'running out of field', Layl decided to land on the grass, and put the B-17

The finish for Fireball – *chin turret torn off, engines askew, a dinghy sprung from its stowage and her back broken. A sad end for a lusty lady.* (Russell J. Zorn.)

down some 400 yards from the upwind end of the runway. Skidding on wet turf, *Fireball* was unable to stop before crossing the perimeter track and crunching heavily into a heap of concrete rubble. Five of the crew suffered minor injuries, and the many-missioned career of their B-17G was ended.

Another multi-mission aircraft with its own claim to Eighth Air Force fame was *Blind Date,* B-17F 42-30195 of the 388th BG – the last 'F' variant used for standard, daylight operations. A stalwart through 66 missions, *Blind Date* had seen two crews complete combat tours and the bomber, a celebrity at Knettishall, was breaking-in the recently-assigned Lt Harold Rensch and crew. Her demise came on 7 October 1944, when heading for an oil objective at Bohlen. Shortly after take-off the number one engine caught fire, and Rensch executed an excellent belly landing near the Suffolk village of Walpole.

Uninjured, her crew hastily departed to warn residents in nearby Bramfield Road

Blind Date *acquired another 54 mission symbols and a niche in Eighth Air Force history before her violent demise near the Suffolk village of Walpole.*

Two engines from Blind Date *were blown into the surrounding countryside when her bomb load detonated.*

that ten 500 lb bombs were now cooking in the blazing aircraft. There followed the rapid evacuation of eight houses, and police closed two roads as black smoke billowed over the countryside and flares and ammunition spurted noisily from the wreck. The biggest sound effect did not come for a surprising two hours. At 10.30 a.m. nine bombs detonated in a violent roar that sent pieces of B-17 teeming down for hundreds of yards. At 2.30 p.m. personnel from 6218 Flight, RAF Bomb Disposal, rendered safe the only unexploded bomb and allowed villagers home. Fortunately damage to their houses was superficial, mainly consisting of broken windows and missing tiles.

In Norfolk on 26 October another property, Caston Hall, narrowly escaped damage when the torn-off tail units of two 452nd BG Flying Fortresses thumped to earth on the driveway. Both rear gunners escaped, and one of them Sgt Louis

'... Still a green combat crew ... '. Standing L to R: Ben Parchinowicz, Marvin Knapp, Jackie Bishop, Wendell Moore, Clayton Edde (not on board) and Louis Correia. Kneeling, L to R: Robert Specht, Francis Maurer, Paul Gross and Anthony Calabrese. Eight of the fliers seen here perished over Norfolk. (Louis Correia.)

Correia, recalls: 'It was only our fourth mission, and we were still a green combat crew . . . I was naturally in my position of tail gunner. Suddenly I felt the 'plane shudder, and I saw a ball of flame go by me – I am facing the rear all this time – and I shouted into the mike: "Hey! What's going on?" There was no answer. Then there was a much louder crunch, and both 'planes were entangled in a terrible collision. I was lucky, as was the other tail gunner. Both tail sections broke off as though they were matchsticks. I was rocked back and forth as the tail section kind of swung to and fro on its fall to the ground.

'They used to say never parachute without your shoes, so I had mine on a piece of bailing wire tied to the strap of the parachute. Well, wouldn't you know, that damn wire and shoes fouled up the 'chute, and I had one hell of a time to get the 'chute to finally open.' Lou suffered slight injuries on landing, as did S/Sgt Harry J. Betts from the other bomber. They were the only survivors from two nine-man crews.

Lou's B-17G, serial 43-37906, was piloted by Lt Robert C. Specht and assigned number six position in the lead element. Shortly after it had assumed position, the formation hit prop wash which caused Specht's B-17 to wallow out of control. Dropping sharply, the aircraft hit B-17 43-38696, piloted by Lt Wallace C. Bragg, who was flying low element lead, just under the lead section. The initial impact broke the tail from Bragg's bomber and Specht's ship pulled up, momentarily separating from the other B-17 before stalling back on to it. In the formation nearby was navigator Michael Prestia, who recorded in his diary: 'Thursday 26 October 1944. Today's target was a parts manufacturer for tanks, trucks, guns and aircraft at Hanover . . . At assembly we witnessed a violent mid-air collision over Deopham Green and just above 16,000ft . . . both ships exploded in a huge, orange fireball. Wreckage filled the sky, and all the crews nearby were extremely agitated. Our ship was about two miles away and just entering the formation. The radio waves were filled with warnings, orders and counter-orders, and all ships spread out until we could recover our nerve.'

The effect below was just startling. Deopham Green Flying Control reported: 'Great plumes of black smoke three or five miles due west of the airfield. Fire Department and medics were immediately notified and instructed to send equipment.'

A mixed load of high explosive and incendiary bombs left little of Bragg's B-17. (Russell J. Zorn.)

Louis Correia's shoes nearly caused his death as he tried to escape from the falling tail turret. (Russell J. Zorn.)

Nearer the incident, 17-year-old Ron Lincoln, a roundsman's assistant, was delivering oil and hardware. 'I heard a roar of engines and then they came nose-down through the clouds, both minus tails, which came following down after, and then two parachutes.'

Each aircraft was carrying five 500 lb M64 General Purpose and five 500 lb M17 aimable cluster incendiary bombs. One high-order detonation occurred on impact, followed by two lesser explosions. Reaching the scene, firemen attempted to deal with the fires but were ordered to withdraw because of the risk of further explosions. The centre-sections of both B-17s burnt to ashes, leaving only the blackened carcasses of eight engines lying forlornly on fields near Caston Hall.

Fortunately the bombs failed to explode on 11 November 1944, otherwise young Roderick Martin might not have been around to tell the tale. Just before lunch he and his chums were playing in a field at Easton, Suffolk, only yards from Roderick's home, 2 Verandah Cottages. High above, 385th BG Flying Fortresses were assembling for targets in Germany, unheeded by the children below. Lieutenant Arthur C. Naylor was flying right wing of the high element. His friend, Robert A. Krahn, was maintaining a tidy position on the left wing, and clearly saw what happened. As they climbed through 16,000 ft Krahn heard Naylor call in to report a fire in his right wing. Leaking oil had ignited, and lost oil pressure meant that Naylor was unable to feather the propeller. Seeping behind the engine firewall, burning oil ate away the B-17's aileron controls, nullifying efforts to set up the automatic flight control equipment (AFCE) before baling out. Krahn watched his friend move out of formation and hold the B-17 steady for his crew to jump. The departing airmen were counted by others in the formation, anxious for their comrades. One . . . two – tail gunner – . . . three . . . two from the nose. Soon, eight 'chutes

Then and now. Left, Caston Hall on 26 October 1944, with the tail section of Bragg's bomber nearest the camera and that of Specht's ship beyond the dislodged shed. Right, The same spot nearly 50 years later. (Russell J. Zorn/Ian McLachlan.)

B-17G 42-31764 landed at Leiston with battle damage in July 1944. Her call letter at the time was 'R'. (Russell J. Zorn.)

Verandah Cottages were threatened by unexploded bombs. The face at the window may be that of young Roderick Martin. (Russell J. Zorn.)

The wrecked tail section of 42-31764, now coded 'Q', attracts the attention of local children, who would long remember the drama enacted at Easton that day. (Russell J. Zorn.)

had opened, and only Art Naylor was left. Looking across, Krahn saw Art's legs protruding from the forward hatch as he prepared to jump. Then the B-17 exploded.

Seeing the first parachute, Roderick and his pals stood enthralled by the drama, counting parachutes. To Roderick, the bomber seemed to dive and explode – other accounts say it became inverted before disintegrating. Tumbling from the debris came Naylor's body and 12 500 lb M64 bombs, one of which exploded in a nearby park. A large section of wing and fuselage containing three bombs thudded to earth only 50 yards from the frightened youngsters. All three bombs were in a dangerous condition, but none exploded. Other bombs fell clear of the wreck, and the heavy, sinister shapes lay threateningly close to Easton. One hit a tree in the park, shearing the striker from the nose fuse but leaving the firing pin in position. This bomb lay close the village, causing several homes to be evacuated. Too dangerous to move, and incapable of being made safe, the bombs had to be detonated *in-situ,* causing some damage to the church and nearby dwellings.

Roderick's family hastily vacated Verandah Cottages because RAF Bomb Disposal units faced serious difficulties dealing with the three bombs buried under the wing section. Trying not to disturb the wreckage, they reached and removed all three ANM101 tail fuses, all set for one-fortieth-of-a-second. Even more troublesome were the ANM103 nose fuses, which could not be seen without lifting off the heavy piece of broken Boeing. A crane was called in, and the bomber's structure was securely shackled and gingerly eased off the bombs. With the sand scooped away each fuse was carefully examined, then *very* gently removed, and the bombs were then rolled clear. Verandah Cottages were saved. That night Roderick slept safely in his own bed after a day's adventure he would never forget. Robert Krahn will also never forget that day. He still recalls shared dangers, some joys, and a friendship, like many, many others, made brief by war.

45: Escorts and enemies

THIS CHAPTER CONSIDERS friends supporting and foes confronting the Eighth Air Force bomber. American strategists originally envisaged that altitude and close formation firepower would protect bombers on daylight operations, but the Luftwaffe soon exposed flaws in this concept. Savage combat and crippling losses confirmed the necessity for effective fighter escort.

British-built fighters, mainly Spitfires, provided limited protection for some early missions, but limited range handicapped their contribution. The first American-made fighter of operational significance was the Republic P-47 Thunderbolt, powered by a rugged Pratt & Whitney R2800 radial. In weight and size the P-47 was considerably larger than its contemporaries, but it eventually confounded critics by proving very capable in combat, although it still lacked the required range.

Following the P-47 came the twin-Allison-engined Lockheed P-38 Lightning. Fitted with drop tanks, the P-38 offered an increase in range but was plagued with opera-

A 62 FS, 56 FG late-model P-47D Thunderbolt photographed by Russell Zorn during trials of a smokescreen system devised to protect bombers, but which proved operationally unsound. (Russell J. Zorn.)

Lightnings of 383 FS, 364 FG airborne from Honington in 1944. (Russell J. Zorn.)

tional problems, and was phased out of service for escort duties by October 1944.

Undoubtedly a war-winner, the superb North American P-51 Mustang offered not only range, but the speed and manoeuvrability essential for dealing with Germany's principal interceptors. Powered by a Packard Merlin, it was capable of long-range escort and frequently sought combat in regions hitherto out of reach.

Confronting the onslaught of Eighth Air Force bombers, Germany employed a varied and formidable arsenal. Initially predominant were two fighters, the Messerschmitt Bf 109 and Focke-Wulf Fw 190. Like their American counterparts, each evolved through a range of variants, but generally kept pace with the opposition until pilot attrition and lack of fuel took their toll.

With fighter opposition diminishing, Eighth Air Force bomber crews faced

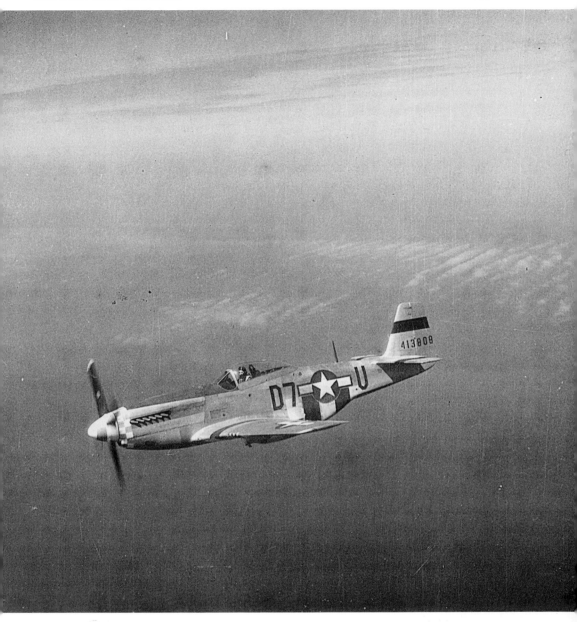

A P-51D of the 503 FS, 339 FG.

increasingly efficient flak. Germany invested considerable manpower and technical resources in anti-aircraft guns and associated radar apparatus. The choking, fearful helplessness of flying into flak, and the impersonality of death so randomly distributed, haunted even the staunchest airman.

Finally, the politically unfavoured activities of German intruders created additional tension for Allied airmen. Fortunately, there were few Eighth Air Force excursions into the intruder's nocturnal domain but, when it did strike, the Messerschmitt Me 410 'Hornet' proved that it could sting the unlucky Liberator or Fortress.

The Messerschmitt Bf 109, one of Germany's most capable fighters. (J. Vasco.)

A Focke Wulf 190 – a highly respected adversary feared by American fliers.

A 105 mm flak gun in action at Munster. (Wilfried Beer.)

Used as an intruder by KG51, the Me 410 created mayhem over Mendlesham.

Appendix

THE FOLLOWING APPENDIX provides additional information on aircraft and incidents for researchers and historians.

Chapter 1
10 November 1943 10:40
Brome, Suffolk
B-17F 42-5793
813 Squadron, 482 Bombardment Group
13 killed
  Lt Arthur J. Reynolds: pilot
  Lt John K. Russell: co-pilot
  Lt Sheldon V. McCormick: navigator
  Lt Alfred L. Rolnick: Bombardier
  Tech Sgt Amos H. Behl: engineer
  Sgt Laurie C. Evans: waist gunner
  Tech Sgt Robert B. Holmes: radio operator
  Sgt Leslie N. Boling: ball turret gunner
  Sgt William H. Landers: waist gunner
  Sgt Andrew J. Allison: tail gunner
  Sgt John D. May: radio operator
  M/Sgt Robert G. Levi: mechanic
  Cpl Hermann J. Kolousek: mechanic

Chapter 2
13 November 1943 09:08
East Wretham, Norfolk
B-17F-90-BO 42-30213 *Li'L One*
562 Squadron, 388 Bombardment Group
  Lt Robert M. Simons: pilot
  Lt Alvin Marcus: co-pilot
  Lt Robert L. Gudgel: navigator
  Lt John D. Pond: bombardier
  Sgt Ira L. Mooney: top turret gunner/engineer

S/Sgt Erwin W. Rehder: radio operator (slightly injured)
Sgt Antonio J. Giangreco: ball turret gunner
Sgt Robert H. Pardue: right waist gunner
Sgt William R. Thompson: left waist gunner
Sgt Charles W. Hash: tail gunner

Chapter 3
30 November 1943 09:05
Wormingford, Essex
B-17F 42-30096 *Liberty Belle*
549 Squadron, 385 Bombardment Group
4 killed
  Cpt Robert C. Smith: pilot (serious injuries)
  Lt James D. McKee: co-pilot (KIA)
  Lt Nathan Ungar: navigator (KIA)
  Lt Charles A. Stevens: bombardier (KIA)
  S/Sgt Samuel S. Litt: top turret gunner/engineer (KIA)
  Tech Sgt Edwin F. Randig: radio operator
  S/Sgt Troy M. Roberts: ball turret gunner
  Tech Sgt George L. Lilburn: right waist gunner
  S/Sgt Henry C. Lohff: left waist gunner
  S/Sgt Louis G. Lonsway: tail gunner

Chapter 4
13 December 1943
Snetterton Heath, Norfolk

B-17F-90-BO 42-30160 *Dottie J. 2nd* AW-E
377 Squadron, 96 Bombardment Group
Four killed
  Lt George Fabian: pilot (injured)
  Lt Thomas J. Scanlon: co-pilot (injured)
  Lt John A. Boyd: navigator (KIA)
  Lt Robert P. Hughes: bombardier
  (injured)
  Tech Sgt Joseph M. Tonko: top turret
  gunner (injured)
  Tech Sgt Joseph M. Tonko: top turret
  gunner (injured)
  Tech Sgt Truman P. Starr: radio opera-
  tor (KIA)
  S/Sgt James W. Mabry Jr.: ball turret
  gunner (KIA)
  S/Sgt Frank Alioto: waist gunner (injured)
  S/Sgt Robert P. Larobardier: waist gunner
  (KIA)
  S/Sgt Jay E. Epright: tail gunner (injured)

Chapter 5
30 December 1943
St Mary-in-the-Marsh, Kent
B-17F 42-37820
333 Squadron, 94 Bombardment Group
  Lt Donald D. Sharp: pilot
  Lt Thomas P. Sheedy; co-pilot
  Lt Frederick W. Irwin: navigator
  Lt Orin D. Gurley: bombardier
  S/Sgt Edward Deutsch: top turret
  gunner/engineer
  S/Sgt August J. Lobone: radio-
  operator
  S/Sgt John L. Fees: ball turret
  gunner
  S/Sgt William C. Nall: right waist
  gunner
  S/Sgt Kenneth F. Majeska: left waist
  gunner
  S/Sgt Joseph Miksic: tail gunner

Chapter 6
5 January 1944 07:04
Shrub Farm, Larling, Norfolk
B-17F-40-DL 42-3268 *Carol Jane* MZ-Z
413 Squadron, 96 Bombardment Group
Ten killed
  Lt James, M. Marshall: pilot
  Lt Richard E. Kostral: co-pilot
  Lt Forest M. Holland: navigator
  Lt John M. McCain: bombardier
  S/Sgt Alfred J. McKay: top turret

gunner/engineer
Tech Sgt Theodore Romanini: radio oper-
ator
S/Sgt Wesley W. Schmidt: ball turret
gunner
S/Sgt John J. Conlin, Jr.: right waist
gunner
S/Sgt Otto C. Scheidegger: left waist
gunner
S/Sgt Kelsel C. Close: tail gunner

Chapter 7
24 January 1944 07:14
High London Farm, Shelfanger, Nor-
folk
B-17F 42-3307 *Skipper* EP-N
351 Squadron, 100 Bombardment
Group
One killed
  Lt Arch J. Drummond: pilot (slightly
  injured)
  Lt Claude E. Schindler: co-pilot
  (slightly injured)
  Lt Frank J. McGuire: navigator
  (injured – burns)
  Lt Maurice G. Zetlan: Bombardier
  (KIA)
  Tech Sgt Sidney A. Cary: top turret
  gunner (injured)
  Tech Sgt Talbert E. Spenhoff: radio
  operator (injured)
  S/Sgt John R. Pendleton: gunner
  (injured)
  Sgt Steven M. Szekely: gunner
  (injured)
  S/Sgt Guthrie H. Head: right waist
  gunner (injured)
  S/Sgt Nicholas Perovich: tail gunner
  (injured)

Chapter 8
2 February 1944
Butt's Lane, Willingdon, East Sussex
B-24D 41-24282 *Ruth-Less*
67 Squadron, 44 Bombardment Group
Ten killed
  Lt James O. Bolin: pilot
  Lt Orville L. Wulff: co-pilot
  Lt Edward J. Ackerman: navigator
  Lt Harold W. Schwab: bombardier
  Tech Sgt James H. Bales: top turret
  gunner/engineer
  Tech Sgt Chester W. Yurick: radio

operator
S/Sgt James L. Wilson: gunner
S/Sgt Ralph E. Strait: gunner
S/Sgt Aubrey J. Maloy: gunner
S/Sgt George M. Dewald: gunner

Chapter 9
5 February 1944 14:00
Dymchurch, Kent
B-17F-70-DL 42-3501 MZ-K
413 Squadron, 96 Bombardment Group
  Lt Donald O. Kasch: pilot
  Lt Leroy E. Allen: co-pilot
  Lt Eugene F. Schadler: navigator
  Lt Roger D. Buhla: bombardier
  S/Sgt Joseph R. Gerba: engineer
  S/Sgt Robert E. Stott: radio operator
  Sgt Norman R. Wilcox: gunner
  Sgt John P. Lawsky: gunner
  Sgt Guy S. Wert: gunner
  Sgt Boles C. Masys: gunner (injured)
This crash killed a British soldier, Pte
Joseph Hampson, 4th Battalion Somerset Light Infantry.

Chapter 10
13 February 1944
RAF Detling, Kent
B-17G 42-39901 *Star Dust*
385 Bombardment Group
  Lt Leonard C. Swedlund pilot
  Lt George H. Guscatt, Jr.: co-pilot
  Lt Rex M. Cantrell: navigator
  Lt Fred D. Berlinger: bombardier
  (serious injuries)
  Sgt Jackson G. Osborne: engineer
  Tech Sgt Charles E. Day: radio operator
  S/Sgt Ernest A. Mazer, Jr.: ball
  turret gunner
  Sgt John P. Brutenback: right waist
  gunner
  Sgt Charles R. Thompson: left waist
  gunner
  S/Sgt Grendell Hawes: Tail gunner

Chapter 11
12 March 1944
RAF Friston, East Sussex
B-24 42-7507 *Heaven Can Wait*
68 Squadron 44 Bombardment Group
  Lt Samuel H. Bowman III: pilot
  Lt James M. Rossman: Co-pilot
  Lt William A. Young: navigator

Lt Charles S. Gordon: bombardier
S/Sgt Kenneth S. Dropek: engineer/top
turret gunner
S/Sgt Bernard D. Creedon: radio operator
Sgt Patrick J. Commisa: ball turret
gunner
Sgt Thomas P. Curry: waist gunner
Sgt Michael Tarzia: waist gunner
Sgt Donald H. Ennis: tail gunner

Chapter 12
19 March 1944
Station 157 Raydon, Suffolk
B-17G 42-31968 *Miss Irish*
100 Bombardment Group
  Lt John P. Gibbons: pilot
  Lt Robert Dykeman: co-pilot (KIA
  29 July 1944)
  Lt Everett M. Johnson: navigator
  Lt Sterling B. Blakeman: bombardier
  Tech Sgt Ira L. Arnold: top turret
  gunner/engineer (KIA 29 July 1944)
  Tech Sgt Edward Walker, Jr.: radio
  operator (KIA)
  Tech Sgt Bernard L. Spragg: ball
  turret gunner (POW 29 July 1944)
  Tech Sgt Frank W. Buschmeier: left
  waist gunner (POW 29 July 1944)
  Tech Sgt Archie Bunting: tail gunner
  Tech Sgt Myron J. Ettus: right waist
  gunner

Chapter 13
12 April 1944 00:55
Great Glemham, Suffolk
B-17G 42-97556
413 Squadron 96 Bombardment Group
Three killed
  Lt Donald M. MacGregor: pilot
  (fracture left tibia, lacerations)
  Lt Isaac L. Hightower: co-pilot (multiple lacerations)
  Lt Francis P. Uihlein: navigator-radar
  (serious injuries)
  Lt George A. Pietrucha: navigator
  (KIA)
  Lt John J. Petrowski: bombardier
  (KIA)
  Tech Sgt Paul W. Morgan:
  engineer/top turret gunner (lacerations
  and burns)
  Tech Sgt Howell H. Thompson: radio
  operator (KIA)
  S/Sgt Arthur L. Flint: waist gunner

(fracture left tibia, burns)
S/Sgt James M. McLean: waist gunner
(fracture right tibia and fibia)
S/Sgt Jesse L. Graham: tail gunner (general
lacerations)
Tech Sgt Emmett L. Matthews: ground personnel (multiple lacerations)
Cpl Nyle Smith: ground personnel (hip and
leg wounds)

Chapter 14
21 April 1944 14:15
Hoxne, Suffolk
B-17G 42-39971 *Little Chum*
729 Squadron 452 Bombardment Group
Six killed
   Lt Dixon I. Wands: pilot (KIA)
   Lt John D. Gattrell: co-pilot (KIA)
   Lt William H. Wroblewski: navigator
(minor injuries)
   Lt Charles W. Lovelwell: bombardier
(KIA)
S/Sgt Leroy H. George: engineer/top
turret gunner (KIA)
S/Sgt Warren H. Hickey: ball turret
gunner (KIA)
Tech Sgt David W. Boyd: radio opera-
tor (KIA)
S/Sgt Ralph Goschey: right waist
gunner (minor injuries)
S/Sgt Charles E. Anderson: left waist
gunner (minor injuries)
S/Sgt Kenneth W. Seibert: tail gunner
(minor injuries)

Chapter 15
23 April 1944
Coopers Farm, Lawshall, Suffolk
B-17G 42-102405
332 Squadron 94 Bombardment Group
Nine killed
   Lt Norman P. Skinner: pilot (KIA)
   Lt Kenneth R. Storey: co-pilot (KIA)
   Lt Jack T. Webb: instructor pilot
(KIA)
S/Sgt Samuel J. Tudisco: engineer/top
turret gunner (KIA)
S/Sgt Harry P. Sonnet: radio opera-
tor
Sgt William J. Copeland: left waist
gunner (KIA)
S/Sgt Benjamin J. Leone: right waist
gunner (KIA)

Sgt Joseph W. Brownlee: ball turret
gunner (KIA)
Sgt John F. Cooney: tail gunner
Sgt Thomas A. McKeon: passenger
(KIA)
Pte Donald E. Morgart: passenger (KIA)

Chapter 16
19 May 1944 11:10
Old and New Buckenham, Norfolk
B-17G 42-38145
730 Squadron 452 Bombardment Group
Two killed
   Lt William C. Gaither: pilot
   Flt Off Ernest M. Demaray: co-pilot
   Lt John W. Stull: navigator
   Lt Roger M. Soth: bombardier
Tech Sgt Edward H. Sullivan: radio
operator (KIA)
Sgt George C. Williams: engineer/top
turret gunner (KIA)
Sgt John F. McCallum: ball turret
gunner
S/Sgt Joseph Lovett: waist gunner
Cpl George Mondell: waist gunner
(minor injuries)
Sgt Robert Sellstrom: tail gunner
B-17G 42-31242
563 Squadron 388 Bombardment
Group
(collision with above aircraft)
   Lt Donald G. Salles: pilot
   Lt Homer Andrews, Jr.: co-pilot
   Lt Jack L. Barcus: navigator
   Lt Thomas S. Matthews: bombardier
S/Sgt Donald L. Robison:
engineer/top turret gunner
S/Sgt Gervis F. Hartle: radio opera-
tor
Sgt Norman F. Powell: gunner
Sgt Rocko D. Garzarelli: gunner
Sgt Harold B. Knoche: gunner
Sgt Frank P. Serio: gunner

Chapter 17
20 May 1944 07:20
Kentwell Hall, Long Melford, Suffolk
B-24H 42-52743
837 Squadron 487 Bombardment Group
Six killed
   Lt Everett F. Goethe: pilot (KIA)
   Lt Ernest T. Carmen: co-pilot (KIA)
   Lt Louis P. Moentenich: navigator

(KIA)
Lt James W. Hartley: bombardier (major injuries)
S/Sgt Darrell M. Dustman: engineer (KIA)
Tech Sgt Stanley M. Allen: radio operator (major injuries)
Sgt James L. Shackleford: nose turret gunner (KIA)
Sgt Joseph J. Puglia: top turret gunner (major injuries)
Sgt Ned Vukemanevich: ball turret gunner (KIA)
Sgt William Jefferies: tail gunner (injured)

Chapter 18
6 June 1944 21:02
AAF Station 134 Eye, Suffolk
B-24H 42-94884 *Lizzie Belle*
848 Squadron 490 Bombardment Group
    Lt Harry G. Holland: Pilot
    Lt Charles Baffo: co-pilot
    Lt Joseph P. Viskell, Jr.: navigator
    Lt Thomas F. McMahon: bombardier
    S/Sgt Paul J. Schmitt: radio operator
    S/Sgt Robert G. Murphy: engineer
    Sgt George G. Gaydos: right waist gunner
    Sgt Marvin W. Tobin: left waist gunner
    Sgt Ernest L. Minter: ball turret gunner
    Sgt. Thomas G. Spurgetis: tail gunner

Chapter 19
7 June 1944 23:48
Joe's Road, Wetheringsett, Suffolk
B-24H-20-FO 42-94911
4 Squadron 34 Bombardment Group
Three killed
    Lt Wilmer J. Dresher: pilot
    Lt Francis C. Rowley: co-pilot
    Lt Antoni H. Grabowski: navigator (KIA)
    Lt Ken Humphrey: bombardier
    Sgt J. Golden: nose turret gunner
    Sgt Robert D. Erisch: tail gunner (KIA)
    S/Sgt Carrol E. Forister: radio operator
    S.Sgt Willard Johnson: ball turret gunner (KIA)
    S/Sgt Jack Blackham: engineer/top turret gunner

Sgt William R. Reschke: waist gunner

7 June 1944 23:50
Nedging, Suffolk
B-24H-15-CF 41-29572
18 Squadron 34 Bombardment Group
Three killed
    Lt Stanley M. Brain: pilot
    Lt Robert L. Buenger: co-pilot
    Lt Richard H. Stevens: navigator
    Lt Donald J. McCarthy: bombardier
    S/Sgt Junior Craft: engineer/top turret gunner
    S/Sgt Stuart A. Stygall: radio operator (KIA)
    Sgt Ernest A. Tipton: gunner (KIA)
    Sgt Paul R. Schopf
    Sgt Al Davids: gunner
    Sgt Chet Nowakouski: gunner (KIA)
    *Staff Sergeant Stygall was assigned to Lt Brain's crew on 28 March, 1944 but may have been with another crew on 7 June 1944.

7 June 1944 23:50
USAAF Station, 156 Mendlesham, Suffolk
B-24H-15-FO 42-52738
391 Squadron 34 Bombardment Group
Six killed
    Lt Hazen D. Eastman: pilot (KIA)
    Lt Paul W. Arthaud: co-pilot (KIA)
    Lt Ross S. Minge: navigator
    Lt Elmer D. Wilson: bombardier
    Tech Sgt George Mucha: engineer/top turret gunner (KIA)
    S/Sgt Robert F. Kruse: radio operator (KIA)
    S/Sgt Everett C. Baird: gunner (KIA)
    Sgt Charles D. Kilne: gunner
    S/Sgt Leslie Van Horne: gunner (KIA)

Chapter 20
25 June 1944
British Airstrip B2, Bazenville, France
B-17G 42-97082 *Mission Mistress*
410 Squadron 94 Bombardment Group
    Lt Raymond J. Graves: pilot
    Lt Vernon R. Kreger: co-pilot
    Lt C. Walder Parke: navigator
    Lt Al Silva: bombardier
    Tech Sgt Ray Cable: engineer/top turret gunner
    S/Sgt Henry B. Lence: radio operator

Sgt Clifford Eby: waist gunner
Sgt Norman Ratliff: waist gunner
Sgt Roland G. Attaway: ball turret gunner
Sgt Manuel Grant: tail turret gunner
(wounded)

6 January 1945 08:30
Mount Farm, Bury St Edmunds,
Suffolk
Aircraft as above
Five killed
  Lt Jack W. Collins: pilot (KIA)
  Lt Robert J. Doran: co-pilot
  Lt Gordon F. Henry: navigator
  (KIA)
  Sgt Clinton R. Hallman Jr.: togglier
  (KIA)
  Sgt James F. Tate: engineer/top turret
  gunner (KIA)
  Sgt Ony N. Carrico: ball turret
  gunner
  Sgt Cecil H. Schermerhorn: waist
  gunner
  Sgt Raymond J. Von Bokel: radio
  operator (KIA)
  Sgt Nicholas A. Urda: tail gunner

Chapter 21
19 July 1944 07.30
Thurston, near Bury St Edmunds,
Suffolk
B-17F-125-BO 42-30851 *Little Boy Blue*
560 Squadron 388 Bombardment
Group
Eight killed
  Lt Walter H. Malaniak: pilot (KIA)
  Flt Off Aaron L. Brinkoeter: co-pilot
  (KIA)
  Flt Off Leo D. Ramos: navigator
  (KIA)
  Lt Amos L. Force: bombardier
  (KIA)
  Tech Sgt Ronald Grey: radio opera-
  tor (KIA)
  Tech Sgt Norris W. Thomas:
  engineer/top turret gunner (KIA)
  S/Sgt John McClusky: ball turret
  gunner (KIA)
  S/Sgt Harold V. Hagerty: right waist
  gunner
  S/Sgt James H. Bennett: tail gunner
  S/Sgt William W. Klemm, Jr.: left
  waist gunner (KIA)

19 July 1944
USAAF Station 138 Snetterton Heath
B-17G 43-37623
413 Squadron 96 Bombardment Group
(Collision with B-17F 42-30851)
  Lt Ralph M. Colflesh: pilot
  Lt Elmer H. Wenzel: co-pilot
  Lt Thomas P. Kialy: navigator
  Lt John Proudfoot: bombardier
  Tech Sgt Bernard J Kelley: radio operator
  Tech Sgt Thomas L. Wallace:
  engineer/top turret gunner
  S/Sgt Clement N. Bergeron: ball turret
  gunner
  S/Sgt Walter R. Stewart: right waist
  gunner
  S/Sgt Denver B. Isaac: left waist gunner
  S/Sgt Charles T. Hutton: tail gunner

Chapter 22
27 July 1944
Hadlow, Kent
B-24 42-94930
34 Bombardment Group
  Lt Gerald Holmes: pilot (injured)
  Lt Dale Granger: co-pilot
  Lt Charles Grzelak: navigator
  (injured)
  Lt Henry Lambert: bombardier
  Tech Sgt Kivett Ivey: engineering/top
  turret gunner (injured)
  Tech Sgt Claude Gibbs: radio opera-
  tor
  S/Sgt Lee Weaver: waist gunner
  (wounded)
  S/Sgt Henry Jensen: nose gunner
  S/Sgt Harry Petersen: tail gunner
  S/Sgt Ed Berry: ball turret gunner

Chapter 23
6 August 1944 18:30
Frog's Hall, Thelnetham, Suffolk
B-17G 43-37528
549 Squadron 385 Bombardment
Group
  Lt Donald J. Noe: pilot
  Flt Off Glenn G. Souik: co-pilot
  Lt William J. Feuerstein: bombardier
  (KIA October 6, 1944)
  Lt Danford D. Milligan: navigator
  Tech Sgt John Gomez: engineer/top
  turret gunner

S/Sgt George W. Runge: radio operator (wounded)

S/Sgt Jack Thomas: ball turret gunner (wounded)

S/Sgt William Espolt: waist gunner (wounded)

S/Sgt Tony Forchione: tail gunner

Chapter 24
13 August 1944 08:40
Factory Lane, Roydon, Norfolk
B-17G 43-38051
848 Squadron 490 Bombardment Group
Four killed

Capt Norman Cosby: pilot

Maj Henry D. Peterson: Aircraft Commander

Lt Elmer I. Crowder: observer (co-pilot)

Lt Dominic A. Pulli: navigator (KIA)

Lt Andrew Korothy: bombardier

Tech Sgt James B. Bristow: engineer/gunner

Tech Sgt Kenneth T. Bagnell: radio operator (KIA)

S/Sgt Paul I Hoban: ball turret gunner

S/Sgt Lawrence L. Barnett: left waist gunner (KIA)

Tech Sgt Milton Rayberg: right waist gunner (KIA)

13 August 1944 08:40
Thelveton, near Diss, Norfolk
B-17G 43-37618
848 Squadron 490 Bombardment Group
Seven killed (collision with 43-38051)

Lt John J. Ketas: pilot (major injuries)

Lt Richard L. Ransom: co-pilot (KIA)

Lt Arthur R. Bright: navigator (KIA)

Lt Clifford A. Ratliff: bombardier (KIA)

Tech Sgt Crawford D. Weaver: engineer/gunner (KIA)

Tech Sgt Charles R. Noblin: radio operator (KIA)

S/Sgt Patsy L. Terling: gunner (KIA)

S/Sgt Paul Bowling: ball turret gunner (KIS)

S/Sgt Edwin F. Hosey: tail gunner (minor injuries)

Chapter 25
11 September, 1944
Harty Ferry, Isle of Sheppey
B-17G 43-37823 *Now An' Then*

XR-V 349 Squadron 100 Bombardment Group

Lt Ferdinand J. Herres: pilot

Lt Edward H. Fehrenkamp: co-pilot

Lt Alvin F. Ringhofer: navigator

Lt Burroughs E. Conover: bombardier

Tech Sgt Robert N. Mulgrew: radio operator

Tech Sgt James Morrow: engineer/top turret gunner

S/Sgt Duell B. Barnes: ball turret gunner

S/Sgt Nester J. Nesser: waist gunner

S/Sgt Andrew R. Main: tail gunner

Chapter 27
15 October 1944 06:39
Woodhall Farm, Sudbury, Suffolk
B-17G 43-38137 H8-N
835 Squadron 486 Bombardment Group
Nine killed (including one civilian, Raymond Smith)

Lt Clarence B. Herrman: pilot (major injuries)

Lt Robert N. Etter: co-pilot (KIA)

Lt Vernon A. Mierhenry: bombardier (KIA)

Lt William M. Annan: navigator (KIA)

S/Sgt John H. Sartain: engineer/gunner (KIA)

S/Sgt Robert R. Stone: radio operator (KIA)

Sgt John W. Jackson: waist gunner (KIA)

Sgt Joseph K. Cook: tail gunner (KIA)

Sgt Ralph M. Spaulding: ball turret gunner (KIA)

Chapter 28
7 November 1944 14:55
Coast Guard Cottages, Felixstowe, Suffolk
B-17G 42-97561 *Batchelor's Heaven*
100 Bombardment Group
Six killed

Capt Stanley A. Clark: Command pilot (KIA)

Lt John T. Dyatt: pilot (KIA)

Lt Ralph C. Bohlsson: navigator (severe burns)

Lt Harry Tennebaum: Lead navigator

Lt Preston J. Wallace: bombardier

Sgt Cornelius J. Romano: tail gunner (severe burns)
Sgt Nelson McClain: radio operator
Sgt August Kienitz: waist gunner
Sgt Donald A. Gustavson: engineer/gunner (KIA)
RAF casualties:
LAC Archibald Cyril Coward: clerk (KIA)
LAC Leslie Patrick Orrom: General duties (KIA)
Cpl David Postlethwaite: armourer (KIA)
Flt Lt Duckworth King (burns)

Chapter 29
21 November 1944
Bryant's Bridge near Snetterton Heath, Norfolk
B-17G-70-BO 43-37764 *Boyd's Boids*
337 Squadron 96 Bombardment Group
  Lt John K. Boyd: pilot
  Lt Robert H. Ashley: co-pilot
  Lt William J. Carey: navigator
  Tech Sgt Louis T. Wallace: togglier
  Tech Sgt Nicholas A. Corleto: radio operator
  Tech Sgt Ernest T. Moriarty: engineer/top turret gunner
  S/Sgt George E. Ritter: ball turret gunner
  S/Sgt Phillip A. Palazzo: waist gunner
  S/Sgt Dale A. Parcher: tail gunner

Chapter 30
30 November 1944 16:52
Battlies Corner, Rougham, Suffolk
B-17G 42-97985
332 Squadron 94 Bombardment Group
Nine killed
  Lt Owen W. Winter, Jr.: pilot (KIA)
  Lt Charles F. Kennedy, Jr.: co-pilot (KIA)
  Lt Richard H. Lambert: navigator (KIA)
  Lt David R. Benz: bombardier (KIA)
  Sgt Phillip Goldfarb: radio operator (KIA)
  Sgt Carmon B. Singletary: top turret gunner (KIA)
  Sgt John M. McCarney: ball turret gunner (KIA)
  Sgt Elmer E. Paris: tail gunner

(KIA)
Sgt Reuben E. Olson: waist gunner (KIA)

30 November 1944 16:52
Rougham, Suffolk
B-17G 44-8177
333 Squadron 94 Bombardment Group
(Collision with 42-97985)
  Lt Neil Pratt: pilot
  Command pilot (name withheld)
  Lt Francis J. McClellan: navigator
  Lt William S. Brallier: bombardier
  Lt Robert R. Smith: bombardier
  Lt Norman Hochberg: co-pilot (tail gunner)
  Tech Sgt Paul J. Kane: radio operator
  Tech Sgt Arthur R. Miller: top turret gunner
  S/Sgt Ervin M. Pattison: right waist gunner
  S/Sgt Junior McCarty: left waist gunner

Chapter 31
27 December 1944 08:35
Parham, Suffolk
B-17G 42-107010
569 Squadron 390 Bombardment Group
Nine killed
  Flt Off James E. McGuire: pilot (KIA)
  Fly Off Hamilton H. Swasey: co-pilot (KIA)
  Tech Sgt Albert V. Banning: navigator (KIA)
  M/Sgt John F. Crahan: togglier (KIA)
  Tech Sgt Pleasant D. Ralston Jr.: engineer/gunner (KIA)
  Tech Sgt Dominick Licata: radio operator (KIA)
  Sgt Devore Murdock: ball turret gunner (KIA)
  Sgt Francis R. Tornabene: waist gunner (KIA)
  Sgt James L. Trotter: tail gunner (KIA)

Chapter 32
31 December 1944
USAAF Station 153 Parham (Framlingham)

B-17G 44-8273
570 Squadron 390 Bombardment Group
Lt Robert Penovich: pilot
Lt W. M. Hayes: co-pilot
Lt Roy N. Golder: navigator (injured)
Tech Sgt Benjamin J. Holman:
engineer/top turret gunner
John N. Gleason: togglier (serious
injuries)
Tech Sgt Richard E. Myers: radio operator
S/Sgt Maurice Stanton: ball turret gunner
Wilmer B. Rhodes: waist gunner
S/Sgt Lloyd H. Chapman: tail gunner

Chapter 33
31 December 1944 07:10
Little Cornard, Sudbury, Suffolk
B-17G 43-37910 C-3R
832 Squadron 486 Bombardment Group
Lt Virgil G. F. Raddatz: pilot
Lt Kenneth C. Hart: co-pilot
Lt William T. Winship: navigator
Lt Frederick F. Koehn: navigator
Lt Robert J. Corman: bombardier
S/Sgt Aloysius J. Ontko:
engineer/gunner
Sgt Harry L. Tekler: radio operator
Sgt William H. Wilcox: waist gunner
Sgt Herman P. Taylor: ball turret
gunner
Sgt Robert C. Holan: tail gunner

Chapter 34
5 January 1945
RAF Station Hawkinge
B-17G 42-97528 *Mary's Sister*
563 Squadron 388 Bombardment Group
Four killed
Lt James F. Reuther: pilot (injured)
Lt Raymond Helminiak: co-pilot
(injured)
Lt H. W. Swanson: navigator (KIA)
Tech Sgt J. Haskett: togglier (KIA)
Tech Sgt Ray Ward: radio operator
(injured)
Tech Sgt F. P. Thielsks: engineer/gunner
(KIA)
S/Sgt Virgil Koon: tail gunner (KIA)
S/Sgt Marlin H. Smith: ball turret
gunner
S/Sgt A. Kiss: waist gunner

Chapter 35
5 January 1945 14:35
Bury St Edmunds, Suffolk

B-17G 43-38050
849 Squadron 490 Bombardment Group
16 killed (collision with 43-38111)
Lt Harold Adelman: pilot (KIA)
Lt Charles S. Elder, Jr.: co-pilot (KIA)
Maj Edward F. Blum: instructor pilot
(minor injuries)
Lt Arthur A. Saye: navigator (KIA)
Lt Harold K. Hatrell: bombardier (minor
injuries)
Cpl Donald N. Turrle, Jr.: radio operator
(KIA)
Cpl Virgil W. Walton: engineer (KIA)
Tech Sgt Harvey C. Smetzer: instructor
radio operator (KIA)
Lt Ernest F. Langholz: instructor navigator
(injured)
Tech Sgt Harold S. Bennett Jr.: instructor
engineer (KIA)

B-17G 43-38111
849 Squadron 490 Bombardment Group
Lt Donald L. Wood: pilot (KIA)
Lt Paul E. McGee: instructor pilot (KIA)
Lt John J. Smith: co-pilot (KIA)
Lt Forest M. Redman: navigator (KIA)
Flt Off Warren J. Allen: instructor naviga-
tor (KIA)
Tech Sgt Clifford A. Kwasigroh: instructor
radio operator (KIA)
Sgt Charles L. Todt: engineer (KIA)
S/Sgt Edward A. Sarazewski: radio opera-
tor (KIA)
Tech Sgt Elmer R. Hammond: instructor
engineer (KIA)

Chapter 36
10 January 1945 08:04
Rookery Farm, Monewden, Suffolk
B-17G-60-VE 44-8304
862 Squadron 493 Bombardment
Group
Four killed
Lt William H. Butler: pilot (KIA)
Lt Sidney B. Jones: co-pilot (KIA)
Lt Robert E. Gaustad: navigator
(injured)
Lt Carlyle E. Bradbury: bombardier
(major injuries)
S/Sgt Ray H. Beeles: engineer/top
turret gunner (KIA)
Tech Sgt William H. Stepp: radio
operator
Sgt Edward A. Campbell: ball turret
gunner

Sgt Arthur J. Doblas: waist gunner
Sgt August B. Muenzer: tail gunner (KIA)

Chapter 37
28 January 1945 09:14
Near USAAF Station 468 Rougham
B-17G 44-8600
331 Squadron 94 Bombardment Group
Four killed
  Lt Wilmar G. Weiss: pilot (KIA)
  Charles V. Weber: co-pilot (injured)
  Lt Leon V. Rondeau: bombardier (KIA)
  Sgt Ralph K. Peeples: crew chief (KIA)
  Sgt Paul J. Pidgeon: radio operator (injured)
  Pte Junior G. Holienbeck: waist gunner (KIA)
  Sgt Henry J. Ollerdessen: ball turret gunner (injured)
  Sgt Wayne M. Ward: tail gunner (injured)

Chapter 38
29 January 1945 09:05
North and South Lopham, Norfolk
B-17G 43-38746 BX-G
338 Squadron 96 Bombardment Group
18 killed
  Lt Alex Philipovitch: pilot (KIA)
  Lt John C. Hubbard: co-pilot (KIA)
  Flt Off Statten H. Gooden: navigator (KIA)
  Flt Off Martin P. Schmidt: bombardier (KIA)
  Tech Sgt Richard J. Zander: radio operator (KIA)
  Tech Sgt Charles H. Tibbats: engineer/top turret gunner (KIA)
  Sgt Robert K. Smith: ball turret gunner (KIA)
  Sgt Jamselm R. Flora: waist gunner (KIA)
  Sgt William F. Brauner: tail gunner (KIA)

B17G 44-6137 AW-J
337 Squadron 96 Bombardment Group
(Collision with 43-38746)
  Lt George J. Peretti: pilot (KIA)
  Lt Gerald Stambaugh: co-pilot (KIA)

  Lt Ernst S. Throne: navigator (KIA)
  Sgt Robert I. Good: togglier (KIA)
  Sgt Marnard A. Faux: radio operator (KIA)
  Sgt Gordon C. Shaul: engineer/top turret gunner (KIA)
  Sgt Noble E. Ellington: ball turret gunner (KIA)
  Sgt Clarence C. Hagler: waist gunner (KIA)
  Sgt Robert R. Stone: tail gunner (KIA)

Chapter 39
6 February 1945 07:40
Prickwillow, Cambridgeshire
B-17G 43-37894
849 Squadron 490 Bombardment Group
Four killed (2 civilians)
  Lt John W. Hedgecock: pilot (minor injuries)
  Lt Eaden M. Whiteman Jr.: co-pilot (minor injuries)
  Flt Off John T. Roschen: navigator (minor injuries)
  Lt Albert Elias: bombardier (minor injuries)
  Sgt Arthur J. Fleischer: radio operator (serious hip injury)
  Sgt Jacob Zuckerman: engineer/top turret gunner (minor injury)
  Sgt Pete Nicoliasen: waist gunner (seriously injured)
  Sgt Edward T. Tijan: ball turret gunner (KIA)
  Sgt Paul I. Estep: tail gunner (minor injuries)

Civilian casualties:
  Miss Pamela Turner – killed
  Miss Josephine Legge – killed
  Mrs Edith Legge – major injuries
  Mrs Gladys Howe – serious injuries
  Mr Reg Howe – serious burns

B-17G 43-37806 *Miss Fortune*
388 Bombardment Group
(Collision with 43-37894 or 490 BG)
  Full crew not known, but the pilot was Lt George Thompson, and the co-pilot was Lt Wettersten (KIA)

Chapter 40
6 February 1945 08:07
Hill Farm, Darsham, Suffolk

B-17G-75-BO 43-38054 *Lil Edie*
851 Squadron 490 Bombardment Group
  Lt Lawrence M. Flannelly: pilot (minor injury)
  Lt Walter C. Cansdale: co-pilot (minor injury)
  Lt Herman F. Pinkleman: navigator (minor injury)
  Sgt Joe W. Huttlin: togglier (minor injury)
  Sgt Clifford A. Gross: engineer (minor injury)
  Sgt James C. Gardner: radio operator (minor injury)
  Sgt Leon D. Hatch: ball turret gunner (minor injury)
  Sgt James T. Underwood: tail gunner (seriously injured)
  Sgt George W. Irwin: waist gunner (minor injury)

Chapter 41
24 February 1945 07:50
Near USAAF Station 136 Knettishall
B-17G 42-97873 *Sack Happy*
563 Squadron 388 Bombardment Group
  Lt Maurice F. Radtke: pilot
  Lt Warren B. Headrick: co-pilot
  Lt William E. Meade: navigator
  S/Sgt Louis J. Steele: radio operator
  S/Sgt Irwin R. Nelson: engineer
  S/Sgt Norman Snyder: togglier
  S/Sgt Billy F. Hardgrave: ball turret gunner
  S/Sgt Carl W. King: waist gunner
  S/Sgt George V. Rose: tail gunner

Chapter 42
12 May 1945 01:20
Shelfanger, Norfolk
B-17G-80-VE 44-8790
418 Squadron 100 Bombardment Group
One killed
  Lt Wade D. Pratt: pilot (serious injuries)
  Lt Harold L. Rintoul: co-pilot (serious injuries)
  Lt James T. Brand: navigator (killed on duty)
  Tech Sgt Anthony Szott: engineer (serious injuries)
  S/Sgt Vincent Ferranco: radio operator (serious injuries)

  S/Sgt Robert G. Guidi: ball turret gunner (serious injuries)

Chapter 43
8 June 1945 14:00
Craig Cwm-Llwdd, Wales
B-17G-40-DL 44-6005
509 Squadron 351 Bombardment Group
20 killed
  Capt Joseph C. Robinson
  Capt Joseph A. Glover, Jr.
  Lt Howard R. Hibbard
  Lt Richard E. Higley
  M.Sgt John Q. Montgomery
  Tech Sgt Paul Lucyk
  S/Sgt Robert E. Smith
  S/Sgt Santo A. Caruso
  S/Sgt Teed O. Smith
  Sgt Boyd P. Dodds
  Sgt Edwin R. Birtwell
  Sgt Sheldon R. Coons, Jr.
  Sgt Camille F. Devaney
  S/Sgt Herbert D. Autenreith
  Cpl Calvert G. Poole
  Tech Sgt Silvio A. Rossi
  S/Sgt Wallace E. Amerod
  Sgt Chester R. Bass, Jr.
  Sgt Dale L. Carlson
  Lt Hartley

Chapter 44
18 February 1944
RAF Manston, Kent
B-24 42-7559 *Kelly*
445 Bombardment Group
  Lt Emmett O. Watson: pilot
  Lt Otis L. Rhoney: co-pilot
  Lt Milton Perlman: navigator
  Lt Perry A. Freda: bombardier (wounded)
  Tech Sgt Paul Fiore: engineer
  S/Sgt Marvin Alford: ball turret gunner
  S/Sgt Thomas Moore: waist gunner
  S/Sgt Sidney M. Moore: tail gunner
  Tech Sgt John F. Hadle: radio operator
  Lt W. Robinson: bombardier

1 May 1944
USAAF Station Mendlesham
B-17G 42-31237 *Alexander's Ragtime Band*

550 Squadron 385 Bombardment Group
Lt Russell A. Novotny: pilot
Lt Fred M. Hageter: co-pilot
Lt Franklin P. Murdock: navigator (baled out over Continent)
Lt Ernest O. Lundgren, Jr.: bombardier (baled out over Continent)
S/Sgt David C. Miller: top turret gunner (baled out over Continent)
Tech Sgt George A. Langer, Jr.: radio operator (baled out over Continent)
Sgt Lloyd A. Winegarner: ball turret gunner (baled out over Continent)
Sgt Raymond E. Smith: tail gunner (baled out over Continent)
Sgt Emile E. Smedley: right waist gunner (baled out over Continent)
Sgt Roger. R. Clark: left waist gunner (baled out over Continent)

30 May 1944 13:25
USAAF Station 137 Lavenham, Suffolk
B-24 42-52745 *Virgin Vampire*
838 Squadron 487 Bombardment Group
Lt Bernard J. Majerus: pilot
Lt Joseph S. Chorola: co-pilot
Lt James F. Kearney: bombardier
Lt James F. Kercheval: navigator
S/Sgt Joseph E. Robinson: engineer
Sgt Edward H. Fee: radio operator
Sgt Charles E. Stevens: nose turret gunner
Sgt Haskell Y. Grandy: top turret gunner
Sgt George W. Stones: ball turret gunner
Sgt Donald E. Denbech: tail gunner

30 May 1944 — collision with 42-52745
B-24 41-29482
839 Squadron 487 Bombardment Group
Lt Arlon F. Ziegler: pilot
Lt George C. MacKenzie: co-pilot
Lt Robert A. Klink: bombardier
Lt John R. Pearson: navigator
Tech Sgt Donald P. Mann: engineer
S/Sgt Francis D. McCann: radio operator
Sgt John M. Goodwin Jr.: nose turret gunner
S/Sgt Stanley M. Goldstein: waist

gunner (minor injury)
S/Sgt James D. Bond: ball turret gunner (minor injury)
S/Sgt Robert M. Allard: tail gunner

22 June 1944
Denge Beach near Dungeness
B-24J 42-94782 *Off Limits*
18 Squadron 34 Bombardment Group
Lt Guy M. Gipson: pilot
Lt Franklin A. Draper: co-pilot
Lt Raymond F. Pariseau: navigator
Lt Alvin D. Lichtenstein: bombardier
S/Sgt Donald E. Mann: engineer/gunner
Tech Sgt Richard J. Peters: radio operator
S/Sgt Edward S. Pendowski: ball turret gunner
Sgt William P. Stevens: top turret gunner (injured)
Sgt Gideon W. Swick, Jr.: tail gunner
Sgt Joseph W. Lisowski: nose turret gunner

17 July 1944 09:35
Friston, Suffolk
B-17G 42-102977
349 Squadron 100 Bombardment Group
Lt Joseph Trapnell IV: pilot
Lt Melvin L. Kodas: co-pilot
Lt Harold L. Heyneman: navigator
S/Sgt Bryon R. Greene: toggler
Tech Sgt Murray W. Holditch: engineer
Tech Sgt John P. Cooper: radio operator
S/Sgt Adam C. Stoppel: waist gunner
S/Sgt Robert Patrick: waist gunner
S/Sgt William A. Geigle: ball turret gunner
S/Sgt Clare R. Harnden: tail gunner

24 August 1944 13:45
Holt, Norfolk
B-24J-160-CO 44-40443
4 Squadron 34 Bombardment Group
Maj Joseph O. Garrett: pilot
Lt William K. MacKay: co-pilot (MIA)
Lt Gordon T. Watson: bombardier (MIA)
Lt John C. Gallagher: navigator

(MIA)
Lt Thomas J. Hogan: navigator (MIA)
Tech Sgt Corrafine Corrales: radio operator (MIA)
S/Sgt Burton C. Holtzman: nose turret gunner (MIA)
S/Sgt Bernard Sabbath: ball turret gunner (MIA)
S/Sgt Clifford R. Smith: waist gunner (MIA)
S/Sgt Saul Spivak: ball turret gunner (MIA)

9 September 1944 08:30
USAAF Station 119 Horham
B-17G 42-31876 QW-Q *Fireball*
412 Squadron 95 Bombardment Group
  Lt Billie B. Layl: pilot
  Lt Theodore L. Bennett: co-pilot
  Flt Off Maurice J. Schwartz: navigator (minor injury)
  Lt George G. Goldstein: bombardier
  S/Sgt Billy B. Morgan: radio operator (minor injury)
  S/Sgt Benjamin F. Powell, Jr.: engineer (minor injury)
  Sgt Lonnie Freeman: gunner (minor injury)
  Sgt Eugene H. Russell: gunner
  Sgt Guillermon A. Vasquez: gunner (minor injury)

7 October 1944 08:40
Holly Tree Farm, Walpole, Suffolk
B-17F-90-BO 42-30195 *Blind Date*
388 Bombardment Group
  Lt Harold E. Rensch: pilot
  Lt James M. Fraser: co-pilot
  Lt George Miner: navigator
  Lt Donald Sjaardema: bombardier
  Sgt James Buckles: engineer
  Sgt Herbert G. Jacobs: radio operator
  Sgt Gollen: waist gunner
  Sgt Mitchell: gunner
  Sgt Checcia: ball turret gunner

26 October 1944 11:25
Caston Hall, Norfolk
B-17G 43-38696
730 Squadron 452 Bombardment Group
Eight killed

Lt Wallace C. Bragg: pilot (KIA)
Lt Harlan P. Humphrey: co-pilot (KIA)
Lt Irvin Eisenstadt: navigator (KIA)
Lt Robert C. Willis: bombardier (KIA)
Tech Sgt Robert C. Bray: engineer/top turret gunner (KIA)
Tech Sgt Albert L. Halvorsen: radio operator (KIA)
S/Sgt Melvin J. Cecil: ball turret gunner (KIA)
S/Sgt Henrey S. Calosso: waist gunner (KIA)
S/Sgt Harry J. Betts: tail gunner (injured)

B-17G 43-37906
730 Squadron 452 Bombardment
Eight killed (collision with B-17G 43-38696)
Lt Robert C. Specht: pilot (KIA)
Lt Francis F. Maurer: co-pilot (KIA)
Lt Paul A. Gross: navigator (KIA)
Lt Anthony Calabrese: bombardier (KIA)
Sgt Benjamin J. Parchinowicz: top turret gunner (KIA)
Marvin S. Knapp: radio operator (KIA)
Sgt Wendell B. Moore: ball turret gunner (KIA)
Sgt Jackie P. Bishop: waist gunner (KIA)
Sgt Louis Correia: tail gunner (injured)

11 November 1944 10:15
Easton, Suffolk
B-17G 42-31764
551 Squadron 385 Bombardment Group
One killed
  Lt Arthur C. Naylor: pilot (KIA)
  Lt Carl L. Cunningham: co-pilot (minor injuries)
  Lt Robert S. Ruben: navigator (minor injuries)
  Lt Henry E. Stumberg: bombardier (major injuries)
  Tech Sgt Steven J. Pawelko: top turret gunner
  Tech Sgt Francis J. Abdella: radio operator
  S/Sgt Lloyd C. Bahton: ball turret gunner
  S/Sgt Wayne S. Tackaberry: tail gunner
  S/Sgt Carl R. Slaton: waist gunner

Index